Stanislav Balík/Vít Hloušek/
Lubomír Kopeček/Jan Holzer/
Pavel Pšeja/Andrew Lawrence Roberts

Czech Politics: From West to East and Back Again

Stanislav Balík
Vít Hloušek
Lubomír Kopeček
Jan Holzer
Pavel Pšeja
Andrew Lawrence Roberts

Czech Politics: From West to East and Back Again

Barbara Budrich Publishers
Opladen • Berlin • Toronto 2017

All rights reserved. No part of this publication may be reproduced, stored in or introduced into a retrieval system, or transmitted, in any form, or by any means (electronic, mechanical, photocopying, recording or otherwise) without the prior written permission of Barbara Budrich Publishers. Any person who does any unauthorized act in relation to this publication may be liable to criminal prosecution and civil claims for damages.

You must not circulate this book in any other binding or cover and you must impose this same condition on any acquirer.

A CIP catalogue record for this book is available from
Die Deutsche Bibliothek (The German Library)

© 2017 by Barbara Budrich Publishers, Opladen, Berlin & Toronto
www.barbara-budrich.net
ISBN   978-3-8474-0585-6
eISBN   978-3-8474-0974-8

Das Werk einschließlich aller seiner Teile ist urheberrechtlich geschützt. Jede Verwertung außerhalb der engen Grenzen des Urheberrechtsgesetzes ist ohne Zustimmung des Verlages unzulässig und strafbar. Das gilt insbesondere für Vervielfältigungen, Übersetzungen, Mikroverfilmungen und die Einspeicherung und Verarbeitung in elektronischen Systemen.

Die Deutsche Bibliothek – CIP-Einheitsaufnahme
Ein Titeldatensatz für die Publikation ist bei der Deutschen Bibliothek erhältlich.

Verlag Barbara Budrich   Barbara Budrich Publishers
Stauffenbergstr. 7. D-51379 Leverkusen Opladen, Germany

86 Delma Drive. Toronto, ON M8W 4P6 Canada
www.barbara-budrich.net

Jacket illustration by Bettina Lehfeldt, Kleinmachnow, Germany
Picture credits: photo: © CTK (cover photo), Demonstration, Wenceslas
   Square in November 1989
Printed in Europe on acid-free paper by
paper&tinta, Warsaw

Contents

Introduction: Czech exceptionalism – *Andrew Roberts* 7

1. The birth of modern Czech politics: 1848–1918 – *Vít Hloušek* 15
2. Politics in interwar Czechoslovakia – *Jan Holzer* 33
3. Czech lands under dictatorships and totalitarian regimes 1938–1989 – *Jan Holzer* 55
4. The Velvet Revolution: the causes and process of the decline of communist power – *Stanislav Balík* 85
5. The Velvet Divorce: the end of Czechoslovakia – *Lubomír Kopeček* 99
6. Czech political institutions and the problems of parliamentary democracy – *Lubomír Kopeček* 115
7. Electoral systems and an obsession with elections – *Stanislav Balík* 147
8. Reshuffling the party system: from non-politics to anti-politics – *Pavel Pšeja* 161
9. Market reforms, society and the main features of Czech capitalism – *Lubomír Kopeček, Stanislav Balík* 183
10. Europeanising and Westernising – *Vít Hloušek* 213
11. Five ways of looking at Czech politics – *Andrew Roberts* 231

References 249

List of abbreviations 273

Tables and figures 277

This book was written and published with the support of the specific research grants from the Faculty of Social Studies at Masaryk University (MUNI/A/1110/2015, MUNI/A/1113/2015, MUNI/A/1342/2014).

Introduction: Czech exceptionalism

Andrew Roberts

Why should outsiders care about the Czech people and their politics? Though the country styles itself the heart of Europe, its objective importance is hard to see. It is the 85th largest country in the world by population (between Benin and Portugal), the 116th by area (between UAE and Serbia), the 40th by GDP per capita (just behind Greece and Estonia), and the 50th by total GDP (between Qatar and Peru).[1] By almost any standard measure, the Czech Republic is an ordinary country – not too big or too small, not too rich or too poor.

But the Czech Republic does have reason to claim our attention. Czech politics presents in refined form some of the major forces shaping the modern world – whether nationalism, democracy, multiculturalism, the dilemmas of being a small state, communism, state division, economic reform, and coming to terms with the past. By virtue of being in the heart of Europe, the Czech lands have experienced in the most direct way possible the vicissitudes of the past two centuries. Czech politics can thus serve as a microcosm for understanding these world-historical forces.

This chapter, however, will argue that Czech politics has an even stronger claim on our attention. In many ways, the Czechs are not just a microcosm or an exemplar, but a trailblazer and a model. Czech politics has pioneered new and unprecedented ways of dealing with just about all of the phenomena described in the previous paragraph. At the least the Czechs show us new possibilities, and at the most they reveal better ways forward. For those who wish to understand politics, it is not just interesting but essential to know something about the Czech experience. This introduction will attempt to make the case for the study of Czech politics by describing this Czech exceptionalism and what it teaches us about politics.

The birth of the Czech nation in the 19th century is in many ways typical of Europe of the time. Czech nation builders closely followed the example of their German neighbours in building an imagined community based on language and culture and relying on print media and schools to spread their message. But the result of these struggles was very different than elsewhere.

Most importantly, Czech nationalism was far less militant and far more flexible than the nationalism of its peers. Indeed, most of the early nationalists were content to remain a part of the Habsburg Empire, and Czech resistance to imperial rule was almost entirely passive up to the very end. Czech nationalism

---

1 These rankings are approximate and vary across sources.

is even one that does not take itself too seriously – witness national icons like the Good Soldier Švejk or the fictional inventor Jára Cimrman.

What explains this? One factor may be that Czechness was created for a fairly well-off people living in a relatively liberal empire. Life was good enough, so why rock the boat too much. Regardless of the cause, Czech nation building challenges the stereotypical view of militancy and violence that came to be associated with nationalism, particularly in peripheral countries. It shows the possibility of an ethnic nationalism without virulent xenophobia or armed struggle.

The creation of the independent state of Czechoslovakia in 1918 had its own peculiarities. Czech nationalism did not lead directly to a Czech state. Instead, Czechs found themselves a part of a multi-ethnic state that included Germans, Slovaks, and Hungarians. While this did, of course, lead to conflict, the newly-formed Czechoslovak Republic was far more functional than one might expect. It is going too far to see interwar Czechoslovakia as an ideal of interethnic harmony, but the state was unique for its time and place in protecting the civil rights of minorities and giving them political representtation. And it did this under less than ideal circumstances. Interwar governments frequently had to deal with ethnic provocations from both inside and outside the country. All, of course, did not end well, but for two decades one of the most diverse countries in Europe worked. It was peaceful and prosperous and democratic.

Even more interesting is the way the leaders of the state created a new "ethnicity", the Czechoslovak. There was nothing natural or obvious about this designation. Czechs and Slovaks had last been united in the 10th century and for most of modern history Czechs had been ruled from Vienna while Slovaks were under the thumb of Hungarians. Their ethnic identities and national mythologies had also emerged separately. Yet, most Czechs ultimately embraced the Czechoslovak state and even the Czechoslovak identity. This was not a case of either/or, they were both Czechs and Czechoslovaks. In short, Czech politics can teach us lessons about the possibility of multi-ethnic democracy and even the mutability of ethnic identity.

Another exceptionalism from this era was Czechoslovak democracy. While all of its neighbours were succumbing to communism, military rule, or fascism, Czechoslovakia continued to hold free elections. Although revisionist accounts point to the blemishes on interwar democracy, there is little question that it met the basic standards of democracy for the time. To get a sense of the achievement, consider how many democracies today are completely surrounded by authoritarian regimes. Mongolia might be the only current example. And the international environment of the time was far less supportive to say the least. The reasons for the survival of democracy are still debated. One explanation might be the absence of forces who had the ability and desire to seize power – the army had new leadership, the nobility had been stripped of its titles and much of its property, and neither communism nor fascism fit a country that was predominantly middle-class and Slavic. Again, interwar Czechoslovak politics can teach us lessons about the possibilities of democracy under very inauspicious circumstances.

The fall of this republic at Munich has become a historical touchstone because it raises debates about how to deal with expansionist dictators. The dilemma of appeasement versus pre-emptive strikes is well-known. Besides this issue in international relations, Munich also lays bare the dilemma of small states. Chamberlain has been derided, probably too severely, for his appeasement of Hitler, but what about Czech leaders who decided to surrender without a fight? Should they have fought even after their allies had abandoned them or after they had ceded the Sudetenland? They would have lost, but they could have put up a fight (they had a large armaments industry and before Munich good fortifications on the borders) and this might have had positive consequences for their national character. Or were their leaders correct in seeing the writing on the wall and avoiding bloodshed and even greater repression? Regardless of the correctness of this choice, it is hard to name many small countries who have taken the decision to lay down their arms without a fight like the Czechs did.

The communist takeover represents another unique aspect of Czech politics. Communists won a plurality in mostly free elections after the war. This put them in a position to lead the government and by 1948 they were able to seize power in a mostly legal way and with the support of much of the population. Czechoslovakia may thus be the first and only case of communism coming to power through democratic means and with considerable popular support. This has its reasons – the disappointment of Munich, liberation by the Red Army, and skilful manipulation by the Communist Party – but it does present a very different perspective on communism in the satellite states than the standard vision of Soviet imposition.

Though communist rule mostly followed the Soviet model in terms of ideology and institutions, the Czechoslovak experience shows a reversal unknown elsewhere. Whereas the typical Soviet satellite saw a hard-line period followed by a gradual thaw, Czechoslovakia experienced a revival of hard-line rule after Stalinism had receded. The thaw here of course culminated in the Prague Spring and the second hard-line period occurred after the Soviet invasion and was called normalisation. This latter period from 1969 to 1989 took the country back to the ideological rigour and cadre politics of the fifties but in a less violent way.

It also created a type of communism that was more or less unique (East Germany may be the only other example). Linz and Stepan (1996) call it "frozen post-totalitarianism" and Kitschelt et al. (1999) label it "bureaucratic authoritarian communism". Its uniqueness lay in the combination of Stalinist politics with an advanced economy and a near complete loss of faith in communist ideology. That hard-line communism could be reimposed under these conditions and that cynicism and opportunism were enough for communism to work after a fashion again tell us something new about the nature of political regimes.

The postcommunist period has provided the Czech Republic with new ways to show its exceptionality. One can begin with the revolution itself. It has been given the moniker "velvet" in part because of how easy it was. After a clash between police and a regime-sponsored parade, the seemingly most stable regime in the region simply melted away. Though a rapid transition was not uncommon in the region, the contrast between before and after was easily the most extreme in Czechoslovakia. The country went from the depths of totalitarianism to a democratic poster child led by a former dissident almost overnight. Indeed, Czechoslovakia had the greatest one-year improvement in Freedom House scores in the more than forty-year history of the index.[2]

It was not just the speed and thoroughness that distinguished the Czech transition. Many scholars have argued that the fall of communism brought little that was new. No new isms emerged. These countries simply overthrew communism and replaced it with standard-issue liberal democracy. Krapfl (2013), however, argues that Czechoslovakia did bring new ideas into the revolutionary tradition. These were the ideals of humaneness and dignity which had never before been at the centre of a revolution. The Czech lands and dissidents like Havel were ground zero for these ideas which have since gone on to enrich the democratic lexicon in other democratic transitions.

Like the democratic transition, the breakup of Czechoslovakia created a new model for state division. It is hard to think of another state breakup that was so smooth and amicable as to deserve the title Velvet Divorce. This was not because both sides wanted divorce. A majority in both nations wanted to stay together even though passions had been inflamed by the time the decision was made. Yet just as Yugoslavia was descending into chaos, the ability of Czech and Slovak politicians to negotiate an end to a state that existed for 70 years was exceptional and suggests that secession and state division may

---

2 This results from summing together the political rights and civil liberties scores. Its improvement in the Polity index was the third largest in the entire dataset.

not be quite so difficult and painful as existing theories predict. Indeed, it was not just the division that was painless. Ever since, relations between the two countries have been more or less problem-free. Each considers the other its strongest ally.

Economic reforms are another area where the Czech way was unique. This is not the basic point about the unprecedented nature of the transformation from communism to a market economy which is worth mentioning in its own right. Other states in the region had to overcome similar obstacles.

What distinguishes the Czech Republic is the role of the public in these reforms and its methods of privatization. At the start of the transition most would-be reformers worried that the public would come to oppose reform as soon as they began to lose the guaranteed employment and low prices that they had become accustomed to. What makes the Czech Republic exceptional was not just that the public endorsed the initial reforms – this occurred, albeit to a lesser extent, in other postcommunist countries as well – but that it kept electing supporters of the free market – a market without adjectives in Václav Klaus's terms – long after other countries had turned to social democrats and former communists to express their disapproval. It took the Czechs eight long years to make such a move and even then it was far from decisive.

The other aspect of reform that set the Czechs apart was their way of divesting themselves of the enormous amount of property owned by the state. The standard prescription was to sell these properties to the highest bidder. The Czechs, however, pioneered two methods that had never really been tried before and have never been replicated to the same extent. The first was restitution of property to its former owners from whom it had been seized. Despite the manifest justice of this approach, it had generally been considered infeasible and uneconomical until the Czechs tried it. The second was voucher privatization. Every Czech citizen could purchase inexpensive vouchers which they could use to become owners of state-owned enterprises, thus creating a citizens' capitalism. Though the success of both methods has been questioned, the Czechs did show the world that there was more than one way to skin a cat.

Finally, the Czechs have broken ground in coming to terms with an authoritarian past. Most postcommunist countries have found some way of dealing with those who collaborated with the communist regime. Few, however, have gone as far as the Czechs. Not only did the Czechs give us the term now used for the practice of purging collaborators – lustration – but they were the first to pursue it and have taken it farther than any other country. The Czech policy of requiring occupants of high public office to submit evidence that they had not collaborated with the secret police has vetted far more people, introduced far tougher sanctions – exclusion from office – and extended far longer in time than any other country. Naturally, it has its defects such as banning the innocent along with the guilty, but it did open new horizons for coming to terms with the past.

Every nation is exceptional in its own way. One could likely produce a similar, though perhaps not quite so long, list of exceptional experiences or policies for many other countries. And one could equally write of the ways that the Czech Republic is a typical country both in general and for its particular time and place. As suggested earlier, one could portray the Czechs as exemplars of such processes as nation and state building, multi-ethnic discord, totalitarian rule, democratic transition, economic reform, and coming to terms with the past. Yet, the descriptions above suggest that unique events did happen in the Czech lands and that they are worth studying.

One of Vaclav Havel's (1993) books was entitled *The Art of the Impossible*. Czech politics gives a sense of this art by uncovering possibilities that have been absent elsewhere in the world, possibilities that are thought to be impossible. They include the possibility of a relatively benign and peaceful nationalism, the possibility of creating a multi-ethnic identity, the possibility of a democratic and multi-ethnic state under inauspicious conditions, the possibility of laying down one's arms when faced with a more powerful foe, the possibility of democratically chosen communism, the possibility of a hard-line communist regime even after people and elites had lost faith in communism, the possibility of a rapid and peaceful democratization and state breakup, the possibility of a popular (in both senses of the word) transition to the market, and the possibility of coming to terms with a brutal past through a comprehensive policy of lustration. These possibilities were not always good ones – though they were often better than the more conventional alternatives – but they should be of interest to any student of politics who wishes to understand how societies are and can be governed. That, in short, is the case for caring about Czech politics.

***

The aim of the chapters that follow is to explore many of the issues outlined above. They are not intended to make the case for Czech exceptionalism as I have above, but simply to provide a better understanding of Czech politics. They represent the work of political scientists and so the emphasis is on conceptual and causal analysis. While the book does attempt to describe the basic who, what, where, and when of Czech politics over the last two centuries, it is not a history per se. Rather its focus is on conceptual understanding – for example, of regime types, party systems, and institutions – and causality – the main forces behind the course of political events in the Czech lands and the consequences of these events.

The book is divided into two parts. Part I focuses on Czech politics up to 1989. Chapter 1 analyses the formation of the Czech nation, Czech politics under the Habsburg Empire, and the creation of an independent state. Chapter 2 focuses on politics during the democratic First Republic (1918–1938) which has been mythologized as a paradise lost and has served as an inspiration for much of current politics. Chapter 3 covers the half century of non-democratic or partially democratic regimes from 1938 to 1989 with most attention on Nazi and Communist rule. All of these chapters describe the political traditions that influence politics to this day. Chapter 4 explains the fall of communism and the creation of a new democracy. Chapter 5 considers the roots and process of the breakup of Czechoslovakia.

Part II analyses the quarter century of democratic rule since the fall of communism in 1989. Chapter 6 describes the new Czech constitutional order – its main institutions, their powers, and their effect on Czech politics. Chapter 7 focuses on elections and electoral systems as the country has now become the site of near constant elections. Chapter 8 deals with political parties and the party system, especially the recent breakdown in both. Chapter 9 tackles the thorny issue of economic reforms and economic policy. Chapter 10 describes the foreign affairs of the Czech Republic with a particular focus on NATO and the EU. Chapter 11 concludes with a larger view of the last two centuries of Czech politics.

The authors wish to thank Oldřich Krpec of Masaryk University for his valuable comments and Michal Kubát of Charles University for his careful review of the manuscript. Štěpán Kaňa's excellent work as translator warrants our deepest gratitude. Finally, we wish to express our appreciation to Masaryk University (MUNI/A/1110/2015, MUNI/A/1113/2015, MUNI/A/1342/2014) for its generous financial support of this project. Our hope is that this book inspires debate and helps to bring Czech politics closer to the centre of research in political science.

1. The birth of modern Czech politics: 1848–1918

Vít Hloušek

The task of understanding the Czech political tradition prior to the founding of the Czechoslovak Republic in 1918 is not easy for a historian, let alone a political scientist. The issue is not only finding a suitable starting point in time; more important is the fact that throughout the nineteenth and twentieth centuries, Czech history has frequently been politicised and subject to various, often antithetical, interpretations. Understandably, this chapter cannot promise to be completely objective and neutral, but it will seek to describe Czech political developments until the end of World War I by employing a perspective that sheds light on the capabilities and deficiencies of Czech society and its political elites. The patterns that emerged before 1918 served as a basis for the many types of regime and society that followed.

1.1. Czech society and the Czech national revival: a difficult transition from serfs to citizens

A useful place to begin is Rokkan's conceptual map of Europe. He attempted to categorize the distribution of European nations and ethnic groups which sought to construct a modern nation at the threshold of the nineteenth century (Rokkan 1999b: 135–147). Although Rokkan's model is primarily focussed on a 'Europe of Celtic, Latin and Germanic peoples', its usefulness goes beyond that. The conceptual map places European states and regions along two axes. The 'West-East' axis combines economic and territorial (geopolitical) criteria (centre vs. periphery, strength of city network), whereas the 'North-South' axis is determined by Catholic (South), mixed (centre) and Protestant (North) areas. This second axis differentiates the conditions of nation-building, whereas the 'West-East' axis emphasises those of state-building.

Rokkan's map shows that the most successful and earliest nation-states were to be found in the European geopolitical centres: Catholic France, Spain and Portugal; the religiously mixed Netherlands; and Protestant Britain, Denmark and Sweden. Unsuccessful nations, by contrast, were located on the peripheries of European politics. As a religiously and linguistically mixed territory and part of the Habsburg Empire, the Czech lands faced an uneasy path towards the establishment of a full political nation. This was to various degrees a result of disputes between its Czech- and German-speaking populations, opposition to Czech national aspirations from the Catholic Church, and the fact that Protestants, drawing from German culture, were not necessarily supporters of Czech nationhood (as they sometimes were in Western European countries).

Of key importance for both the Czech and the wider Central European experience was the process of modern nation building, often described in Czech historiography using the somewhat imprecise, but poetic and nationalistically tinged expression *národní obrození* – national revival or renascence. The term suggests the pre-existence of a Czech nation in a distant past. Czech national mythology interprets the Battle of White Mountain as the symbolic beginning of Habsburg rule and the suppression of Czech nation-hood. The nation gradually revived itself, beginning in the late eighteenth century.

This story is not, however, the historical truth. Modern nations are the product of historical developments, which could have taken – at some stages at least – alternative paths. As Jiří Kořalka (1996: 19-66) reminds us, in the early-nineteenth-century Czech lands there were no fewer than five alternative (and not necessarily exclusive) national-political collective identities: Austrian (a patriotism linked with the Habsburg dynasty); Greater German (a nationalist idea that brought together the German-speaking citizens of the Habsburg monarchy with those of what would later become Germany); Slavic (which sought the future of Czech existence in a close alliance with other Slavic ethnicities, relying largely on a political leadership role for Russia); Bohemian (based on territorial rather than linguistic differences – by analogy we might also speak of Moravian patriotism, involving both the Czech- and German-speaking inhabitants of Moravia); and, finally, Czech (which emphasised the ethnic and linguistic construct of the Czech nation). Not all of these notions were of equal relevance. The dynastic Austrian and Bohemian identities, disregarding as they did linguistic differences, enjoyed the support of very narrow social bases of civil servants and certain intellectuals. Slavic patriotism was more of a political tactic than a truly shared identity. And so the Czech and German linguistic nationalisms emerged during the nineteenth century as clear winners. Czech nationalism spanned the territorial boundaries of the historical lands of Bohemia and Moravia, whereas German nationalism extended beyond the borders of the Habsburg monarchy.

During the first half of the nineteenth century, the Czechs were becoming a fully-fledged modern nation.[1] They underwent a process typical of most of Europe at the time, with Herder's linguistic and ethnic notion of nation and German nationalism serving as paradigms.

As Miroslav Hroch (1999) has argued, the Czech national movement enjoyed a good starting position in that it could refer to the long tradition of independent statehood in the medieval and early modern period. Indeed, early advocates of Czech nationhood frequently based their arguments on historical rights. Scholarly interest among the Czechs in their language, history and ethnography emerged at the turn of the eighteenth and nineteenth centuries. In the context of the Habsburg monarchy, this was relatively early. The interest of scholars during the Enlightenment was soon complemented by, and later replaced with, political demands. The period until the mid-1840s was a time of cautious national campaigning by patriotic activists on behalf of Czech cultural and political ideas.[2] The campaign won the support of more and more Czech speakers. With the revolution of 1848, Czech nationalism became a truly mass movement, which gradually built up a Czech social structure and formulated more radical demands – not just nationalist but also democratic.

As suggested above, geopolitics was a factor influencing to what degree Central European political systems were able to democratise themselves. Of equal weight were events that were connected with attempts to establish democratic and liberal ideas not only in Central Europe, but on the whole continent. The Revolutions of 1848 were, naturally, a symbolic moment. Unlike their predecessors in the 1820s and 1830s, they immediately influenced the nations in Habsburg-ruled Central Europe. And, unlike the exports of the French Revolution, in this case the reception in Central Europe of the new political currents was favourable.

The year 1848 was a milestone on the road to modern democratic politics in Central Europe. In terms of the preconditions for the liberalisation and democratisation of political and social life, the Revolutions of 1848 separated Central (Habsburg) Europe from Eastern (Romanov) Europe and South-

---

[1] For non-ruling ethnic groups like the Czechs, building a modern nation involved three processes: (1) overcoming cultural and linguistic inferiority by cultivating and developing a literary language and a national culture; (2) overcoming political subjugation by obtaining the right to participate in political decision-making; and (3) abolishing the inferior social standing of their members vis-à-vis the ruling nation (Hroch 1996: 10–11).

[2] The important Czech historian Jiří Štaif (2005) describes Czech national leaders of the pre-March 1848 period as 'a cautious elite'.

Eastern (Ottoman) Europe, which never received the ideas of the revolution. The year 1848 was also important in that it was still the era of *risorgimento* nationalism, when demands for the liberalisation and democratisation of political life went hand in hand with calls for national, cultural and political emancipation. The tendencies to Germanise, to replace Slavic languages with German both in intellectual endeavours and daily life, failed to prevent the progress of the nation-building project among the Czechs, but as a result these projects were clearly pitted against the Germans or, symbolically, against Vienna (Claval 2000).

An even more important legacy of the revolution was that it started the process by which serfs were transformed into citizens. The revolution in fact abolished for some time the prerogatives of the aristocracy, many of which were not restored during the neo-absolutist period of 1849-1860. An August/September 1848 Act that abolished serfdom paved the way for the gradual political socialisation and mobilisation of rural populations, then still the decisive majority of the population.[3] The revolution ushered in a modern society in the Czech lands. Nevertheless, one of the fundamental traits of this society was the plebeian character of Czech society. As a result of Habsburg rule and Germanization, the Czechs lacked an aristocracy and upper stratum. This meant that Czechs viewed excessive political and social differences with much suspicion and were only too eager to listen to the proponents of exaggerated egalitarianism. The trend that culminated in the communist takeover in February 1948 therefore had deep historical roots.

1.2. Was Czech society exclusively Czech? Nationalist disputes and their cultural and political consequences

From today's perspective, the Czech Republic is a relatively homogeneous country, where religious identities and disputes are of low importance, nationalist and ethnic issues are politicised only to a very modest degree, and

---

3 The 1910 census showed that the proportion of people working in the primary sector of the economy (39 %) was still higher than that of those working in the secondary sector (37%) – despite the fact that the Czech lands were the most industrially developed part of the monarchy (Kořalka 1996: 117).

Czechoslovakia could be peacefully dismantled.[4] It must, however, be noted that the path towards this homogeneity was only taken from the 1930s onwards, and the process was violent, including the elimination, expulsion, and assimilation of minorities. Before 1918 the society of the Czech lands was diverse in linguistic, national and religious terms. This variety produced cultural exchange along with very strong social and political tensions.

Leaving aside the phenomenon of the great migrations of peoples in antiquity, an overview of the evolving multinational society in the Czech lands needs to begin in the Middle Ages. In the twelfth century, immigrants from Germany began to colonise the peripheries of Bohemia, Moravia and Silesia. The Germans gradually became the largest minority and politically the most important. Their arrival was strongly supported by the Přemyslid royal dynasty, as they settled in and cultivated hitherto uninhabited regions of the Czech lands, in particular the borderlands. Thanks to this German colonisation and the geographical and cultural proximity of Germany, German models influenced many of the institutions of Czech medieval and early modern politics and society.

This did not, however, mean that relations between the Czechs and the Germans were always cooperative. From the very beginning, relations oscillated between cooperation and conflict. The Reformation was a critical juncture: the dispute between Catholics and Protestants temporarily pushed the Czech-German rivalry into the background (Brokl 1999: 49-52). This led to a relatively short period at the turn of the sixteenth and seventeenth centuries when humanist ideas flowed freely between Czech and German societies and across religious spheres. Enforced re-Catholicisation after the Battle of White Mountain (1620) destroyed the developing dialogue between religions and nations, increased tensions between the Czechs and the Germans and, last but not least, deprived Czech society of its historical aristocracy. The aforementioned Czech plebeianism was thus grounded in the specific structure of Czech society. From the end of the eighteenth century, the endeavours of Czechs to catch up with, and if possible get ahead of, the developmentally more 'progressive' Germans provided a permanent and dominant impetus to nascent modern Czech politics. Its programme was to 'redress' White Mountain. This not only inspired Czech politics, but also nourished and radicalised competition and animosity between Czechs and Germans. Contact and

---

4 The 2001 census showed that 94 % of the Czech Republic's population were of Czech (90 %), Moravian, or Silesian nationality.

confrontation with the German element was in practice the strongest inspiration for Czech national activists (Křen 1996).[5]

On the German side, attitudes towards the Czech lands had long been ambivalent. The ethnically Czech population could hardly be considered a fully-fledged part of the German nation-building process, but the Czech lands were clearly understood as a geographical part of the German cultural and political space. The well-known Czech historian and politician František Palacký was invited alongside ethnic Germans to represent Bohemia and Moravia at the Frankfurt Parliament (1848). His no less famous letter, in which he refused the invitation and emphasized instead Czech participation in the Habsburg monarchy and compromise within the ethnically fragmented commonwealth, created a framework for the statehood efforts of the Czechs and their distinctiveness vis-a-vis the German element in the Czech lands in particular and the Habsburg monarchy in general, a framework that remained in place until almost the beginning of World War I.

Constitutionalisation, liberalisation and the gradual democratisation of governance transformed the struggle between Germans and Czechs on economic and political levels. Economic nationalism and the slogan *'svůj ke svému'* ('each to his own [folk]') limited commercial relations in the Czech lands, The Imperial Council *(Reichsrat)* and the regional diets of Bohemia, Moravia and Silesia long suffered from nationalist struggles. This climate was not propitious for peaceful compromises and a number of attempts to do so in Bohemia from the 1870s onwards met with failure. Indeed, the institutions of Bohemia (its diet, *Landtag*, and committee, *Landesausschuß*, which served as the governing bodies) were temporarily suspended in 1913 as nationalist rivalry between Czech and German parties effectively paralysed them. In Moravia, such developments had been avoided thanks to the Moravian Compromise of 1905 *(Ausgleich)*, but the price paid was the *de facto* division of Moravian self-government into Czech and German parts.

The Jewish population, which mostly resided in urban areas, further increased the diversity of the Czech lands. Prague and Brno had their first continually-inhabited Jewish quarters in the eleventh century but, until the eighteenth century, Jews did not enjoy full civil rights. They were subjected to frequent pogroms, attacks, and economic and administrative discrimination.

---

5 The famous Czech historian Josef Pekař remarked in 1929: '[I]f we are further advanced than other Eastern nations in economic and industrial capability, in administration, discipline and diligence, we owe it especially to our German education' (reprinted in Pekař 1995: 509–510).

The majority group perceived them as foreign and the gradual process of Jewish emancipation only began with the reforms of Emperor Joseph II. In terms of political rights, emancipation was complete with the adoption of a fundamental and universal catalogue of civic rights and freedoms in the constitution of December 1867. Thus, Jewish emancipation became a part of a more general process by which the neo-absolutist understanding of the populace as subjects was transformed into a constitutionally-defined citizenship. The emancipation process had overturned the religious ostracism of the Jewish population, but did not in itself signal the achievement of independent political representation for Jews. Linguistic differences overrode religious-ethnic differentiation: richer, urban, Jews participated in the politics of the German liberals, whereas those in small towns and villages who spoke Czech tended to seek political representation in Czech parties (Pěkný 2001).

Thus, in terms of political salience, the national conflict in the Czech lands was largely reduced to a rivalry between Czechs and Germans. Despite attempts at reconciliation made by some aristocrats and conservative bourgeois politicians, Czech-German relations continued to worsen, and national bonds were emphasised to the detriment of civic and democratic principles. The Czech and German communities in the Czech lands carried their nationalist dispute into the era of the so-called First Republic. Their dangerous tendencies towards ethnic homogenisation were preserved too. Later these tendencies much simplified the onset of both 'brown' and 'red' totalitarianism.

1.3. The Czech lands as part of Cisleithania: the consistent constitutionalisation and the inconsistent liberalisation of political institutions

National strife carried over into political life and complicated – sometimes even paralysed – the functioning of political institutions. The Habsburg monarchy could hardly be described as a pioneer in liberalising and democratising its political life. Nonetheless, developments in the last third of the nineteenth century laid down the foundations of a modern administrative state and gradually democratised the political system. These were the foundations on which the interwar Czechoslovak state was also able to build. The following brief overview focuses on constitutional developments in the

Empire, the particularities of the Cisleithanian parliament and government, and the political institutions of the lands of Bohemia and Moravia.[6]

The first phase of the constitutionalisation of the Habsburg monarchy was connected with the revolutionary wave of 1848-1849. At the outset the process looked promising. The Pillersdorf Constitution was imposed in April 1848, taking as its model the Belgian liberal constitution of 1830. It guaranteed fundamental civic rights and anticipated universal male suffrage, but it also preserved the specific position of the Emperor and was inconsistent in its separation of powers. Its main problem, which frequently reappeared in Habsburg constitutionalism, was its limited territorial validity, as it did not apply to Hungary and the Lombardo-Venetian Kingdom. Disputes over internal autonomy within the Habsburg monarchy, which led to the establishment of the dual monarchy of Austria-Hungary in 1867, also provided the context for the aspirations of the Czech national movement to secure self-rule for the Czech lands within the monarchy. In the end, neither the Pillersdorf Constitution nor the much more liberal constitution adopted by the Kremsier (Kroměříž) parliament (Brauneder and Lachmayer 1992: 117–119) came into effect, and in March 1849 the Stadion Constitution was imposed. Compared to the earlier two, it was clearly regressive. It corresponded to the gradual exhaustion of the revolutionary wave.

These constitutional experiments were finally put to rest with the St. Sylvester's Day Patents of 31 December 1851, which suspended the validity of the Stadion Constitution and paved the way for the neo-absolutist period of the so-called Bach regime, named for the repressive Minister of the Interior. Although the revolutionary constitutional attempts essentially failed, what was achieved was a fundamental modernisation of public administration, including its central offices, whose symbolic culmination was the establishment of the Council of Ministers as a collective form of government in March 1848 (Baltl and Kocher 1997: 195–196). Liberalism established itself as an important economic doctrine and was gradually put into practice. The political and nationalist aims of the Czech (and German) liberals, however, remained unfulfilled (Jászi 1961: 86–99).

The gradual dismantling of the neo-absolutist regime was a consequence of Austria losing the Franco-Austrian War in 1859. The October Diploma (1860) and the Schmerling (also called February) Constitution (1861) restored

---

6 Cisleithania refers to the Austrian half of the dual monarchy. The Hungarian half was termed Transleithania. The Leitha River marked part of the boundary between the two.

limited constitutionalism. Among other achievements, they opened the way for the establishment of provincial assemblies or diets in the individual crown lands, thus allowing Bohemian, Moravian and Silesian provincial politics to develop (Hye 1998: 58–72). This was far from liberal governance, however, not least due to the highly discriminatory electoral system, in which those who paid the highest taxes were allowed to dominate: there were four classes of electors, or curias, and the system was strongly biased towards the representation of the landed gentry.[7] Furthermore, the system of constituencies that was adopted and the way these were drawn allowed large-scale gerrymandering, the main consequence of which was the over-representation of German-speaking areas (Valenta 2002: 66–67). Among other illiberal and undemocratic elements, the monarch held executive power, there was neither a constitutional court nor a catalogue of fundamental rights, ministers were not accountable to the parliament, and the separation of powers was inconsistent. The demands of the individual nations and parts of the monarchy were, again, insufficiently addressed, which led in practice to a dysfunctional political system.

The Austro-Hungarian compromise (*Ausgleich, kiegyenlités*; Galántai 1985) led to the adoption of the December Constitution (1867). A positive development was that it was not imposed, but adopted jointly by the monarch and parliament. The constitution was based on a combination of the principles of monarchical legitimacy and the sovereignty of the people. It established a true separation of powers, reintroduced both the catalogue of fundamental rights and the constitutional court, and consistently subordinated the activities of the state and its bodies to the rule of law. It did include a provision for emergency legislation, the notorious Article 14, which allowed the ruler to issue emergency decrees with the power of the law. This was frequently used in practice as the fragmented House of Deputies was often paralysed by abstention or obstruction.[8]

The constitution introduced a bicameral Imperial Council with a House of Lords and a House of Deputies. The latter would be elected indirectly by provincial diets. Many of the diets were paralysed by national strife and the obstruction that went with it (Bohemia was particularly renowned for this

---

7 To be fair, in its favouring of rich voters, the Habsburg monarchy was certainly not an exception in Europe at the time (Rokkan 1999a: 252–253).
8 Czechs, Moravians, Tyroleans, Romanians, Italians, and Slovenians practised abstention for significant periods of time.

practice), so the principle of direct election was gradually introduced beginning in 1868.[9] In an attempt to overcome the negative consequences of obstruction, an emergency electoral law was adopted in 1873. It allowed the government to hold a direct election whenever a deputy was not exercising the duties of his office. These laws were a direct response to the deliberate Czech policy of abstention.

The struggle for universal suffrage flared up in the early 1890s, but electoral reform did not take place until Count Badeni's draft was adopted in 1896. This added a fifth curia for most of the male populace. The reform increased the number of voters in Cisleithania from 1,732,000 to 5,333,000 (Baltl and Kocher 1997: 225–226). However, suffrage was limited to men aged over 24 and soldiers and police officers were denied the franchise. Suffrage once more topped the agenda in 1905, when the demand for equal suffrage crystallised.[10] Beck's electoral reform, which came into effect in January 1907, responded to these events (Pernes 2005: 282–296). It introduced universal, equal, and direct male suffrage by secret ballot, but still limited to those over 24 and excluding soldiers and police officers.

Governments in Cisleithania were peculiar. They were not answerable to parliament, but only to the Emperor. For that reason, the make-up of a government did not necessarily correspond to a parliamentary majority (indeed, given the fragmented party spectrum, majorities were hard to form), and governments sought to create rather heterogeneous coalitions in parliament or simply ruled using Article 14.

With the exception of the troublesome years 1865–1867, the German Liberals (the so-called constitutional party) ruled for almost two decades from 1861 onwards. This, however, does not mean that the cabinet was closely linked with the liberal faction (or factions) in the Imperial Council. In fact, the individual cabinets preferred to keep their distance from parliamentary factions, espousing alternately a liberal, conservative, federalist or centralist profile, depending on specific points of the policies being carried out (Brauneder 1987: 30–31). Liberals were then replaced by the government led by Count Eduard Taafe (1879–1893), who was renowned for his attempts to

---

9 With the exception of the fourth curia, where the elections were still indirect, these elections took place through special electoral colleges.
10 Employees of the railways waged an unusual campaign in support of universal suffrage: they worked to rule, thus causing chaos on the railways (Urban 1982: 524).

rule in a non-partisan manner, which in practical terms meant replacing politics with administration.

At the turn of the nineteenth and twentieth centuries, governments followed each other in quick succession. Practically all of them fell due to an inability to find any reasonable compromise between Czechs and Germans, with both nationalities engaging in obstruction. The situation quieted down somewhat during the government of Ernst von Koerber (1900–1904), which ruled technocratically, sought to ignore language issues, and focussed on economic development. The year 1905 was once again turbulent due to the question of equal suffrage. It was followed by a series of largely caretaker governments which continued into the years of World War I.

In the context of Czech representation, one must mention the practice of appointing a Czech *Landsmannminister* to the government. Though not present in every government, this minister without portfolio represented the Czech nation, but his position was complicated, as he had to balance the pressures for Czech political representation against the demands of the cabinet.

Provincial politics, that is, provincial diets and governments, provided a more important locus in which a Czech political culture and elite (or more precisely, elites) could be created and socialised. The fundamentals of provincial self-governance were already formulated in the constitution of February 1861 and remained in force until World War I. Whatever was not explicitly a prerogative of Cisleithania fell within the jurisdiction of the provinces. Furthermore, in 1907 the provinces obtained further powers in the areas of civil and criminal legislation and a new civil service system. Although provincial self-governance could be suspended, in general the trend of the years 1867–1918 was to strengthen regional and provincial self-government.

The provincial diets were legislatures made up of the so-called 'Virilists', i.e., *ex-officio* members representing specific interests (typically, dignitaries of the Church and university rectors), and elected deputies, who were significantly more numerous than the Virilists. The electoral system was unfair, as it was based on curias (classes) of voters, where membership was determined on the basis of property ownership. The provincial committee served as the executive, but as it was formally a standing committee of the diet, it was composed of sitting deputies. The Emperor appointed the chairs of these committees. A provincial committee acted strictly as a collective body: there were no powers granted to its individual members and decisions were taken in plenum. The scope of their authority consisted of the powers given to provincial self-government. Until the 1890s, the provinces had been quite weak financially, and this changed only when there was a boom in public works. The efficiency of provincial self-government was often hampered by nationalist and party strife. However, even in these cases it was generally true that in the provincial committees themselves the atmosphere was constructive.

In addition to the bodies of provincial self-governance, there were also those of public administration. At the provincial level they were headed by governors and their offices oversaw county offices. Furthermore, there was also a network of provincial and county revenue offices, school boards, and other institutions.

Provincial diets were often victims of passive resistance and the policy of abstention. Thus, in the 1870s, the functioning of the Bohemian diet was complicated by the absence of the Old Czech Party – one of the two Czech parties of the time – and in the second half of the 1880s by the absence of German deputies after they lost their majority in the diet. From 1908 until its closure in the summer of 1913, the Bohemian diet was practically defunct due to obstruction.

In Moravia a political solution for the complicated relationship between Czechs and Germans was found in the Moravian Compromise of 1905. Czech politicians demanded a change to the law governing elections to the diet which would secure adequate representation of the Czech-speaking majority and also expansion of the use of Czech as a language of provincial and local self-governance. The Germans, meanwhile, wanted an arrangement that would provide them with some protection from the Czech majority.[11] After many years of disputes, an agreement was found that secured a relatively peaceful coexistence between the two ethnicities. The compromise consisted of four laws: a new provincial system of government, a new electoral law for elections to the Moravian diet, the *Lex Parma* which addressed language issues and local self-governance (each local authority could choose the language in which it would conduct business, and a minority representing 20 % or more of the populace had the right to have the business conducted in its own language); and the *Lex Perek*, which regulated education in Moravia according to the language criterion, splitting the provincial, county and local school boards between Czechs and Germans. The new electoral law introduced registers of voters according to ethnicity, ensuring a fixed number of Czech and German

---

11 At the turn of the century, Moravia consisted of 28 % German speakers and 71 % Czech speakers. Germans were not concentrated in one area, but scattered throughout the Czech population.

deputies in both the existing curias of towns and villages and the newly introduced universal curia. In the diet the deputies would be split into Czech and German curias, while the curias of the large landowners and those of the business and trade chambers remained intact. Neither Czechs nor Germans could command a clear majority in the diet and it was necessary to seek cross-curia support in order to adopt laws. The advantage of the compromise was that it allowed for stable governance and showed that agreement was possible. However, the price paid for this peace was high – the *de facto* ethnic separation of Czechs and Germans in Moravia.

To sum up the constitutional and political developments and the political system that resulted, we can use the thresholds of democratisation model developed by Stein Rokkan (1999a: 246–247). The Czech polity had to cross these thresholds on its way to modernity. The first, the threshold of legitimation, which provides the freedom to express oppositional political views, was set high. The first attempt to cross it during the revolution of 1848–1849 failed and the Czechs then had to wait until the early 1860s. This fact, together with the insufficient differentiation and the acute nature of the nationalist conflict, led to the long-term concentration of Czech political representation in a single National Party, as we shall see below. The revolution also brought a failed attempt to cross the threshold of incorporation, the introduction of universal male suffrage. The subsequent path towards the achievement of universal suffrage was based instead on the British model of gradual, evolutionary reform. The thresholds of representation (a proportional electoral system) and of executive power (a government answerable to parliament) were crossed only after the creation of the First Republic in 1918. Still, it can be argued that the essential elements of modern competitive mass democratic politics were already established before World War I. In this sense, the heritage of Cisleithania provides a key part of the explanation for the greater longevity of democracy in interwar Czechoslovakia (and in Austria where it lasted until 1934) than in most other Central European countries. However, it must be added that the political culture that became established was somewhat parochial, focussed as it was on the national struggle, and often encouraged conflict over consensus. Over the last decades of the Habsburg monarchy, this process was further complicated by socio-political differentiation and the rise of mass parties. Very much manifest in the Czech lands, this process is the subject of the next section.

1.4. Czech society, parties, and politics before World War I

A key feature of political life in Cisleithania before World War I was the growing importance of political parties, as instruments both of political struggle and of the political socialisation of citizens. To describe the specific relationship between parties and their voters in situations where the voters typically constituted relatively distinct social groups or *milieux*, the metaphors of camps or pillars are frequently used. How was such a camp- or pillar-based political culture created? In Cisleithania, the dominant political force since the 1860s was the German liberal bourgeoisie, who not only had specific political demands, but also a specific political culture. Though influenced by liberalism in the economic meaning of the term, they were from the outset characterised by relatively strong German national feeling and an elitist stance towards the further expansion of political participation. Other political parties (and the citizens they represented) had to fight for their place in the sun.

The issue of expanding the franchise in Cisleithania provides a good illustration of the rivalries that accompanied the rise of new mass political parties. The only way other groups could gain more political space for themselves was to obtain political concessions from the ruling stratum – either by protest or by acts of defiance – and such efforts took time. Political parties such as the Social Democrats, the Christian Socialists, and naturally the Czech and Moravian parties defined themselves as separate from the dominant liberal political culture, which was viewed in the Czech environment not only as a brake on upward social mobility and the political emancipation of the lower social classes (this was true of the whole of Cisleithania) but also as a political force aimed against Czech national needs. In this sense, the process by which the Czech camps or pillars established themselves was a *response* to social and political events.[12]

As already indicated, the camps and their parties served as mechanisms of political and social modernisation. The large network of activities supporting each movement ranged from explicitly political endeavours (the party and its organisation, its periodicals and other printed matter, and affiliated trade unions) to economic activities linked with the party (consumers' or producers' cooperatives) to social and apparently non-political activities that strengthened the collective experience and mentality of its supporters (gymnastics and sports

---

[12] John W. Boyer, an American historian, even argued that these camps conceived of politics as 'social aggression and ideological conquest' (Boyer 1986: 165–166).

associations, reading and educational clubs, etc.). To exaggerate slightly, a well-functioning camp offered its supporters not only political representation, but also comprehensive social integration 'from the cradle to the grave'.

In this respect, one can observe in Bohemia and Moravia similar processes to those unfolding in German-speaking countries. Nevertheless, these processes did not split society in Bohemia and Moravia into such distinct entities that would warrant the use of the concept of a pillar. Hence scholars usually speak of camps, with political Catholicism and the Social Democrats being closest to the pillar structure. Other parties that created camps were the Agrarians, the Young Czechs together with the Old Czechs (the national-liberal camp) and the National Socialists. The remaining parties did not have the same capacity to integrate citizens. The seemingly academic difference between a pillar and a camp is, nonetheless, not insignificant, and consists precisely in the degree of social, cultural and intellectual integration of these entities' members (Malíř 1996).

Originally, Czech provincial politics was concentrated into a single National Party (the so-called Old Czech Party), though multiple currents existed within it from the outset. From 1863, a radical wing began the process of becoming the Young Czech Party, which officially became independent in December 1874 (its formal name was the National Free-Thinking Party). Its programme, written by Julius Grégr, combined the values of civic liberties, historical Czech law from which it derived a claim to the political autonomy of the Czech lands, and a distinctive Central European liberalism, which allied with and sometimes subordinated itself to nationalism. The Young Czechs provided the liberal, openly anti-clerical, counterpart to the conservative-liberal Old Czechs. In terms of the social make-up of their politicians and supporters, there were no significant differences between the Young and Old Czechs. Both were parties of educated Czech bourgeoisie *(Bildungsbürgertum)*. The Young Czechs too were internally heterogeneous and further political currents gradually broke away from the party.

Though originally limited, the spectrum of parties in the Czech lands (comprising aristocratic 'parties' of large landowners, German Liberals, Old and Young Czechs, and the politically insignificant Social Democrats, whose attitude to the national question was conciliatory) started to differentiate itself from the 1890s onwards. Influenced by Leo XIII's encyclical *Rerum Novarum*, the Catholic Church changed its hitherto passive stance on modern party politics and now called for explicit political activity on the part of Catholics, who in turn created Catholic political parties and associations. Thus, the Czech

Catholic camp came into being. In 1894 the Christian-Social Party for Bohemia and Moravia was founded, and in 1896 Mořic Hruban established the Catholic National Party in Moravia. In autumn 1896, the Archbishop-Count Adalbert Josef Schönborn founded the conservative Catholic Association in Bohemia, which in 1897 became the National Catholic Party in the Kingdom of Bohemia. Factionalism was typical of the Catholic camp, as was a certain differentiation between political Catholicism in Bohemia and Moravia (Fiala 1995: 186–191). The supporters of the 'clerical' parties, as they were also called at the time, hailed from various social strata, both urban and rural. What they shared was their religious feeling, stronger than the norm in the majority of the population, and the fact that they were socialised within the Catholic Church and the associations linked with it.

The first step towards the establishment of the agrarian camp was taken by Alfons Šťastný, who in 1891 founded the Bohemian-Moravian Agricultural Party. Šťastný's radical agrarianism was not, however, very successful, and it took the birth of the Association of Czech Farmers (from 1899 the independent Agrarian Party) to represent the interests of peasants and Czech agricultural businessmen and make agrarianism a relevant political force.

As far as the nationalist current of opinion was concerned, in February 1898 the Radical Constitutional Party emerged from the wreckage of the radical nationalist progressive movement, specifically as a continuation of its strongly anti-socialist faction. Originally, the Radicals emerged from the Young Czech Party. This Radical Party was unique in rejecting the idea that Czech statehood could only be implemented within the framework of the Habsburg monarchy. There were also other small, politically insignificant parties. The Czech People's Party was significant as the home of Tomáš Garrigue Masaryk, later the Czechoslovak president. During World War I and shortly thereafter, most of these small, conservative, liberal and nationalist parties merged with the National Democracy Party.

In April 1898 the National Socialist Party was founded for the territories of Bohemia, Moravia, Silesia and Upper and Lower Austria. It sought to combine non-Marxist socialism with radical Czech nationalism. Workers, however, tended to prefer the Social Democrats, whose camp was the strongest, particularly in Bohemia. The Czechoslovak Social Democratic Workers' Party was founded in 1878. The initial rupture between the so-called revisionists and revolutionaries was largely healed at its conference in Brno in 1880, but in the following year an anarchist wing split away. The Czech Social Democratic Party was the second largest and most important political party in

Cisleithania. In December 1887 it adopted a new programme and, following a rift, re-joined the all-Austrian party. In 1910 the Czech Social Democratic Party suffered a schism over the national question, and at its congress in Brno in May 1911, the Czech Social Democratic Workers' Party in Austria (the so-called autonomists) broke away and managed to take control of the Czech social democratic movement.

In Moravia, Czech party politics up to 1890 had been limited to the National Party in Moravia (the Old Czechs), which, however, was internally divided into multiple factions (conservative, liberal, farmers, and Catholic). In 1891 the Young Czechs in Moravia founded the Moravian People's Party, which was able to cooperate with the Moravian Old Czechs better than their counterparts in Bohemia. The emancipation of Catholic parties has already been discussed above in connection with Bohemia. It needs to be added that the influential Catholic politician Jan Šrámek was able to build a mass party, and the Catholic camp was clearly the strongest in Moravia for a long time. Social Democrats also built a mass party in Moravia. In 1904 the Agrarian Party became fully independent, and by 1910 it managed to build up a mass membership. The position of the National Social Party in Moravia was much weaker than in Bohemia. After 1905 the Moravian progressives also became organisationally independent. Compared to Bohemia, Moravia was distinctive due to the relatively strong position of the Tradesmen's Party, established in Přerov in 1908 to represent tradesmen and small businesses.

The elections to the Imperial Council in 1907 and 1911, held under universal male suffrage, revealed the degree of public support for the individual parties. In the Czech lands the strongest parties were the Social Democrats (in Bohemia), the clericals (in Moravia) and the agrarians (strong in both lands); the National Socialists and Young Czechs were also relevant. Other parties were either not represented in the Imperial Council at all or had only one deputy.

To sum up, the evolution of party-political life in the Czech lands before World War I was diverse and complex. Multiple party systems were established, divided along provincial (Bohemia, Moravia, Silesia) and national (Czech, German and, in Silesia, also Polish) lines. There was coordination between Czech and German parties in Bohemia and Moravia, and some parties, especially the Social Democrats and the National Socialists, reached across the boundaries of the historical lands. Nonetheless, political life before 1914 can be described as very differentiated, a feature that was to some extent replicated in the political culture of the First Czechoslovak Republic. The concept of cleavage, developed by Stein Rokkan (1999a and 1999b) to describe the situation in Western Europe, can also be applied to the pre-WWI Czech party system. The cleavages in this case included those of owners vs. workers (on which the Social Democrats and National Socialists established themselves), urban vs. rural (the Agrarian Party) and church vs. state (the clerical parties). The centre vs. periphery cleavage was overarching, as it united all Czech parties (with the exception of the minority wing of the internationalist Social Democrats) in their struggle to have Czech national demands fulfilled. However, except for the Constitutional Radicals, all Czech parties took the existence of the Habsburg monarchy as a given in their plans for Czech statehood. With the exception of the exile of Masaryk and Beneš, the domestic political elite were until late 1917 unwilling to abandon the idea of winning autonomy within Austria-Hungary.

1.5. Czech society in the context of Central Europe

From 1850 to the start of WWI, Czech society witnessed a number of remarkable developments, which are particularly conspicuous when compared to those in other Central European locations. Unlike in Transleithania, Russia, or the Ottoman Empire, Cisleithania experienced a true, though rudimentary, democratisation, a modernisation of public administration, and a liberalisation of economic life. Compared to other nations, the Czechs managed to create a complete social structure (which, however, lacked a native aristocracy), including political, economic, and cultural elites. Political party life was also developing, but was limited by two factors. First, liberalism was subordinated to a nationalist policy. This had the consequence that those political institutions that protected minority opinions were underdeveloped. National unity was taken as a priority, and this made Central European democracy less mature and more vulnerable than in most countries of Western Europe. Second, national strife and the acute nature of the centre vs. periphery cleavage polarised public opinion and political elites alike. This ultimately subjected the quality of politics to nationalist rivalries, even if that meant sacrificing liberal-democratic values. Despite the remarkable achievements of interwar Czechoslovakia in building its political institutions, the combination of these two tendencies ultimately left its mark in the demise of interwar Czechoslovak democracy and the sequence of non-democratic regimes that followed.

2. Politics in interwar Czechoslovakia

Jan Holzer

With the official proclamation of the independent Czechoslovak Republic on 28 October 1918 (*Republika československá*, RČS), Czech politics achieved a goal which it had been focussed on for more than half a century: its own sovereign, internationally recognised state. This achievement was dependent on the demise of the Austro-Hungarian Empire which, in one possible interpretation, was merely an obscurantist medieval relic in the European political system. In this interpretation, the creation of Czechoslovakia confirmed the arrival of a hoped-for age of progress. In another interpretation, the Empire was a difficult to replace stabilising element whose importance stretched beyond Central Europe. In this interpretation, the creation of Czechoslovakia signalled the arrival of an era of turbulence. Both interpretations have some validity.

In any case, RČS, or the First Republic, as it was later called, was granted only two decades of existence (from October 1918 to September 1938).[1] That is much less than Tomáš Garrigue Masaryk, its Founder and President-Liberator, had dreamt of. These were two decades of political disputes, party wrangling, nationalist friction, social conflict and, ultimately, an increasing feeling of helplessness in the face of the dramatic international developments in the second half of the 1930s. And yet, despite all this, the First Republic produced the myth of a golden age for the Czech nation, a myth that has survived all the non-democratic regimes that followed. What was and continues to be the source of this myth? Was it the achievement of historical justice – that the First Republic was culturally and linguistically *Czech,* and hence *national* and *ours* (and not Habsburg or German)? Or was the source in its politics – that the First Republic was *democratic* and *liberal* (and not authoritarian or totalitarian, Nazi or communist)? Whatever the case, the figure of Tomáš Garrigue Masaryk is, without a doubt, the key that unlocks our understanding of the First Republic.

---

1 For detailed accounts of the whole period, see Kárník (2000, 2002 and 2003) or Olivová (2000).

2.1. The idea of the Czechoslovak state

T. G. Masaryk's conception of the so-called 'Czech question' as a practical problem demanding concrete political action was his undisputable contribution to modern Czech history. This insight, delivered on the cusp of World War I, was preceded by years during which Masaryk, a university professor, presented himself more as a classic academic than as a politician. He had enjoyed a privileged position in what was called the dispute about the meaning of Czech history (Havelka 1995 and 2006), a set of philosophical, historical, sociological and theological arguments and discussions focussed on the modern existence of the Czech nation, the renewal of its statehood and the position of Czechs in Europe. This dispute provided an alternative arena in which the Czech polity could constitute itself, since, in the opinion of its elites, Czech politics was not afforded adequate space within Austrian politics. Masaryk both received and landed many blows in this debate.[2] Above all, he formulated the opinion that the story of Czech politics was not inevitable, that, moreover, it was uncertain whether it was (and would be in the future) the story of the *Czech nation*, and whether it would be a fully-fledged *political* story, i.e., the story of a *Czech state*. In addition to producing his own theory of the Czech question,[3] Masaryk won recognition as a deputy in the *Reichsrat* in Vienna (without, however, obtaining political power that he could potentially leverage) and ultimately, at the threshold of the war, decided to go into exile with the aim of convincing Western elites about the viability of the project of a Czech/Czechoslovak state.

It is remarkable how Masaryk's notion of the Czech question, conceived at the outset as a purely academic project, translated itself into the specific political construction of the First Republic, its institutions and officially declared mentality. In other words, it is appropriate in the Czechoslovak case to speak about a specific *idea of the state*. It is, however, also indisputable that this was a normative conception and one which in its characteristics was exclusive and selective. Each of the individual traits of Masaryk's doctrine of the state created tensions and conflicts. What, then, were these traits?

---

2 A canonical part of Masaryk's attitude towards modern Czechness was his critical distance from the prevailing opinion in such cases as the dispute over the genuineness of the manuscripts of Dvůr Králové and Zelená Hora and the anti-Semitic campaign connected with the alleged ritual murder of Anna Hrůzová (Soubigou 2004).
3 See Masaryk's book of the same name: *Česká otázka* (Masaryk 1894).

The first characteristic of the Czechoslovak state, the republican idea,[4] was the cornerstone of Masaryk's project. Its practical implementation was dependent on the disintegration of Austria-Hungary, which was to demonstrate the final end of an era dominated by traditional, multinational monarchies. By contrast, new and established nation states were to symbolise the triumph of the progressive doctrine of national liberalism. They appeared as natural constituents of a new world order. They seemed predestined to realise the contemporary political, civic and nationalist calls for democracy. Masaryk's philosophy of Czech history thus brought together the particularistic claim for national emancipation with the universal ideal of a world revolution. Indeed, the Czechs were to be, in the spirit of their own renowned Hussite reformation tradition (Malia 2006: 37–59), the bearers of universal (or at least European) values of humanity and democracy.[5]

The wave of nation-state construction was, therefore, to provide the proof that there was a space in which a modern political vision could be realised, one that negated as many of the characteristics of the Habsburg era as possible. Before 1914 the idea of a nation state was first and foremost articulated by the Czech national-liberal camp, whose elites were responsible for the construction of the Czechoslovak state immediately after it was declared.

There was, however, another potentially powerful political camp which laid claim to a role in this national-republican political work: Czech socialism, represented by the Czechoslovak Social Democratic Workers' Party (ČSDSD). ČSDSD was divided between a reform wing, which accepted the priority of the national emancipation process, and a radical wing, which insisted on a Marxist, internationalist interpretation of socialist doctrine. The reform wing of ČSDSD became one of the foundational parties in the new republic and participated in government coalitions whose common denominator was their willingness to respect the Masarykian idea as the embodiment of Czechoslovak democracy. The radical wing, by contrast, understood the establishment of the First Republic as a necessary yet intermediate step, that is, as the culmination of a *bourgeois* revolution, after which the socialist camp should proceed to realise a *socialist* revolution, the transition from a capitalist socio-economic

---

4 The concept of 'republicanism' must be understood here as expressing the distinction between a republic and a monarchy. Thus, republicanism could be, but was not necessarily, democratic, as it could have been spearheaded by aristocratic elites. In the Czech case, republicanism was primarily a programmatic expression of political distance from Vienna and the Habsburg monarchy.

5 Jan Patočka called it 'elementary democratism', Karel Kosík 'plebeian democratism'.

formation to a classless one. Their slogan – 'Without the Great October Socialist Revolution, there would be no independent Czechoslovakia' – reveals where they found inspiration.

This dispute came to a logical conclusion in autumn and winter 1920, in a clash, which was the first turning point in the history of the First Republic. It is usually described as the 'battle for the People's House' (*boj o Lidový dům*), but from the perspective of European history the designations 'battle for the Czech Soviet Republic' or 'battle for the Czech Republic of Soviets' would be more exact, as this was the Czech equivalent of the efforts of the young Soviet Union to install Soviet republics in Central Europe (for example, in Hungary, Slovakia and Germany). The course of events in Czechoslovakia was relatively banal and the conflict less dramatic than in other countries, as the capacity and decisiveness of the Czechoslovak Republic's elites proved much greater than the radical left had expected. However, the effects of this clash were far-reaching and systemic: in May 1921, the radical wing split off from ČSDSD and founded the Communist Party of Czechoslovakia, which was to become one of the most successful communist parties in Europe and a strong anti-system actor on the political stage of the First Republic (Fiala, Holzer, Mareš and Pšeja 1999).

In consequence, ČSDSD became a small party able to win at most ten percent of the vote in elections, but one that strongly supported the republican substance of Czechoslovak statehood. Four (and later five) parties claimed allegiance to this substance: besides ČSDSD, the Czech National Socialist Party (ČSNS), the liberal National Democratic party and the Republican Party of Smallholders, popularly known as the Agrarians. When, later, the Catholic camp represented by the Czechoslovak People's Party (ČSL) joined them (see below for the chain of events), the Republic and the idea of republicanism obtained a devoted base on which the First Republic would stand politically for its duration. The electoral potential of this base, however, had its limits: in order to be able to produce the key condition of a democratic model, a parliamentary majority, it had to sacrifice ideological coherence.

2.1.1. Parliamentary democracy

In Masaryk's conception, the republican idea went hand in hand with the ideology of democracy. Masaryk believed that the Czech nation was predetermined to be a historical bearer of democracy, which would not only serve as a counter to authoritarian reaction, but would represent a moral order standing above politics and encompassing society as a whole. Precisely in this sense, then, Masaryk believed that if the new Czechoslovak state were to have a future, Czechoslovak society would have to develop democratic values. Paradoxically, the initial political debate about the form the state would take – the form that was to embody these values – was, in the end, entirely pragmatic, based on self-interested wrangling over the powers given to the various state authorities and the relations between them.

How, then, did the Czechoslovak democratic regime look? A parliamentary democracy was adopted because the presidential model seemed to the elites of the time to be potentially undemocratic, as it was in theoretical contrast with the desire to give all power to the people. Masaryk preferred a strong presidency along the lines of the US model, with the president as the head of the executive, and indeed this conception won its way elsewhere in Central Europe.[6] That is why, having returned home from exile in December 1918, Masaryk criticised the interim constitution which limited the powers of the president (who required the countersignature of the responsible member of the government) and insisted that the powers of the president be strengthened, especially vis-a-vis the government. This he achieved through a constitutional amendment that allowed him to appoint and remove the government and its individual ministers.[7] The amendment also broadened the president's ties with the government by giving him the option to participate in government meetings, to chair these meetings (but not to vote), and to be in contact with individual ministers.

The constitution of February 1920, which codified the constitutional model of the First Republic, nevertheless ultimately respected the established practices of a parliamentary system in its definition of the position of the president. Though the president appointed the government, the government was accountable to the Chamber of Deputies which could vote no-confidence in the government, and most executive power was given to the government. The only unusual aspect of the constitution was an article that explicitly excluded Masaryk from the limitation that no individual may be president for more than two consecutive terms.

---

6 The Weimar constitution in Germany gave the Reich president extraordinary powers. In Austria's and Poland's constitutional systems efforts to strengthen the position of the president were frequent, and in Hungary the monarchy in fact lasted until November 1921 (with a vacant throne and a regent).

7 This power was originally given to the Chamber of Deputies, the lower chamber of parliament (called the National Assembly).

In sum, T. G. Masaryk could not realise his vision of the president's role within the constitutional system. Hence, he had to look for less obvious methods and procedures, and the other actors within Czechoslovak politics quickly accommodated themselves to his approach. This situation corresponds to the conviction widely held by political scientists that the text of the constitution rarely provides sufficient information for a full understanding of the political system in question. It was no different with the First Republic.

2.1.2. Anti-Catholicism

The third component in the idea of the new Czechoslovak state was anti-Catholicism, a trait that naturally followed from Masaryk's framing of a new Europe in terms of progress and tolerance, which he pitted against the Catholic traditionalism of the old Europe. Masaryk's 'idealist-teleological' conception of Czech history owed much to the philosophy of the 'Father of the Nation', the historian František Palacký, and found inspiration in the Hussite movement and the Unity of the Brethren, represented by figures such as Petr Chelčický and Jan Amos Comenius. This was not a secularised, anti-Christian doctrine. Masaryk's conception of brotherhood brought together national and Christian dimensions and was, above all, strongly anti-institutional, critical of the close connection between the Catholic Church and the House of Habsburg-Lorraine.

This was one of the most contentious of Masaryk's arguments, and one that was subject to much criticism both scholarly and political during the Austrian era. Historians reproached Masaryk for his discontinuous and selective reading of Czech history and his obviously political motives. The Catholics, meanwhile, simply presented the reverse view: Hussitism was an era of decline. Czech history peaked with the Holy Roman Emperor, King Charles IV of Bohemia; and its heroes were the Czech saints, St Wenceslaus and St Adalbert of Prague.[8]

Here the special position of the Catholic Church in the interwar Czech lands deserves attention. In 1921 82.0 % of the inhabitants of the Czech lands professed to be Roman Catholics, 5.2 % claimed allegiance to the second

---

8 There was another type of criticism, one that questioned the necessity of a grand historical narrative. Instead, it advocated the tradition of 'small Czech history', which relied on ordinary people and their non-heroic tenacity. Even this attitude produced a reaction: it was attacked for philistinism, indolence, čecháčkovství (a term based on a pejorative diminutive of 'Czech', with connotations of a petty-minded outlook), provinciality, even defeatism – allegedly typical products of the Habsburg era.

largest church, the Czechoslovak (later Hussite) Church, 2.3 % to the Evangelical Church of Czech Brethren, and 7.2 % indicated 'no religion'. The atmosphere of the time encouraged people to leave the Catholic Church: by 1930 only 78.5 % of the population claimed to be Catholics, 7.3 % were members of the Czechoslovak Church, 2.7 % claimed allegiance to the Evangelical Church, and 7.8 % indicated 'no religion'. Furthermore, even Catholic priests understood that the number of unbelievers was impossible to determine accurately and that not all of those recorded in parish registers were truly believers.

Today the Czech Republic is the most secularised European country with the lowest proportion of inhabitants professing to believe in God in general, as is apparent not only from the censuses cited but also from Europe-wide surveys of values (e.g., the Eurobarometer Poll 2010, according to which 16 % of the population in the Czech Republic explicitly believed in God in 2010, the lowest figure from all EU countries; *Special Eurobarometer, biotechnology* 2010: 204). The explanation often given by observers from both outside and inside Czech society is the influence of the communist past. Yet a glance at the realities of the First Republic (and also the preceding era) shows that modern secularism is the consequence of the specific character of Czech anti-clericalism in the second half of the nineteenth and the first half of the twentieth century (Balík et al. 2015).

Initially, the new elites of the First Republic simply did not count on any significant involvement by the Czech Catholics within the new nation. However, this perspective soon proved to be too restrictive. Electoral support for the doctrine of political Catholicism, represented by the ČSL and amounting to about 10 per cent of the vote, was too precious to be driven away from the national camp. Nevertheless, it took several years before the elites of ČSL managed to embed themselves firmly in the politics of the First Republic. Credit here is due to the party chair Jan Šrámek who agreed to drop his demand for ending the separation of church and state. Nevertheless, the Catholic camp was never able to win Masaryk's trust.

2.1.3 Czechoslovakism

The last characteristic trait of the Czechoslovak state was the doctrine of *Czechoslovakism* which saw Czechs and Slovaks as a single people. Unlike republicanism and democracy, which corresponded to general trends in European politics, this was a specifically Czech stratagem. It had been almost absent from Czech politics in the Habsburg era. This is not to say that the topic of Czech and Slovak mutuality had not previously existed; but it did not extend to the vision of a common state. Previous constitutional arguments referred exclusively to the rights of the *Czech* state, rooted in its distinctive history.

During his World War I exile, Masaryk found himself in an unenviable situation. His efforts to convince Western elites of the advantages stemming from the disintegration of Austria-Hungary and its replacement by nation-states collided with the reality of Central European nationalities. Ethno-political data suggested that in terms of national variety, the new Czechoslovak nation would merely be a replica of the Habsburg Empire. This complicated Masaryk's negotiating position in which Viennese oppression of the Czechs was a major argument. Thus, the artificial construct of a Czechoslovak nation – a political myth *par excellence* – was born. Its main advantage was that it created a convincing Czechoslovak national majority as opposed to a minority of Czechs ruling over ethnicities.

Though originally a pragmatic manoeuvre, at the point when the independent state was founded, Czechoslovak fervour began to be transformed into a veritable ism. That is, it became a political doctrine that transformed the fiction of a single (Czechoslovak) nation into a legal doctrine, confirmed by the February 1920 constitution and not subject to discussion.[9] The new state began to conceive of itself as an exclusive arena from which non-Slavic ethnicities, especially Germans and Hungarians, were excluded. The irredentist movements of these two groups, which Czechoslovakia had to overcome in the first years of its existence, exacerbated the situation. However, parts of the Slovak polity also had a problem with the myth, as they simply did not wish to become Czechoslovaks.

The doctrine of Czechoslovakism was a problematic trait of the First Republic, one that illustrated the limits of political loyalty to the idea of the Czechoslovak state. This led to the classic political problem, the conflict between ideals and the actual practice of governance.

---

9   See the preamble to the constitution: 'We, the Czechoslovak nation...' and its article 129 that stipulates the fundamentals of linguistic rights: 'The Czechoslovak language is the official state language of the republic...'

2.2. Governance in the First Republic

It makes sense to base a commentary of the First Republic's politics on a comparison with the realities of other interwar European political regimes. On the one hand, Czechoslovak democracy resisted until the mid-1930s the temptations of authoritarian rule (see Chapter 3) to which many of its neighbours succumbed. On the other, it exhibited a number of problematic tendencies throughout its existence. Indeed, the cumbersome governance model of the First Republic, which represents an underexplored topic in political science and particularly political theory, paradoxically contributed to the survival of the Czechoslovak democracy, as it blocked the rise of any non-democratic political actor who might seek to seize power. Such actors were nevertheless present on the Czechoslovak political scene, and as there were no relevant proponents of a monarchical restoration,[10] the actors who desired a transformation into totalitarianism were gradually to become the most dangerous opponents of the regime.

2.2.1. Coalition governance and anti-system opposition

The preceding sections indicated that there were five relevant political parties in Czechoslovak politics after 1918. The Agrarians, the Social Democrats, the National Socialists, the People's Party and the National Democrats constituted the backbone of the First Republic's political system. They represented the crucial social strata, especially of Czech, but also partially of Slovak, society: farmers, the working class including its various subgroups, Catholics, and tradesmen. The generally low level of social stratification aided the cohesion of the Czech polity, which furthermore felt the need to define itself in opposition to national minorities and their political representatives. The political ideologies or doctrines for which the parties were vehicles (rural conservatism, reform Marxism, nationally-oriented socialism, Catholic conservatism, and liberal nationalism) were not employed rigidly in practical politics and permitted the creation of coalitions. The electoral system, whose electoral formula and lack of a threshold maximised the principle of

---

10 Consider the minimal role played by the aristocracy in the building of the Czech polity in the second half of the nineteenth century and the lack of any connections whatsoever between the ancien regime and the army of the First Republic, which was built after 1918 without a significant reliance on the Austrian past.

proportionality (Balík et al. 2003: 55–56), contributed to the large number of parties present in parliament. In 1920, 1925 and 1929 there were 16 parties in the Chamber of Deputies and in 1935 14 parties. Altogether these factors led to a rigid political system and to pressure on those actors not included in the 'Czechoslovak' project to radicalise.

Four models of coalition government can be identified during the two decades of the First Republic: (1) an all-national grand coalition (for example the very first government led by Karel Kramář from November 1918 to July 1919), which is typical for an embryonic post-revolutionary stage; (2) a red-green coalition between socialist parties and the Agrarian party (two governments led by Vlastimil Tusar in 1919 and 1920); (3) a civic (also called gentlemen's) coalition (*panská koalice*) between right-wing parties, such as that led by Antonín Švehla from October 1926 to February 1929; and (4) a broad (concentration) coalition, starting with František Udržal's government from December 1929 to October 1932. Indeed, this was the only type of government that could have been formed after 1929.

Out of these coalition models there was only one, the so-called gentlemen's coalition, which had a distinct position on the left-right axis. In this case, several traditional government parties – specifically, the Agrarians, the National Democrats and the People's party – decided in 1926 to govern without the socialist parties. These were replaced in government by the German Christian Socials and the German Agrarians alongside a key Slovak political representative, Hlinka's Slovak People's Party (HSĽS). For the first (and last) time, a government was formed not on the basis of loyalty to the idea of the Czechoslovak state as defined above – an idea defended, unsurprisingly, only by Czech/Czechoslovak parties – but on the basis of proximity of ideologies and programmes.[11] This 'right-wing' government, associated with the only real opponent to President T. G. Masaryk, the Agrarian Antonín Švehla, was not a particularly successful one (Dostál 1989, Miller 2001). Despite that, it was a political revelation, as it was a manifestation of the efforts to enlarge the support base of Czechoslovak politics by including non-Czech parties. This meant that the socialist parties (ČSDSD and ČSNS), although loyal to the state and its system of government, were in political opposition. Yet it also involved a revolt against the original idea of the Czechoslovak state.

---

11 Some parties established themselves as Czechoslovak, i.e., they constructed their organisational network in both the Czech and the Slovak section of RČS.

Masaryk's narrowly-conceived construct of the Czechoslovak state prevented the emergence of a loyal opposition that would be able to alternate with the existing government without jeopardising the regime. The First Republic produced no fewer than two parties which commanded a significant share of votes, but whose programmes entirely negated the idea of the First Republic. The Communist Party of Czechoslovakia (KSČ) came second in the 1925 parliamentary elections with 13.2 % of the vote, and the Sudetendeutsche Partei (SdP) won the 1935 elections with 15.2 %. KSČ represented ideological anti-system opposition. It was the vehicle of an internationalist doctrine disloyal to a bourgeois republic (Rupnik 2002). SdP represented an ethnic anti-system opposition. It preferred a nationalist doctrine disloyal to a republic based on Czechoslovakism.

In any case, the duration of the gentlemen's coalition was short and the Czechoslovak consensus was soon renewed, which testified to the rigidity of the interwar Czechoslovak political system. Free and pluralistic elections were held in the system and were contested by actors operating in an open political field.[12] However, following elections, similar coalitions were always formed, not so much despite but rather irrespective of the results of elections. Opposition pressure did not lead to government alternation. As a result, the system became increasingly rigid in terms of personnel, ideologies, and party programmes. Some ministries became party fiefdoms. Furthermore, the leaders of the five parties loyal to the Czechoslovak idea established the so-called *Pětka* (the Five), an association without grounding in the constitution whose purpose was to pre-negotiate compromises ahead of parliamentary discussion. The parliament then essentially served only as an arena in which the declaration of this consensus was voiced. This meant that other political actors in the First Republic were not afforded space in which to articulate their objections, which soon led to criticisms that Czechoslovak politics was carried out in private and increased disillusion with the performance of the political elites. In Europe as a whole, similar tendencies led to the emergence of a variety of non-democratic regimes both totalitarian and authoritarian. Czechoslovak politics, by contrast, resisted such temptations for a surprisingly long time.[13]

---

12 Excepting the 1920 parliamentary election in which non-Slavic parties could not yet take part.
13 Surprisingly, there has not been a sustained discussion about the causes of the vitality of Czechoslovak interwar democracy including comparisons with other contemporary Central European countries. This chapter points out some of the limits of Czechoslovak democratic governance; yet it is evident that the traditionally authoritarian actors (the army, aristocracy, and large landowners) held little power in the First Republic (with the partial exception of large

2.2.2. Caretaker governments and the critique of political partisanship

The first of what were called caretaker governments *(úřednické vlády)* was appointed in September 1920 after the so-called red-green coalition fell apart. It relied on the parties of the former all-national coalition plus the Tradesmen's Party. Thus, in the very first years of the First Republic, another remarkable phenomenon was introduced into its political system, and one that was to accompany it until its demise.

Caretaker governments are typically formed to govern in situations of crisis. In the First Republic, they also reflected the parties' mistaken belief that they could avoid responsibility for certain unpopular measures and once these were adopted revert back to coalition government. This was true of the first caretaker government, which steered the ship of state through the dramatic events of late 1920 and the unsuccessful attempt on the part of the revolutionary-left wing of the Social Democrats to unleash a revolution that would lead to the Bolshevisation of Czechoslovakia. The second caretaker government (from March to October 1926, with J. Černý again as the prime minister) opened the space for the formation of the gentlemen's coalition in October 1926. The caretaker-technocratic government of Jan Syrový during the Munich crisis (22 September to 4 October 1938) was obviously connected with the political crisis created by the Munich Agreement and the end of the First Republic.[14]

In the politics of interwar Czechoslovakia, a caretaker government represented a means of establishing a wider consensus in politically complicated times. To what extent it met the standards of interwar democracy continues to be intensely debated to this day (Hloušek and Kopeček 2013: 40–43). These caretaker governments were not unconstitutional. They were, however, a phenomenon at variance with the spirit of parliamentarianism as expressed in the February 1920 constitution.

---

landowners who were represented by the Agrarian Party). The temptations of totalitarianism were to prove the crucial challenge to Czechoslovak democracy.

14 The post-Munich cabinet was not fully technocratic, involving as it did four political ministers without portfolio along with Jozef Tiso, the minister responsible for administering Slovakia, who acted as the Slovak government, and Andrej Bródy, the minister for administering Carpathian Ruthenia, who acted as the government of the latter. Thus, there were, on the one side, Czech technocrats and, on the other, Slovak and Carpathian-Ruthenian politicians. See Hloušek and Kopeček (2012: 40–43).

The caretaker governments also demonstrate another typical feature of the Czechoslovak political system: they strengthened the position of the president who appointed them.[15] Thus, they served to resolve conflicts between the president on the one hand and parties on the other, as the solution preferred by the president was typically adopted. Although even these governments depended on the support of the Chamber of Deputies, their activities were only subject to limited control; this strengthened the bureaucracy. Hence they were not only a practical instrument for crisis resolution, they were also an expression of mistrust in partisanship and in the functionality of the classic model in which parties/coalitions alternate in power.

This brings us to the theme of traditional Czech scepticism of partisanship. Criticism of political parties and their leaders was typical of the First Republic. These debates cast a long shadow over the Second Republic and the post-war Third Republic, both of which limited party pluralism. The understanding that, in a plural society, partisanship is essential had always clashed in the interwar era with a unifying, defensive conception of modern Czech politics. Czech politics had always had a fundamental point of departure, which was beyond discussion. In the nineteenth century, it was the theme of nation-building and the search for what was referred to as the Czech nation's just place within the Austrian monarchy. During the First Republic, a positive attitude towards independence was considered incontestable.[16] Yet the phenomenon of political partisanship seemed opposed to all of this and aroused fears that a truly *partisan* political system would be realised, in which everyone took sides, i.e., favoured the interests of a 'mere' part of society and its 'particular' interests.

The chief representative of the partisan conception was the Agrarian Party, whose doctrine of farmers' conservatism represented a significant segment of the Czech electorate. Although he was a difficult-to-replace (and essentially willing) participant in most governing coalitions, the long-standing chair of the Agrarians, Antonín Švehla, sought to establish his party as a classic political actor, one that preferred competition, conflict, and the defence of its own interests. The potential of this conception, but also its limits, were shown in the gentlemen's coalition. Yet during the second half of the 1930s, the Agrarian

---

15 A vote of no confidence in the government (which was unusual in the First Republic) meant the government handed in its resignation to the president, who then appointed an administrator of governmental affairs until a new government was appointed.
16 The obligation of loyalty on the part of actors in Czech/Czechoslovak politics was reinterpreted in an existential/defensive vein during the Protectorate and in a class-struggle/Marxist vein during the communist era.

Party started to manifest tendencies inspired by more authoritarian models of governance.

2.2.3. The Castle

Politics in the First Republic was not entirely dominated by political parties. They found a strong adversary in President Masaryk, whose view of 'how to do politics' can be described as another limit on governance. From the early 1920s, the president saw both international and domestic threats as warranting his use of methods that – under the banner of stabilising the situation – exceeded his legal authority and defied the opinions of other actors. Masaryk certainly did not suffer from excessive faith in parties and preferred a select group of elites. He sought to appoint non-partisans as prime ministers, endeavoured to push his allies into ministerial positions, and repeatedly advocated the use of state secretaries – that is, departmental experts working alongside ministers serving as 'political' chiefs.

Masaryk understood that he needed political backing for the promotion of his political interests. Hence the notion of *the Castle* (Hrad) came into use in the early 1920s, a concept first rejected but later used by Masaryk. On a practical level, the Castle was an attempt to create a real counterpart to the party-based Pětka by putting together a circle of public figures who shared Masaryk's idea of the state. These figures comprised his collaborators from exile, often employed in the presidential office, representatives of 'pro-Castle' factions in individual parties, and certain artists (Karel Čapek) and public intellectuals. However, the Castle also had links with socialist trade unions, a number of voluntary associations (the Association of Czechoslovak Legionnaires, the Teachers' Union, Sokol [a sports and gymnastics association], the Slovak Institute, the Oriental Institute, and the Brentano society), non-Catholic churches, financial institutions (e.g., Legionbanka), and the media.

The Castle was essentially an independent element in the politics of the First Republic and one that aspired to become a symbol of the Czechoslovak Republic's idea of the state. The Castle changed its priorities over time in line with this aspiration. Whereas in the 1920s it focussed on domestic conflict with party-political elites, during the 1930s it concentrated on issues connected with Czechoslovakia's position in Europe. It consistently implemented a classic realpolitik strategy, influencing day-to-day political developments, contributing newspaper articles under pseudonymous by-lines, denouncing its opponents and funding its allies. Paradoxically, Masaryk enjoyed the aura of a 'good dictator', an uncritically admired, even deified, ruler (consider the epithets 'demokratický vladař' [democratic prince], 'milovaný vládce' [beloved sovereign], 'tatíček' [Daddy], which were regularly bestowed upon him), which led to criticisms of a monarchist cult of Masaryk and comparison with Franz Josef I (Ferdinand Seibt). Masaryk's indisputably controversial personality was manifest both in the domain of ideas and in practical politics. This was to be demonstrated in what was called the 'Battle for the Castle' after T. G. Masaryk's resignation, a battle that fundamentally transformed Czechoslovak politics (Klimek 1996 and 1998).

2.2.4. The cultural front

The Castle thus represented two important tendencies in Czech political thought: scepticism towards partisanship and political power more generally and a demand that politics be ethical.

What were the origins of this specifically Czech notion of politics, which was later called *non-political?* An explanation can be found in the relationship that Czech society had with culture which provided the environment where the Czech nation constituted itself. The escape to language and culture was a defence mechanism against the pressures of the German population and the Austrian state.[17] As the initiator and vehicle of nineteenth-century national revival, the cultural elite occupied a privileged position. The situation was made easier for them by the fact that they faced little competition. Czech society in the second half of the nineteenth century was unsympathetic to the idea of including aristocratic circles in the Czech national project and,[18] a few exceptions aside, ethnic Czechs lacked career opportunities in the military, diplomacy, or public administration. One does not need to agree completely with the thesis that the Czech character is plebeian.[19] But it is obvious that Czech society as it developed was largely middle-class, involving both urban and rural elements, with writers and tradesmen as typical representatives of its

---

17 Culture later served as a sort of asylum from absolutist rulers (the Nazis and the Communists), as even these powers were not able to exercise total control in the cultural domain.

18 On the theme of possible alternative projects for constructing the polity in the Czech lands, see Kořalka (1996: 90–137) and Řepa (2001).

19 This argument is developed in the polemical essay, *Češi v dějinách nové doby – pokus o zrcadlo,* written by Milan Otáhal, Petr Pithart, and Petr Příhoda and published as Podiven (1991).

elites. These archetypes produced the view of politics prevailing in Czech society, which brought together elements of idealism (what Raymond Aron called the 'extremes of retrospection and utopia') and provincial practical realism. It is among these values that one should seek the development of Czech political thinking and practice.

The conception of politics as described here suited the Czech Marxist left which, since its origins in the 1870s, understood politics as a sphere of ideological conflict – but at the end of this conflict an ideal society without conflict would emerge. The strong position which the Communist Party of Czechoslovakia won in the 1920s was therefore not a sudden historical swing. It expressed the potential of the left in Czech politics generally, a potential that was intertwined with the prevailing left-wing opinions of cultural and media elites. This gave birth to an intellectually canonical view of the public sphere – one that is still valid in Czech society – which linked the only possible democratic politics with the left. It was one of the enduring myths of the First Republic.

2.3. The political crisis of the First Republic

2.3.1. 'Strong democracy'

The conception of politics described in the preceding section was systemically reflected in the model of governance. This occurred in connection with the presidential election of 1935, which can be described – alongside the struggle for the People's House and the gentlemen's coalition – as the third crucial point in the history of Czech politics during the First Republic.

The election was preceded by efforts on the part of Czechoslovak elites to respond to domestic and foreign developments during the first half of the 1930s. It seemed necessary to take action against German and Hungarian irredentism and against the excesses committed by the Communists (especially in parliament) and the fascists (the so-called Kobzinek putsch in Brno-Židenice in January 1933). A secondary motivation was the contemporary economic crisis. The political response was to strengthen the power of the state and limit parliamentarianism, leading to a state of affairs that has been described as *strong democracy* (Broklová 1992; Heumos 1995: 136–139). In June 1933, parliament adopted an act that gave the government extraordinary powers,[20] and this was followed by acts regulating the legal status of political parties,[21] a press act, an extraordinary measures act, an amendment to the act protecting the republic, an act on the prosecution of subversive activities undertaken by public servants, and an act on suspending and dissolving political parties, which was used to ban the German National Socialist Workers' Party (DNSAP). Another 240 economic measures were also adopted. In January 1934 the currency was devalued and a debate opened about establishing a so-called economic parliament, which was redolent of similar ideas appearing in contemporary authoritarian regimes. To put it frankly, Czechoslovak democracy took on some of the characteristics of a police state without this necessarily increasing its ability to act and to act efficiently (consider the results of the 1935 parliamentary election, which was won by the SdP with an irredentist programme).

2.3.2. The presidential election of December 1935

It was under these circumstances that T. G. Masaryk, who was only recently (in May 1934) re-elected president for the fourth time, resigned for health reasons. As his successor he recommended Edvard Beneš, his long-standing ally (their cooperation reached back to the years of exile during WWI) and a member of many governments during the First Republic, in which he served as prime minister or minister for foreign affairs. Beneš had a totally different personality than the vigorous and passionate Masaryk: he was coldly rational, an agnostic, puritan, and social Darwinist, as well as a militant anti-Catholic. His unquestionable advantages included his competence in administration and diplomacy. He revered Masaryk's state idea which was manifested in his foreign policy. Beneš considered Hungary and Poland to be Czechoslovakia's main enemies, describing them as 'feudal' states. In domestic politics he preferred a socialist interpretation of democracy that emphasised equality and collective interest. He had a tendency to favour the methods of *scientific* (i.e., Comtean) politics, which understood politics as an object of ideal-constructivist experiments.

---

20 After the government passed a bill, the parliament could meet within the next fortnight to either approve or reject it. If it failed to act, the bill became a law.
21 It allowed the government to prohibit parties that did not conform to the constitution from standing for election or to ban those parties.

Though often a target of attacks which were really aimed at Masaryk, Beneš had a truly remarkable range of opponents, which included most party leaders. Beneš liked to circumvent or ignore these party elites, as he did not consider domestic politics to be of relevance when choosing his foreign policy line. He was criticised for his authoritarianism, solitariness, kitchen-cabinet politics, building of clientelist networks, and his tendency to denounce opponents.[22]

It was therefore unsurprising that – against Masaryk's recommendation to have Beneš elected the new president – opponents created the *December Bloc* and proposed Bohumil Němec as its candidate. However, the non-socialist parties which assembled in the bloc under the leadership of the Agrarians ultimately recoiled at the possibility that, by supporting a candidate other than Beneš, they would be undermining Masaryk's conception of the Czechoslovak state. This would re-open the Slovak and German questions. It is not surprising that it was a Slovak, the Agrarian politician and prime minister Milan Hodža, who initiated this bloc. The general public, aware of the rise of the non-democratic National Socialist regime in Germany, identified the dispute about the position of the German minority in RČS and the willingness on the part of the Agrarian Party's elites to play the role of mediator for German interests on the Czech political scene with a rivalry between democracy and dictatorship. Any hint of concession was then perceived as a betrayal of national interests. The December Bloc ultimately fell apart before the election proper and there was no battle for the Castle. In the end HSĽS, ČSL, and even the Agrarians did not dare to vote against Beneš.[23]

Yet the calamity was complete. In its effort to secure support for Beneš's election, the Castle managed to reach an unprecedented agreement with the Communists without realising the consequences such a partnership would entail for the future. KSČ could afford to support a 'bourgeois' candidate thanks to the international communist movement's change of strategy: at its seventh congress in June 1935, the Communist International unveiled the popular front strategy, which permitted cooperation with non-communist left and centre parties under the banner of the anti-fascist struggle.

---

22 For a typical example of such pamphleteering literature, see *Kramářův soud nad Benešem* (1938).
23 In the election on 18 December 1935, 440 valid votes were cast: 340 for Beneš, 24 for the Germans, and 76 ballot papers were blank.

Czech/Czechoslovak politics thus joined the ranks of those European countries in which the contemporary left – with its dialectically broad notion of fascism (encompassing everything to the right of centre) – redefined the notions of the left and right and, reshaped European conceptions of politics for decades to come. In the Czech situation this meant that the conservative circles in the National Democratic Party (representing a nationalism different from the official, Masarykian, one), Czech fascism (of negligible capacity), the conservative segment of Czech political Catholicism, and non-Czech political representatives were all tarred with the same brush.[24]

Thus, as elsewhere in interwar Central Europe, one can observe a struggle between authoritarian and totalitarian models.[25] A number of right-wing Central European currents were willing to see in authoritarian arrangements a practical implementation of some conservative values, for instance the hierarchical principle (elitism), corporatism and anti-modernism (traditionalism). From this perspective, fascism could seem to be an ideological current at least partially compatible with conservatism. Like conservatism, it was convinced of the necessity of strong authority, strong statism, and faith in the nation. In Czech politics, such sympathies appeared among certain circles of political Catholicism which stood in opposition to Jan Šrámek's official leadership of the ČSL. For example, the Czech provincial group led by Bohumil Stašek considered the Italian corporatist model a way of implementing the values and ideas expressed in the papal encyclical *Quadragesimo Anno*. Catholic intelligentsia, meanwhile, rejected the Masarykian conception of Czech history as embodying the struggle between Reformation and Counter-Reformation, i.e., as a battle between Protestants and Catholics. A model for these tensions was developed in responses to the civil war in Spain.[26] The diverging views on the events in Spain revealed a fundamental disagreement between two camps within Czech intellectual circles, one social-liberal and the other conservative. Czech conservative leaders were mistaken about the possibility of partnership with fascism. It ultimately became clear that such

---

24 Immediately after the Nazi regime took power, the overwhelming majority of German party representatives in Czechoslovakia expressed inclinations towards the National-Socialist ideology, or at least towards German nationalism. A logical consequence of this was that most of the German minority declared its disloyalty to the Czechoslovak state. See Majewski (2014).
25 Political theory was only able to describe this distinction adequately with the works of Juan J. Linz, in the 1960s and 1970s.
26 Legendary was the polemic between Karel Čapek (written from a liberal point of view) and Jaroslav Durych (from a conservative point of view).

partnerships were precluded by fascism's activism, its insistence on permanent revolutionary change, and its negative attitude towards the role of traditional institutions (Gregorovič 1995). The limits were to be demonstrated in the era of the Second Republic (see Chapter 3). The relationship between interwar non-ideological authoritarian regimes whose legitimacy rested on a specific temperament and ideological fascist regimes continues to be a hotly discussed topic in political theory to this day.

The alliance of the democratic left with the communist movement, cemented by the election of Edvard Beneš as the second Czechoslovak president in December 1935, precipitated a similar discussion: the possibility of partnership between democratic actors and totalitarian movements. This option was to become much more powerful in the ensuing decades of Czech/Czechoslovak politics.

2.4. Political traditions of the First Republic

During the second half of the 1930s, the external context of European politics proved to be a fundamental limitation on the efforts of Czechoslovak elites to defend their state and its democratic regime. The dramatic developments rendered the difference between democracies and non-democracies entirely meaningless. A symbol of this chaos was the Munich Agreement, the international agreement concluded on 30 September 1938, where Germany, Italy, Great Britain and France without the participation of RČS representatives decided that the Czechoslovak territories of the Sudetenland were to be handed over to the Third Reich, and ethnically Slavic populations were to be displaced from those areas with a German majority.

The coerced assent of Prague – which did not manage anything beyond a statement that it did not want to be a cause of war – meant the end of the First Republic. It meant the collapse of its foreign policy ambitions, a loss of much of the country's resources, a change in its international position and a destabilisation of domestic politics. Finally, it also meant the end of the democratic regime and the beginning of six decades in which various forms of non-democratic regime followed one other, as did changing forms of statehood. Masaryk's republic ceased to exist.

But this was also the time that the mythology of the First Republic came into being. Two decades were enough for an incipient 'tradition' of Czech politics to become established and the basic dispositions and limits of Czech political life to be laid down. These traditions were the following: (1) an emphasis on the national element; (2) an uncritical approach to democracy; (3) a disdain for political power; (4) a scepticism towards political partisanship; (5) an emphasis on ethical politics; and (6) a specifically Czech conception of politics reflecting the dispute over the 'Czech question'.

Some of these traditions were discussed above. We turn here to the fifth point, which concerns moral issues and the strong demand for ethical politics. This pillar is the foundation of all the other traditions. The main root of the Czech conception of politics as a struggle between good and evil is the context in which Czech politics was born during the second half of the nineteenth century. It was born out of a rejection of Catholicism and an emphasis on the Reformation (Hussite) identity of the Czech nation, an identity that was unique in Central Europe. This approach had always emphasised the ethically superior dimension of the Hussite 'trace' in Czech history, contrasted with the allegedly 'cynical' approach taken by the political Catholicism of Vienna. Such an analysis, however, robbed the incipient Czech politics of the possibility of greater participation in Austria's reform course, which to the vast majority of Czech political elites seemed overly cautious and drawn-out, if not altogether lacking in legitimacy. The 'noble' motive of struggle for national identity, by contrast, provided Czech politics with abundant legitimacy.

This approach also implied a disdain for political power. An important segment of Czech political elites, including President Masaryk and much of the Czech general public, distanced themselves from the notion of politics as a necessary practical skill and from the understanding of political power and its exercise as resulting from continuous debates and permanent reformulations of objectives, which reflect the plurality of interests and values in modern society. They instead saw politics as a fatal moral clash, requiring absolute measures and strategies. When actually exercised, political power was perceived as suspect, even despicable politicking because of its amorality.

In line with this characteristic, the Czech departure from Austria-Hungary was accompanied by a thoroughgoing negation of previous developments and their characteristic traits. This model of regime change was to repeat itself. From this point of departure, a key characteristic of politics in the First Republic was derived. Left and right had formed not on the basis of natural competition between particular ideologies representing relevant social groups. They developed as mutually alienated and irreconcilable social entities, waiting for the opportunity to put their adversary out of action. This encouraged the notion that it is appropriate to intervene in natural social processes and that intellectuals can identify ideal socio-structural arrangements (see Chapter 3 for more details).

The traditions described above, however, may not have been the result of a free 'choice' made in Czech politics. Such a reading would be suggested by the notion of 'small nation' developed by the Czech historian Miroslav Hroch, who defined the mentality of a 'small nation', its specifics and stereotypes. Unlike a 'state nation',[27] a small nation is the result of a 'successful national movement' in a formerly 'non-governing ethnic group', typically featuring: (1) conflict between social interests, which does not evolve through standard, ideologically-articulated clashes, but is firmly bound up with the national issue; (2) a faster pace of national mobilisation; (3) the feeling that national existence is under threat (suggesting that it does exist as a matter of course); (4) the development of a distinctive culture; (5) a demand for national unity (sometimes articulated aggressively in the imperative for an all-national consensus); (6) a stereotype of a peaceful nation; (7) a unifying view of history; (8) the myth of a simple people; and (9) provinciality (Hroch 1999: 156-163).

Compared to other nation-state projects in Central Europe, one might argue that the First Republic was a successful political performance by an emancipated Czech national society, which created attachments to the idea of democracy and resisted totalitarian and authoritarian temptations during the interwar period. However, future developments were to provide another level of comparison. Whereas the Polish and Hungarian authoritarianism would show obvious resistance to communist totalitarianism, Czech politics, by contrast, would willingly take the totalitarian path.

---

27 That is, nations whose identity developed in parallel with the state-building process. According to Miroslav Hroch, there were seven such nations at the turn of the nineteenth century: France, Spain, the Netherlands, Portugal, Great Britain, Denmark, and Sweden (Hroch 1999: 13).

3. Czech lands under dictatorships and totalitarian regimes 1938–1989

Jan Holzer

The half century in Czech/Czechoslovak politics between 1938 and 1989 might seem too diverse to summarize in a single chapter. The Czechoslovak state endured four different regimes: two of them authoritarian (the Second and Third Republics) and two totalitarian (the Protectorate of Bohemia and Moravia and the communist era). However turbulent these political developments, the mood in society was just as volatile: from a desire to revise the system of the First Republic after the 'Munich betrayal' to the sufferings of war to unprecedented enthusiasm after liberation to a new feeling of darkness and unfreedom. The five decades also confirmed a Czech tradition: regime change does not simply entail a replacement of the preceding political elite; it means the complete negation of the past, a rejection of everything that came before.

Despite all the changes over those fifty years, there was one main factor that provided the impetus for change in Czech politics: Czech communism. For the KSČ, the post-war era represented a historical breakthrough. Its reputation as an extremist force on the fringes of the political spectrum was now a thing of the past. In comparison to the other parties of the First Republic, the KSČ wore a halo as the chief opponent to fascism and it was now responsibly addressing the tasks lying before the Czechoslovak nation. It was thanks to this new renown that the KSČ was able to implement its programme of building socialism after the war. And in 1948, when the party turned the Czech lands and Slovakia into what was effectively a fiefdom, it stood ready to fulfil its 'historical task'.

3.1. The Second Republic

The era of the Second Czechoslovak Republic began with the Munich Conference (30 September 1938), where France, Italy, Germany and Great Britain agreed to cede part of the historical border territories of the Czech lands and Slovakia to Germany, Hungary and Poland. The authoritarian regime of the Second Republic lasted until March 1939, when the Third Reich occupied the rest of Czechoslovakia (the elites of the Second Republic offered no resistance), created the Protectorate of Bohemia and Moravia, and established the independent Slovak State.

3.1.1. Political regime

The Second Republic gradually abandoned the democratic standards of the First Republic. The newly proclaimed model of what was called *authoritarian democracy* was purged of those elements of pre-Munich politics that seemed entirely out of step with the times, namely, a multi-party system and liberal economy. Edvard Beneš's allegedly failed foreign policy was also to be changed entirely. The abandonment of democratic principles during the Second Republic did not, however, imply an overtly totalitarian society: the regime produced no ideology of its own, applied neither a system of terror nor the leader principle, and preserved the independence of the judiciary.

The regime of the Second Republic did, however, admit the possibility of some of these characteristics and even took the first steps towards their realisation. J. J. Linz's notion of a *mobilising, authoritarian regime in a post-democratic society* seems apt to describe the Second Republic.[1] The adjective 'post-democratic' refers to the regime as a reaction to the preceding 'failure of democracy' and the mobilisation element reflects attempts to re-orient society towards saving what was left of the First Republic. Regimes described by Linz's theory typically focus on pragmatism and the technological aspects of governance. They rely on a certain mindset: in the Second Republic this was to include the national community, social justice, morality, and education in a national and Catholic spirit,[2] and the negation of pre-Munich 'Protestantism'. Political and socio-economic harmony was to be restored among the various layers of society. The social institutions protecting the individual from the pressures of society were to be rebuilt. In its attempts at social cohesion, the Second Republic felt it was necessary to restrict some civic rights and freedoms (residence, association, press). Certain minorities – for instance,

---

1 It was not, however, a conscious and intended prelude to the totalitarianism of the Protectorate, as some authors have argued (Rataj 1997). There is a clear discontinuity between the regime of the Second Republic and the Protectorate.
2 Consider the elevation of the St Wenceslas myth, the state's appreciative view of the aristocracy, the attempts to reintroduce religious education to schools, and the demands that atheism and freemasonry be made illegal.

Jews – began to encounter discrimination in their everday activities[3] and there were attempts to control the media (newspapers, cinemas). However, censorship had existed in the First Republic and the new measures did not lead to a complete denial of freedom of expression. The economy was to be more regulated by the state through corporate bodies. Partly in response to the the loss of substantial human and material resources, punitive work camps were introduced and limitations placed on certain trades. The classic signs of totalitarianism in the economy – central planning, a command economy, and limitations on private property – only appeared after March 1939.

3.1.2. Governance

Although according to international law the Munich Agreement was a violation of treaties then in force, Jan Syrový's caretaker government accepted it (though some highly-placed military officers were determined to deploy the army to defend the country) with the argument that it was necessary to observe the commitments towards France and Britain entered into by Hodža's government. As the changes in the country's boundaries had not been ratified by parliament – this contravened the constitution – the legal construct of nullity *ex tunc* was applied after the fact. This meant that the Second Republic never existed *de jure* and its constitutional acts were void. It also legalized the position of Edvard Beneš as the leader of foreign resistance after March 1939.

As far as constitutional bodies were concerned, the changes brought by the Second Republic are best illustrated by the role of the president. It was the resignation of Edvard Beneš on 5 October 1938 that confirmed the fall of the First Republic. Yet it also started a process which led to the second Czechoslovak president becoming the embodiment of anti-fascist exile. Beneš argued that his resignation was coerced and thus null and void, as was the subsequent election of Emil Hácha, the third president of RČS, on 30 November 1938. Hácha's election initially met with a positive response both at home and abroad, but this was only a temporary illusion, and Hácha's life ended in tragedy (see below).

With the adoption of the so-called enabling law executive power was strengthened in a non-standard way at the expense of legislative power. For two years the government obtained the authority to replace laws with

---

3 See the government resolution dated 27 January 1939 on identifying citizens of Jewish origin in public office.

government regulations and the president received the power to issue decrees whose authority was equal to legislation.[4] The National Assembly was weakened. Indeed, the only parliamentary bodies that kept working were the joint standing committee of its two chambers and the committee which oversaw the economy. Parliament also disintegrated in terms of personnel: deputies and senators gradually lost their seats for a variety of reasons,[5] until parliament was reduced to a mere remnant, the so-called *fragmentary parliament (kusý parlament)*, which was not summoned after December 1938. Furthermore, a non-elected, corporatist State Council for the Economy, a kind of 'economic parliament', was proposed. Indeed, in February 1939 the Council was established as an advisory body to the government and parliament on economic, social and financial matters. It comprised one hundred members, delegated by parliamentary chambers, public corporations, and universities. To sum up, the characteristics of parliamentarianism largely disappeared from the political system of the Second Republic.[6]

3.1.3. Party system

The onset of these authoritarian practices had significant repercussions for political parties. The open, multi-party system of the First Republic was alleged to be one of the main causes of Czechoslovakia's problems. The slogan of the day, supported by the majority of the public, was 'simplification' of party politics, a continuation of the view already held before the Munich Agreement

---

[4] The agenda of the first cabinet of the Second Republic – the caretaker government led by Jan Syrový – was focussed on handing over some executive powers to the so-called regional *(krajinské)* governments of Slovakia and Carpathian Ruthenia. It was followed by the so-called government of *national unity* led by Rudolf Beran, which was technocratic in character and focussed on stabilising the position of RČS in foreign affairs but also its internal political situation, with an emphasis on social and economic policies.

[5] First those of the occupied territories if they claimed nationality other than Czechoslovak or Russian (Ukrainian); then the members of the KSČ, which was dissolved by authorities; then those elected in the Uzhhorod electoral district, and finally those elected for the ČSDSD in Slovakia, as the Slovak government dissolved this party.

[6] Regional parliaments also gained autonomy. The Assembly of the Slovak Land (or Region) was elected on 18 December 1938 and that of Carpathian Ruthenia on 12 February 1939. In both elections there was only one candidate list, that of the Slovak People's Party and the Ukrainian National Union respectively.

by the parties of national minorities.[7] Systems with either one or three parties were discussed for some time,[8] but a two-party model soon prevailed. On the right wing of the party spectrum, the unification process, spearheaded by the Agrarian Party, resulted in the creation of the governing Party of National Unity (SNJ) on 4 November 1938. The process of consolidation was not easy, though, as it encompassed not only the anti-Masaryk and anti-Castle right – that is, Czech nationalists and fascists like the National League, National Unity, and National Fascist Community and conservative Catholic circles – but also those currents which respected the ideas of the First Republic – the Agrarian, People's, and Tradesmen's parties (Čechurová 1999). The party that ultimately emerged became the personnel and organisational basis of the new regime. Ideologically it relied on Czech nationalism and a corporatist notion of the state. The SNJ programme envisaged the introduction of a new electoral law that would preclude party fragmentation, the reform of public administration and the resolution of the issue of immigrants and the Jewish question. The programme assumed the creation of a planned economy and the partial nationalisation of agricultural land, but it also counted on the preservation of private ownership and entrepreneurship (albeit in line with state interests). In foreign policy, friendship with neighbours, including Germany, was the preferred line.

The opposition National Party of Work (NSP) was founded somewhat later, on 11 December 1938, on the initiative of the Social Democrats and with the involvement of many members of the National Socialists and a few individuals from the ranks of the KSČ. Its programme was for a social-

---

7 Polish and Jewish parties started to cooperate before the 1935 parliamentary election. In early 1937 the Hungarian parties did as well. In March 1938 the German parties merged with the Sudeten German Party. The activities of the last mentioned were suspended on 16 September 1938 and the German Social Democrats likewise ceased their activities after Munich. Government regulations of December 1938 and January 1939 made the creation of new political parties subject to government approval and defined how parties could be dissolved – the government had to consider the degree to which they jeopardized the public interest. The first affected was the KSČ, which was dissolved on 28 December 1938. The political representatives of the German minority that remained on the territory of the Second Republic considered themselves to be a part of the Reich's NSDAP.
8 Some ČSNS and ČSL elites hoped that the 'concentration' would only occur on the left and the right and that they would be able to preserve their centrist positions. In the end, both merged with the governing Party of National Unity. In ČSL this deepened regional factionalism between the Moravian branch led by the chairman Jan Šrámek and the Bohemian branch led by Bohumil Sašek. In ČSNS a minority of MPs joined the oppositional NSP.

reformist democracy focused on equality and justice and espoused an economy run on Keynesian principles. The NSP strategy presumed that the rule of law would be preserved and that the party would co-operate with the government as a loyal opposition. In this way the NSP tried not to diverge too much from the practices of the First Republic and at the same time to avoid provoking the new regime (Kuklík 1992: 30–92).

The formal nature of the two-party model resulted in the emergence of a number of non-party platforms which maintained a critical distance from the authoritarian model. They included groups concentrated around some journals (*Čin, Národní osvobození, Národní myšlenka*) and non-party groupings (Political headquarters [*Politické ústředí*]), from which the future domestic anti-Nazi resistance started to form as early as spring 1939.

3.1.4. The end of the Second Republic

The end of the Second Republic and with it the illusion that an independent Czechoslovak could continue was linked externally with the increasing pressure exerted by Germany in spring 1939 (Procházka 1981: 107-146) and internally with the autonomist tactics of Slovak political representatives (for example, the Žilina Agreement of 6 October 1938). During the final crisis of March 1939, Slovak representatives proclaimed the secession of Slovakia from the RČS and the construction of an authoritarian 'Ľuďák regime' based on nationalism and conservative political Catholicism.[9] In response to these developments and to the negotiations in Berlin between Emil Hácha and Adolf Hitler, the remaining territory of RČS was occupied on 15 March 1939 and the Protectorate of Bohemia and Moravia was declared. Czechoslovakia ceased to exist.

The Second Republic did not last long enough (not even six months) to develop its own answer to the 'Czech question'. Its elites believed that the post-Munich situation could be dealt with by building an authoritarian regime and isolating its left-wing opponents. They did not, however, cross the threshold into totalitarianism. Rather, they laboured under the illusion that they could defy the changes occurring elsewhere. They did not dream of rebuilding the whole of society according to some grand ideological scheme. As opposed to

---

[9] In parallel the Republic of Carpatho-Ukraine declared its independence, but its territory was ultimately occupied by Hungary.

other authoritarian regimes in Central Europe at the time, the Second Republic had the following characteristics:

a) It relied on a broader social basis, not just the reaction of the middle classes;

b) Although groups avowing fascism were present in the regime, they were not its dominant actors;

c) The motive (or myth) of struggle during the building of the regime was absent. This followed from its non-heroic birth;

d) The regime espoused Catholic social doctrine, a reaction to the favouring of Protestantism in the preceding system.

3.2. The Protectorate

The Protectorate of Bohemia and Moravia began with a decree on 16 March 1939 and ended with the liberation of the Czech lands in early May 1945, from the east by the Soviets and from the west by the Allied armies. The circumstances under which Bohemia and Moravia fell under this occupational Protectorate were unconstitutional and included Hácha's constitutional incompetence, German pressure, and violations of state and international law. In foreign policy terms, it was not a classic 'protectorate', as that would necessitate a legal relationship. It was more of a vassal state whose rights, such as territorial autonomy, were entirely notional.[10] This is one of the reasons why, over the six years of the Protectorate (in a situation where the existence of the nation was under direct threat), Czech politicians only deployed a tactic of containment. For obvious reasons, they were unable to pursue any explicitly anti-German policy.

This was the first time that the Czech lands experienced a totalitarian regime and the regime was unusual in that its protagonists were ethnically

---

10 In Slovakia the constitution adopted on 21 July 1939 confirmed the sovereignty of the Slovak state. In later developments, however, institutions appeared that claimed allegiance to the Czechoslovak state: consider the creation of the Slovak National Council by the so-called 'Christmas Agreement' in December 1943 over the objections of the government-in-exile in London. The activities of the Council, beginning with the Slovak National Uprising, led to a legal dualism.

foreign. All of the classic traits of totalitarianism were present and developed during the Protectorate. There was a single political authority. Censorship completely suppressed freedom of expression and led to what has been called 'journalistic activism', i.e., the accommodation of most journalists to the new situation. The state had total control over the economy and, in its effort to maximise the use of human and material resources, placed limitations on private property. The state had – understandably given the war – a monopoly on weapons. Finally, the population was divided into two unequal classes – the privileged German nationals and second-class Protectorate citizens, who were exposed to terror and omnipresent persecution that primarily targeted the intelligentsia, former members of political parties, and the officer corps. The result was the total suppression not only of political and civic rights and freedoms but also of fundamental rights, as demonstrated by the tragic fates of the Jewish and Romani minorities.

The ideological situation was complex. It is true that ideological elements (the leader principle, the motif of a victorious German race, anti-Semitism) were present and put into practice (consider the so-called final solution to the 'Jewish question' and the activities of the Centre for Jewish Emigration). However, the ideological pillars of the Protectorate – patriotism and social justice – could hardly develop into a complete form of National-Socialist ideology, as the growth of Czech patriotism, albeit 'under the protection of the Reich', was in a logical conflict with the German identity of the occupying elite. In reality, waves of ideological mobilisation tended to take a back seat to the pragmatic necessity of keeping the population in its place.

3.2.1. The regime of the Protectorate and its instruments

In the system of the Protectorate, both the state and the party were German structures, in the form of the Führer and the National Socialist German Workers' Party. The system of Czech institutions, notionally autonomous, was replicated by Reich authorities, which briefed and controlled the former. State President Hácha and the government of the Protectorate had to respect the course set in Berlin, represented in Prague by the Reich-Protector. As the defence of the Protectorate was taken over by the Reich, the positions of foreign minister and national defence minister were abolished in Alois Eliáš's government (the government army created in July 1939 was of only marginal importance). Nonetheless, until 1941 the government and the president proceeded on the basis that some rights would be preserved and through their communications with the government-in-exile in London they co-ordinated domestic resistance, protested against arrests, and interceded with the German authorities on behalf of those held prisoner (Pasák 1998: 350–394).

The arrival of the new acting Reich-protector Reinhard Heydrich in October 1941 changed this state of affairs. Heydrich made himself known by arresting the Prime Minister Alois Eliáš (in January 1942), eliminating the relative autonomy of the Protectorate's authorities, abolishing the dual (German and Czech) administration, and introducing a brutal system of martial law and terror. He also strengthened social legislation and introduced the Curatorium for Youth Education *(Kuratorium pro výchovu mládeže)*, a mass extra-curricular organisation whose task was to educate Czech youth aged 10 to 18 in National Socialist ideology. The new government led by Jaroslav Krejčí was also affected by these changes. The number of ministries was again reduced. The most important portfolios remaining were those of interior and public education. The minister for the latter, Emanuel Moravec, became a symbol of collaboration under the Protectorate. Under these circumstances, Beneš urged Hácha and the government to resign, but Hácha, pressured by the Germans, withdrew his resignation. The exiled government in London ceased its policy of toleration towards Hácha and the representatives of the Protectorate generally. Hácha's health and activity declined and he was used by the German authorities solely for propaganda purposes (Pasák 1977: 82ff.).[11] This situation continued unchanged even after the successful assassination of Heydrich – a unique achievement on German-controlled territory – and his replacement by Karl Daluege in May 1942 and Wilhelm Frick in August 1943. During the last two years of war, the Minister of State of the Protectorate Karl Hermann Frank further concentrated power in his own hands (Maršálek 2002: 45–88).

Soon after the establishment of the Protectorate, a non-party corporatist organisation was created – the National Partnership *(Národní souručenství)* – which practically the whole of the male population joined. After an initial period of defence against pro-German activism, collaborators came to dominate the National Parternship (Vladimír Krychtálek was a leading figure). However, the Partnership was not pro-Nazi (consider, for example, its disapproval of discrimination against Jews). Rather, it was a depoliticised association focussed on culture and public education. Among other groups that sought to represent the Protectorate politically, the most important was the Flag

---

11 Hácha was arrested shortly after liberation and died in a prison hospital in June 1945.

(Vlajka) led by Jan Rys-Rozsévač. However, none of its attempts to distinguish itself (for example, the founding of the Czech National-Socialist Camp in October 1939) won the trust of the Reich and some leaders of the Flag were ultimately persecuted by the German authorities.[12] Other collaborationist organisations (the Czech Union for Cooperation with the Germans and the Czech League against Bolshevism) operated under the direct administration of the occupiers.

3.2.2. Society and domestic resistance

Under the totalitarian rule of the Protectorate, Czech resistance had to go underground. From the very beginning the resistance was divided into two camps, democratic and communist, which differed in both organisation and objectives. The democratic resistance established three organisations: the Political Headquarters, with links to the government-in-exile, led the resistance politically; the Defence of the Nation was a military group well developed organisationally since its membership was recruited from the former officer corps, Sokol, and other social groups; the Petition Committee We Shall Remain Faithfull (PVVZ) represented the left. The initial naive enthusiasm of the resistance disappeared after the brutal response by the Germans to anti-Nazi demonstrations in autumn 1939 and a wave of arrests that affected all these organisations (with the partial exception of PVVZ) in early 1940. For that reason the unified Central Leadership of Home Resistance (ÚVOD) was created in the spring of 1940, but its activities were also soon paralysed. Domestic resistance arose again only in 1943, but even groups such as the Preparatory National Revolutionary Committee, the Czech National Council, and the Preparatory Revolutionary Council (the Council of the Three) did not avoid German retaliation. Hence the state of the democratic resistance at the end of the war was pitiful.

The communist resistance, by contrast, managed to remain active underground despite repeated German attempts to destroy it. Czech communists fully respected the instructions from Moscow, which were often changed: for instance, after the Ribbentrop-Molotov pact was concluded, the communists assumed a restrained attitude towards the Reich. Germany's attack on the Soviet Union, by contrast, allowed them to establish contacts with the non-

---

12 For instance, Rys-Rozsévač, who attempted to lead a campaign against minister Moravec, ended up in the Dachau concentration camp.

communist resistance and renew preparations for a socialist revolution after liberation.

A general problem for domestic resistance movements was that the occupation administration guaranteed to most categories of the population a reasonable material standard of living, even if certain necessities were sometimes lacking. For this reason, the Protectorate did not become the site of a rebellion. Nonetheless, mass demonstrations of loyalty to the Reich should not be overestimated as they were motivated by justified apprehension about the brutal repression that would follow any non-compliance.

3.2.3. The government-in-exile and foreign resistance

Under these circumstances it was the government-in-exile that became the main force seeking to maintain the continuity of Czechoslovak statehood. Two centres were ultimately formed, one in London, the other in Moscow. Despite starting out from opposed ideological premises, these centres not only opened a dialogue, but eventually achieved a remarkable degree of concord. This was to have fateful consequences for post-war developments.

The background to the first attempts to form an interim Czechoslovak government-in-exile was the complicated approach of the Allies to the Protectorate and the Slovak state. The Allies initially refused to grant them legal recognition in March 1939 and then granted *de facto* recognition in May 1939. For this reason in the early days no one, including Beneš, could claim to be the leader in exile. Besides Beneš, the Slovak Agrarian and former Prime Minister Milan Hodža, the ambassador to France Štefan Osuský, and General Lev Prchala all sought to take this role. When in late 1939 Beneš established the Czechoslovak National Committee (ČNV) in Paris, the Hodža-organised Slovak National Council organised an opposition which promoted Slovak autonomist demands and the idea of a Central European federation. Indeed, in January 1940 Hodža managed to bring together politicians opposed to Beneš and created the Czecho-Slovak National Council (Kuklík and Němeček 1999: 39–89). It was only France's defeat, the relocation of the exiles to Britain, and the efforts of Jan Masaryk, the ambassador in London, that definitely placed Beneš at the head of the Czechoslovak foreign resistance.

The main objectives of the government-in-exile in London were first to win Allied recognition for the Czechoslovak authorities in exile and then to co-ordinate the resistance and formulate the political arrangements for post-war Czechoslovakia. The cornerstone of Beneš's conception was to undo the

Munich Agreement and its roots,[13] even if that were to mean a redefinition of the First Republic's political system. This fixation of Beneš defined the solution to all individual issues, including the Slovak question, the punishment of traitors and collaborators, the fate of Germans in Czechoslovakia, his relationship to the Czech and Slovak right, and postwar foreign policy.[14] In order to fulfil Beneš's conception, the exiles in London devised what was called the Provisional Czechoslovak State Apparatus, a quasi-sovereign political structure which at the time of its inception in July 1940 relied in legal terms on its recognition by Britain and on a claim of constitutional continuity with the First Republic.[15] Beneš exercised the office of president-in-exile on the basis of the argument that although he had resigned after the Munich Agreement, his resignation was coerced and therefore unlawful. Thus, the argument went, Beneš remained the head of state, as confirmed by the recognition granted to him by Allied governments. And he should remain in office until a new election could be held (Kuklík 1998: 71–108).

Apart from his symbolic role as Masaryk's successor, Beneš's chief instrument of power was his authority to issue constitutional decrees (Kuklík 1998: 41–70), legal directives that – under normal circumstances – would have to be adopted as constitutional laws. These decrees set such important postwar policies as the confiscation of property and the withdrawal of Czechoslovak citizenship from ethnic Germans and Hungarians, ultimately resulting in what was called the *resettlement* of non-Slavic minorities. The interim government, numbering five ministers with portfolios (foreign affairs, national defence, finance, interior, and social affairs) and three without, focussed mainly on the organisation of the army and military strategy, the management of embassies, and the construction of a provisional state apparatus. The State Council, originally appointed by the president as an advisory body, accepted the role of a quasi-parliament. As a body that claimed to represent all relevant domestic political views, the Council was gradually enlarged by newly arriving exiles, including members of the KSČ. It could not,

---

13 Jan Tesař aptly described Beneš's relationship to Munich as 'complex'; see Tesař (2000).
14 For the extensive memoir literature on this theme see e.g., Beneš (1946b), Drtina (1991), Feierabend (1994, 1994, 1996), Fierlinger (1949), Táborský (1993). For scholarly work see Pehr (2011).
15 Constitutional restoration was achieved by the decree on the restoration of legal order, which declared that legal acts made after 30 September 1938, when the Czechoslovak people was 'deprived of its freedom', were coerced and hence null and void.

however, pass laws or hold the government accountable. To sum up, it was Beneš who dominated the government-in-exile in London.

The Czech communist centre in Moscow became active only after the German attack on the Soviet Union. In line with Kremlin policy, it understood the war chiefly as an opportunity to export revolution into Central Europe. The Soviet Union's increased international influence, due to the Red Army's role in the defeat of Germany, was to become an argument for the KSČ to play a key role in the political and socio-economic transformation of post-war Czechoslovakia. During the war the KSČ formulated its strategy for assuming power and socialising the country (the idea of national committees, nationalisation of property, infiltration of other parties, and the use of certain ministries to achieve a position of power) and convinced the majority of the exiles in London, including President Beneš, that their own conception was compatible with the communist one.

3.2.4. The end of the war

Agreement between the democratic and communist left was confirmed by Beneš's controversial decision to return to the liberated homeland not from the West but by way of Moscow. The government-in-exile in London resigned and on 4 May 1945 was replaced by the Government of the National Front (NF) in Moscow led by Zdeněk Fierlinger, a Social Democrat. The Czech National Council, led by Albert Pražák, which was the official executive body of the domestic resistance and the co-ordinator of the Prague uprising, respected the priority of the government in exile, and on 11 May 1945 handed over its administration to the NF and ceased its activities.

The Czechoslovak state was officially renewed, but with a reduced territory: in its easternmost part, a congress of national committees in Mukacheve on 26 November 1944 elected the Ukrainian National Council which – pressured by the Soviet authorities – submitted an application on behalf of Carpathian Ruthenia to accede to the Soviet Union. Given the international situation, Beneš's government accepted this change to the borders.

Czechoslovakia emerged from World War II as a member of the victorious coalition. However, the international system and the domestic balance of political power had both changed in the meantime. The degree to which the democratic forces led by President Beneš converged with the programme of the radical left suggested political changes and obstacles to Czechoslovakia's return among Western democracies.

3.3. The Third Republic

The Czech and Slovak nations entered the post-war era with the bitter memory of six years of war, but also with strong hopes for a better future. Citizens, however, were not united as to what course should be taken. Some preferred to return to the system of the First Republic, but a significant portion of society, Czechs in particular, wished to radically rebuild Masaryk's state from its very foundations. This vision was not represented by the KSČ alone. An important part of the democratic left also held this view.

3.3.1 The starting points for the reconstruction of the political system

The existence of significant groups in favour of political, economic, national, and ideological reconstruction helped to secure acceptance of a political system imposed by the two groups of exiles (one in London, the other in Moscow). In order to explain the logic of political developments after May 1945, one must therefore start with the general accord between President Beneš's political conception and the vision promoted by the KSČ. From the perspective of the First Republic, this partnership lacked logic, yet it had both strategic and ideological roots.

Beneš's personal qualities and organisational skill contributed signifycantly to the success of the government-in-exile, particularly in diplomacy, and led to the birth of the Beneš myth. He was hailed as the irreplaceable symbol of Czechoslovak statehood. In the long-term, however, his strategy proved deeply problematic. Beneš's interpretation of the 'Munich betrayal' led him to the conviction that Western democracy was in deep crisis and that a thoroughgoing political reconstruction was needed after the war, a conviction he had already articulated openly in his lectures at the University of Chicago in 1939 and later summarised in his book *Demokracie dnes a zítra* [Democracy today and tomorrow] (Beneš 1946a). It is questionable, though, whether Beneš's 'democracy of tomorrow' would, in fact, be a democracy. Beneš's opinions on political partisanship provide a good illustration. Although he declared that the post-war system would be based on the democratic traditions of the First Republic, from the outset he wanted to limit the number of parties. His discussion of two or three parties 'of the so-called left and the so-called right, possibly also a party of the centre' (Beneš 1946a: 314) ultimately led to a four-party model after May 1946, of which three were socialist and one Catholic. Other parties, however deeply they had been involved in Czech and Slovak politics for decades, were banned (they comprised the entirety of the First Republic's right, i.e., the Agrarian Party, Hlinka's Slovak People's Party, and the Tradesmen's Party as well as the parties of national minorities). The ban on the Agrarian Party, the chief political representative of the Czech countryside and a key element in the system of the First Republic, was particularly galling. Beneš initially assured Ladislav Karel Feierabend, the main representative of the Agrarians in London exile, that their party would not be forgotten. However, by the time the president left for negotiations with KSČ representatives in January 1945, he had already decided to ignore his promise (Dostál 1998: 220ff.). The representatives of parties in exile did not oppose the undemocratic limitation placed on the number of parties. In sum, Beneš's post-war political vision introduced an undemocratic regime, which was unable to counter the emerging totalitarian force of Czechoslovak communism.

3.3.2. A pre-totalitarian authoritarian regime

What kind of regime was the Third Republic? It was notionally democratic which was highlighted in the exiles' programme. Their aim was to hold free elections and establish a regular parliament as soon as possible because the interim body that acted as the legislature – the Provisional National Assembly – was a mere shadow of a parliamentary body.[16] Yet the parliamentary election, which only took place in May 1946, deviated from democratic standards. Unlike the 1920 constitution, only a unicameral parliament was elected. In the Czech lands only four parties were allowed to compete. Non-Slavic ethnicities were deprived of their right to vote. Red Army troops present on Czechoslovak

---

16 In office from 28 October 1945 to 25 May 1946, the Provisional National Assembly was created indirectly – by delegation, election by national committees, and through meetings and congresses of electors at the town, district and regional levels. This produced a joint candidate list of the National Front with parity representation of the legal parties. However, due to places being reserved for representatives of all-national organisations, the left actually prevailed in the body.

territory were deployed during the election. Parties' electoral campaigns were also unusual, since a convention was adopted that campaigning would have to be waged in a 'decent' manner. Under this convention, the parties bound themselves not to criticise either the Košice government programme or what were called the achievements of the national and democratic revolution. This meant that issues like the nationalisation of property, stripping the non-Slavic populace of citizenship, the resettlement (expulsion) of non-Slavic people, and constitutional-legal arrangements could not be the subject of electoral campaigning. Thus the point of the election was simply to grant legitimacy to the political course already charted. Indeed, this was confirmed in the second point of the convention which presumed that all four permitted parties would participate in a coalition government after the election.

The election, then, was not free. And the victory of the KSČ (43.3 % of the vote in Bohemia and 34.5 % in Moravia-Silesia) was more symptom than cause of the installation of a non-democratic system in the country. In neither the polity nor its politics was there any official opposition or check on the executive. All permitted parties pledged their loyalty to the government and plurality of opinion received no institutional backing. In terms of policies, the central government gradually accumulated the instruments needed to direct the economy. The property of the middle and upper classes was confiscated by means of two land reforms and large-scale nationalisations which started with banks, industry, mines, and insurance companies.[17] The state used a number of methods to control the media and destroy free social, economic and cultural relations. The Third Republic thus exhibited many elements of the incipient phase of a transition to totalitarianism, warranting the use of Linz's category of pre-totalitarian authoritarianism.

From May 1945 to February 1948, the Czech and Slovak right was systematically ostracised. For the left, by contrast, this was a period of domination in both power and ideology. It took three years to create a new totalitarianism, one that was predominantly domestic in origin. The democratic parties participated in its construction. The Social Democrats initiated the nationalisation of the economy. The National Socialists, in the post-war atmosphere of hatred towards Germans, contributed to the radical solution of the German question: the mass deportation of the German population from

---

17 By 1 March 1947 more than 3,000 enterprises, employing 61 % of industrial workers, had been nationalised (Veber 2008).

Czechoslovakia (the so-called resettlement or expulsion).[18] Although the KSČ was the strongest political actor in the Third Republic, it did not necessarily have to act in a more radical way than the rest of the coalition. The general concord was only questioned by some intra-party factions, for instance, in the Czechoslovak People's Party. Paradoxically, the party centres preferred to take care of their own dissenters so that they would not lose their share of power (consider the expulsion of Helena Koželuhová from the ČSL, see Renner 1999: 37–42). In the ČSNS there was also a dissatisfied faction (Kocián 2002: 111–160), which naively hoped that the influence of Beneš would guarantee that democracy would not be abandoned entirely. This belief was fatefully mistaken. When the democratic camp became more activist in the second half of 1946 and into 1947 in an attempt to counter the increasingly ferocious KSČ campaign (they were creating pro-communist factions in other parties, infiltrating crucial ministries, and slandering their opponents) (Hanzlík 1997), they were unable to find common ground with the Democratic Party in Slovakia, the strongest anti-communist actor of the day. This revealed another systemic limitation of Czechoslovak democracy which had deep roots. Any agreement with the Democratic Party would have to admit a discussion about Czechoslovakism or Slovak autonomy – topics that were politically taboo for the Czech democratic left.

The result of all this was the takeover of power by the KSČ in February 1948. It involved a combination of them obtaining a government majority (following the resignation of several ministers, which President Beneš accepted) and pressure by the mass organisations controlled by the communists (for example, a congress of trade unions) alongside shows of power by the People's Militia, the KSČ's paramilitary corps (Kaplan 1997). This gave birth to a legend about the non-revolutionary, democratic methods of Czech and Slovak communists. They managed to put into practice all the basic tenets of Marxism-Leninism for the takeover of power (exacerbating the crisis, questioning the liberal political and economic model, exploitation of 'useful

---

18 The 'resettlement' had two phases. In the first post-war months, there was a 'wild' expulsion organised by revolutionary guards, based on the principle of collective guilt and involving violence, theft, and murders of German civilians. The second (organised or systematic) phase occurred from January 1946 on the basis of the Potsdam Agreement. The total number of Germans who had to leave due to the post-war 'resettlement' was about 2.6 million. Precise numbers are difficult to establish, and are the subject of intensive discussions between Czech and German historians. For some of the most significant literature on the topic, see Staněk (1991) and Brandes (2002).

idiots'), without having to deploy violence. This was accompanied by a largely supportive general public.

3.4. The communist regime in Czechoslovakia

With the 'victory of February' or, in an alternative interpretation, the 'tragedy of February' (Ripka 1995), a new chapter was opened in Czech and Czechoslovak history, characterised by a totalitarian socio-political system which intertwined the fate of the Czech and Slovak nations with that of the KSČ. The tradition of political pluralism and the rule of law, dating back to Austria-Hungary and the First Republic and already disintegrating during the years 1938–1948, was now forgotten. For the next forty years, Czechoslovakia embarked on a path of 'organised violence' (Hejl 1990) – an attempt to realise the Marxist-Leninist ideal of a socialist society. Unlike elsewhere in Central Europe, this transformation was not imported by the Soviet Union, but drew on the previous activities of the KSČ and the Czech left generally. (The impact of the repressive and propaganda units of the Soviet regime, acting on Czechoslovak territory in co-ordination with the KSČ, was nonetheless important.) True, the international context played an important role. After the post-war disintegration of the anti-Hitler coalition and the construction of two ideologically opposed blocs, Czechoslovakia chose to join the Soviet camp.[19] Or was it made to join? It is exceedingly difficult to answer this question. It is nevertheless apparent that the traditionally pro-Western stance of the Czech polity was much weakened as a result of the Munich Agreement and the distancing of the Western powers from Czechoslovakia in their dispute with the Third Reich over the status of the German minority in Czechoslovakia. Naturally, this furthered the tendency of a significant part of the Czech polity to look East. The Red Army's contribution to the defeat of Hitler's Germany produced, to put it euphemistically, 'the final solution to the German question in Czech politics' and strengthened traditional pro-Slavic sympathies in Czech society.[20] In any case, Czechoslovak society, and its Czech segment in particular, chose its political path largely of its own accord.

---

19 Czechoslovakia joined the Council for Mutual Economic Assistance in January 1949 and the Warsaw Pact in May 1955.
20 Last but not least, it marked the final disappearance of the phenomenon of Central Europe, which – at least symbolically – had balanced the Western and Eastern foreign-policy

3.4.1. Communism as state ideology and as a system of power

The totalitarian regime began to establish itself in Czechoslovakia by the spring of 1948 (Kaplan 1991). In the spirit of the National Front's action programme, the KSČ assumed control over state authorities, took steps towards the elimination of political opposition, achieved the unification of mass social organisations, and started to implement measures that gave the party comprehensive control over the economy. Over the summer the KSČ also took over the presidency: Beneš, who refused to sign the new, so-called May constitution, resigned.[21] In June 1948 Klement Gottwald became the new president of the Czechoslovak Republic. That the KSČ was in charge and a new socialist era had begun was confirmed by the elections to the National Assembly in the autumn in which 89.2 % of the electorate voted for the single list of National Front candidates (actually dictated by the KSČ). The party's hegemony was also illustrated by its assimilation of the Social Democrats and its organisational reunification with the Communist Party of Slovakia – all of this before the end of 1948.

The real ideological and practical intentions of the KSČ were evidenced in its plan to construct socialism as established at its ninth congress in May 1949. The party at the time comprised about 2.3 million members which, as a proportion of the populace, made it the largest communist party in the world. In the programme adopted at the congress, the KSČ asserted that it commanded sufficient support to implement the transition 'from capitalism to socialism', to solidify the power of the working class through the dictatorship of the proletariat, and to achieve the transformation of both the state's institutional structure and the national economy.

In terms of the exercise of power, this implied the creation of a model in which the KSČ was absolutely dominant – a model which expressed its 'leading role' in all aspects of life.[22] At the top of the pyramid of power was the KSČ leadership. The structure of the KSČ was built to replicate public

---

orientations of the Czechoslovak state during the interwar period. Controversial is the issue of the degree to which Central Europe was a real phenomenon (consider the so-called Little Entente) or simply an echo of a sense of belonging to the Austrian-Hungarian monarchy (Trávníček 2009: 5–111).

21 Passed by the Constitutional Assembly on 9 May 1948, the May constitution brought together standard constitutional principles (adopted from the 1920 constitution) and what legal terminology of the times called the new legal 'core of social transformation'. See Gerloch, Hřebejk and Zoubek (1999: 34–36).

22 Formally enshrined only later in the 1960 constitution.

administrative and economic structures. There were party organisations in state-owned companies, agricultural co-operatives, schools, offices, the armed forces, and scientific and cultural institutions – in each case the party body was superior to the corresponding non-party body. The KSČ's supreme body was the Congress, held every five years. The Congress elected the Central Committee, which elected the Presidium (the so-called Politburo) from amongst its members, and this steered the party between the plenary sessions of the Central Committee. It was headed by a general secretary who, together with the Politburo, decided all essential questions. The fundamental principle of the system was democratic centralism, which meant that bodies were subordinate to organisations which elected them and were also obliged to file reports of their activities to superior bodies.

Mass social organisations, active within the framework of the KSČ-headed National Front (NF), were an integral part of the system. The NF also incorporated those non-communist parties who respected the leading role of the KSČ (the Czechoslovak People's Party and the Czechoslovak Socialist Party in the Czech lands and the Party of Slovak Renewal and the Party of Freedom in Slovakia), trade unions, the Socialist Youth Union, the Women's Union and artistic unions. The armed forces – the police, army, and State Security (political police) – were managed directly by the Politburo.

In line with Marxist-Leninist theory, the fundamental task was dealing with potential opposition to the dictatorship of the proletariat with the KSČ at its head. Large-scale political trials affected those groups and individuals who might be expected to deviate from the regime's official line.[23] Although formally legal, the trials were based on an understanding of law as an instrument of the ruling party (Koudelka 1993; Kaplan 1999) and their victims included members of non-communist parties (the execution of the National Socialist MP Milada Horáková attracted international attention) and interest associations, Catholic priests (Bulínová, Janišová and Kaplan 1994), businesspeople and landowners, senior army officers and police officers of the First Republic era, and non-Marxist intellectuals. Repression also affected the Communist Party itself through the principle of the permanent exposure of the 'enemy within'. The most important such case was that of the 'anti-state conspiratorial centre', in which the first secretary of the KSČ Rudolf Slánský was among those sentenced to capital punishment. Trials of lesser party cadres included those of the Slovak 'bourgeois nationalists' in April 1954, one of

---

23 See *Soudní perzekuce politické povahy v Československu 1948–1989* (1993).

whom was Gustav Husák who later became communist president of Czechoslovakia. The trials demonstrated the willingness on the part of the KSČ to use every means, including large-scale repression and judicial murder. A secondary, but not marginal, manifestation of this trend was purges within the state apparatus, which affected about 10,000 people, and the realisation of the promise to fill the public service with proletarian cadres, which involved about 200,000 to 250,000 workers (Kaplan 1992 and 1993).

In the economy, the emphasis of the first five-year plan was on the nationalisation of all industry, the encouragement of heavy industries and the industrialisation of Slovakia, the interconnection of markets among the so-called people's democracies, and a vigorous programme to eliminate private property in cities. In agriculture, the original intention to continue with the distribution of land to small farmers was replaced by mass agitation to entice farmers to 'voluntarily' enter into agricultural cooperatives, and to carry out a collectivisation policy by means of these cooperatives. This line, together with social policies[24] and the fixation of ideological (Marxism-Leninist), cultural (socialist realist), and information monopolies (Kaplan 1994) allowed the party to achieve total control over society.

The death of Klement Gottwald (on 14 March 1953, only a few days after the passing of Joseph V. Stalin) was something of a turning point. He was the most distinctive figure in the history of the Czech communist movement and the politician who managed to establish the Bolshevik line within the KSČ and bring the party to power. However, the figure of Gottwald was also connected with the non-democratic methods which the party used to achieve its successes. With the new President Antonín Zápotocký, the determination to implement the party line irrespective of the circumstances – in particular, the state of the economy – started to wane. The tenth party congress in June 1954 and the elections in November nevertheless confirmed the KSČ's hegemony.

The debate at two sessions of the KSČ's Central Committee in March and April 1956 about the report from the 20th Congress of the Communist Party of the Soviet Union on Stalin's crimes and what was called his cult of personality did not lead to major changes in Czechoslovakia as it did in other countries of the communist camp. Though the report initiated an intra-party debate about the dogmatism of the past, responsibility for past 'deviations' was said to be purely individual. In some social organisations, however, discussions of the

---

24 By introducing such measures as free healthcare, social and health insurance, canteen meals in enterprises, rent and energy price regulation, etc.

personality cult were more radical; the second congress of Czechoslovak writers in April 1956 has become legendary in this respect (Kopeček 2009: 293–304).

The short period of ideological uncertainty ended with a national conference of the KSČ in June 1956, which described the attempt to hold a discussion within the party as a 'revisionist tendency'. The pragmatic social measures that followed prevented an escalation of the situation, and Czechoslovakia did not experience the same unrest as Hungary and Poland. There were several reasons for this. First, the Czechoslovak communist regime could still rely on the support of a significant segment of Czech and Slovak society. The social structure of its supporters had expanded. In addition to the working class and some intellectuals, a significant proportion of new bureaucrats supported the communist regime. As opposed to other Central European countries, those of an anti-communist bent were unable to rely on institutions that were not controlled by the state, such as the Catholic Church. The second half of the 1950s in Czechoslovakia were years of political and socio-economic stability, crowned in 1960 by the adoption of the so-called socialist constitution, which proclaimed the 'victory' of socialism in the country (the word 'socialist' was now added to its official name, Czechoslovak Socialist Republic, abbreviated to ČSSR). Its Article 4, enshrined what was called 'the leading role of the KSČ in society'.

A more serious dispute, one that went beyond the party and involved much of society, especially the Czech part, emerged in the 1960s (Kaplan 2000 and 2002). A 'thaw' in the Soviet Union and a generational conflict within the KSČ led to a political relaxation in the first half of the 1960s. Younger party officials sensed the controversial nature of the 1950s political trials and refused to be held responsible for them, thus exerting pressure on the party leadership. The optimism expressed at the 12th Congress of the KSČ in December 1962 with the development of socialism and the seven-year economic plan was at variance with increasing intra-party tension.

Internal party mechanisms were unable to resolve the deepening conflict between the conservatives and the reformists. The report of a special commission published in August 1963 did lead to the trial verdicts being repealed, and more than 400 people affected (including those involved in the Slánský trial) were judicially rehabilitated. A number of party functionaries were also punished.[25] Yet all of these actions only affected party members. Non-communist prisoners who were released at the same time were not rehabilitated, and for the time being the party ignored society's new mood.

The dispute eventually became personal. That part of the party apparatus which obtained their posts in the 1950s and now felt under threat closed ranks around the party's first secretary Antonín Novotný.[26] Opposition to Novotný, consisting mainly of the party intelligentsia, reinforced their positions in party and non-party bodies and organisations (the Writers' Union, cultural and scientific institutes, universities) and in the media (the editorial boards of Czechoslovak Radio and Television and the cultural and political weeklies of the Writers Union, like *Literární noviny* and *Kulturní život*). The opposition could also lean on the discussion about Marxist thinking in the international communist movement (Karel Kosík, Ivan Sviták and others; Kopeček 2009: 304–348) and on the international success of the Czechoslovak arts, including its new-wave cinema and its national pavilions at Expo 58 in Brussels and Expo 67 in Montreal. All of this lent legitimacy to the opposition's demands, which included the end of primitive egalitarianism and added expert decision-making as well as the abandonment of the official dogmatic interpretation of Marxism-Leninism. The leadership of the Communist Party of Slovakia (KSS), including Alexander Dubček and Vasiľ Biľak, who were unhappy with the suppression of the principle of Slovak parity in the 1960s constitution, also exhibited anti-Novotný tendencies. Finally, this wing in the party was strengthened by the rehabilitation of KSČ officials like Josef Smrkovský who had been persecuted in the 1950s.

The personal successes of the opposition at the 13th Congress of the KSČ, held from 31 May to 4 June 1966, removed the taboo from a number of issues, such as the Slovak question and economic reform in the context of the collapse of the unrealistically optimistic third five-year plan.[27] Ota Šik's proposal for the decentralisation of management, the rehabilitation of the market within the planned economy, giving companies a 'material interest' in the their own

---

25 Former Minister for State Security Ladislav Kopřiva and former Minister for National Defence Alexej Čepička were expelled from the party for abuse of office.
26 Especially the stratum of former workers who became corrupted as they transitioned into the ranks of bureaucracy and obtained higher social status and the members of the People's Militia (the armed corps controlled by the KSČ).
27 The Slovak question came to the fore at the 9th Congress of the KSČ in November 1962, which discussed the unequal position of Slovak bodies in the 1960 constitution, the rehabilitation of the so-called bourgeois nationalists, and the existence of a nationalist wing within the KSS.

performance, efforts at wage differentiation, and decoupling the economy from direct political command as well as proposals for the democratisation of the political system went against the prevailing principle of intertwining economic and political power. A conflict was about to take place.

3.4.2. 1968: a crisis of, or an opportunity for, communist ideology?

The year 1968 was a turning point. In one interpretation, it revealed the limits of communism's public support and the instruments employed by the KSČ. By implication, it also showed communism's inability to reform and the naiveté of the vision in which the KSČ could lead a transition to a pluralist democratic system. In another interpretation, 1968 is taken to prove that Marxist-Leninist theory could be put into practice thanks to the dialectic harmony between the communist and non-communist segments of society.

The conflict[28] escalated between October 1967 and January 1968 at three sessions of the Central Committee (ÚV KSČ). The party split into camps either supporting or opposing Novotný. Those opposed accused him of mishandling the Slovak question and of having usurped power[29] and called for him to resign. Although Novotný attempted to internationalise the dispute and win the support of Moscow,[30] he failed to retake control of the party, and at the January 1968 session of the ÚV KSČ he was replaced as the party's first secretary by a representative of the reformists, Alexander Dubček, whose rise to power is usually taken as the beginning of the Prague Spring.

The fall of Novotný was the result of joint action taken by a heterogeneous coalition, with the so-called pro-reform politicians (Oldřich Černík, Alexander Dubček, Jiří Hendrych, Ota Šik, and František Vodsloň) on the one side and representatives of the pro-Soviet line (Vasiľ Biľak, Alois Indra, Miloš Jakeš,

---

28 Consider the events at the 4th Congress of the Union of Czechoslovak Writers in June 1967 and the so-called Strahov demonstration of Prague university students in October 1967. For more detail see Kaplan (2002: 9–90).
29 Consider the criticism of Novotný's behaviour during his visit to Matica slovenská in Martin on 27 August 1967.
30 Leonid Ilyich Brezhnev said it was a matter for the Czechoslovak comrades to resolve. Generally, it can be said that the relaxation in 1960s Czechoslovak politics was made possible by the contemporary 'thaw' in Soviet politics during the era of Nikita Sergeyevich Khrushchev. In any case, the Prague Spring never became a cause for tension in international relations. The West respected the fact that it was an internal problem of the Soviet bloc.

and Lubomír Štrougal) on the other. In the first three months of 1968 the KSČ largely focussed on a change of personnel in its leadership. The most conspicuous move was the election of General Ludvík Svoboda as the new president of Czechoslovakia on 30 March 1968.[31] In parallel, the party gradually ceased to exercise control over its lower bodies, but more importantly, it failed to respond to the radicalisation of Czech and to a lesser extent Slovak society. Some parts of society understood the developments as an opportunity to redefine the entire communist era. Political parties, particularly the Czechoslovak Socialist Party and the Czechoslovak People's Party, became more active, as did social organisations like the Czechoslovak Union of Youth. They sought to extricate themselves from the National Front's control. There were attempts at the renewal of the Social Democratic Party and new non-communist political organisations were founded (the Club of Former Political Prisoners (K231), the Club of Committed Non-Party Members (KAN), and the Critical Thinking Club). Social movements (such as Scouting) that had been previously banned were revived, and churches were also energised. All of this suggested that the KSČ might lose its monopoly and a pluralist political system would emerge.

The Action Programme of the KSČ, adopted in April 1968, was an attempt to regain the lost initiative. The thesis of this programme – the famous 'socialism with a human face' – sought to emphasise the specificity of the Czechoslovak path to socialism. Because it was an industrially developed country, the mechanical adoption of foreign (which can be read as 'Soviet') models should be resisted. It also criticised centralist and bureaucratic administration. The programme envisaged a new political system combining democracy with scientific management,[32] creating space for social initiative, guaranteeing a plurality of interests (still, however, within the framework of the National Front), allowing democratic discussion, providing guarantees against the arbitrariness of power, and, last but not least, turning Czechoslovakia into a federation. At the same time, however, the social order was expected to consolidate, socialist society to stabilise and regain its discipline, and the state to strengthen its ties with the Soviet Union and the anti-imperialist

---

31 Other possible candidates discussed in the KSČ were Čestmír Císař (the new secretary of the ÚV KSČ for education and culture) and Josef Smrkovský (the new speaker of the National Assembly).
32 In this it referred to Zdeněk Mlynář's work *Naše politická soustava a dělba moci* (1990: 90–104).

forces of peace. Economic policy, in line with Šik's reform, was also internally contradictory. On the one hand, it expected economic growth to come from the opening of the economy to international competition, limiting protectionism and subsidies, implementing structural changes in manufacturing, extending workers' rights in factories, and confirming enterprises' right to trade freely. On the other hand, the plan preserved the planned economy and maintained direct investment, price controls, and state intervention on the 'socialist market'. To sum up, the programme was based on the entirely contradictory ideas of guaranteeing political rights and freedoms on the one hand and consolidating the leading role of the KSČ on the other. Demonstrating the predominance of the Dubček faction at the time, it also reflected the limits of these reformers. Though their support for reform gave them the upper hand politically, they could not violate the KSČ's monopoly on power. It was more of an attempt at a 'third way', popular at the time in the West as well (Pithart 1990).

Public opinion grew more radical, especially after the pamphlet *Two Thousand Words (Dva tisíce slov)* was published.[33] And this again split the party elite. Thanks to liberalisation and the abolition of censorship,[34] Dubček and his supporters rode a wave of public sympathy and enthusiasm among many in the cultural front. However, a part of the party apparatus which had previously supported Dubček began to reject further reform. Furthermore, Moscow renewed its anti-reform pressure on Prague during numerous negotiations.

The result of these developments was the occupation of Czechoslovakia by the armies of five states of the Warsaw Pact on the night of 21 August 1968. Society was shocked, the party in chaos. Those loyal to Moscow failed to put into practice their plan to create a government of collaboration headed by Biľak (the so-called worker-peasant government), but the Vysočany Congress (22 August 1968) quickly summoned by reformers did not reinforce their grip on power either. The 1,192 delegates present were more than three-quarters of those eligible, but few Slovak delegates attended the congress. The Congress took a number of steps and articulated demands. It elected a new Central

---

33 Published on 27 June 1968, its author Ludvík Vaculík pointed out the threats posed by the 'allied countries' and conservatives, and emphasised that the national movement must radicalise by means of strikes, demonstrations, and civic protests. For the text, see Vančura (1990: 143–148).

34 For the media during the Prague Spring generally, see Stropnický (2013).

Committee, whose members included both current leaders and others interned in Moscow. It demanded that all constitutional actors be restored to their posts, condemned the aggression against Czechoslovakia, and insisted that foreign armies leave the country.[35] An extraordinary congress of the Communist Party of Slovakia held on 26 to 29 August 1968 rejected the results of the Vysočany Congress. Still, the new status quo was ultimately defined by negotiations in Moscow, where President Svoboda had to intercede on behalf of Dubček and his interned comrades. The Moscow Protocol confirmed the temporary presence of the Warsaw Pact armies on Czechoslovak territory and bound the KSČ to undergo a change of personnel, halt the activities of anti-socialist forces, and normalise the situation – all under the control of other socialist states. The Prague Spring was over.

The personal dramas of some members of the communist elite subsequently helped to create the illusion that in August 1968 the Communist Party enjoyed the support of the whole nation.[36] Yet their fates are not more worthy of attention than those who had no communist affiliation in February 1948 or in spring 1968 and who interpreted the Prague Spring merely as a power struggle within the KSČ. The wave of national protest against the forces of the occupation, a protest symbolised by the self-immolation of two students, Jan Palach and Jan Zajíc, in early 1969, does not represent support for the reform wing of the KSČ.

There was an about-face in political reforms in autumn 1968. A treaty on the conditions for the temporary stationing of Soviet troops on Czechoslovak territory was signed on 16 October 1968. Czechoslovakia was turned into a federation, which satisfied potential Slovak dissenters.[37] Internally, the KSČ adapted itself to the new political reality. An anti-Dubček faction established itself with the support of former Novotný allies (such as Antonín Kapek), who presented the events of spring 1968 not as a reform process but as the actions of anti-socialist, right-wing opportunist forces within the party. Thus, according to the line that prevailed at the April 1969 session of the ÚV KSČ, the leadership was unable to take sufficient measures to resolve the critical situation and to consolidate the country. In response, Dubček resigned from his

---

35 Proposals to leave the Warsaw Pact, to declare neutrality, and to call a general strike failed to win support.
36 Consider, above all, the refusal by František Kriegel to sign the Moscow ultimatum.
37 The National Assembly adopted an act establishing a Czechoslovak federation on 27 October 1968. The act replaced chapters III to VI of the 1960 constitution.

post of first secretary. Gustav Husák, who replaced him, argued that intra-party unity and the leading role of the KSČ in society must be reinstated in order to restore public order, consolidate the situation, resolve economic issues (especially the mounting inflation), and renew friendly relations with countries of the communist bloc (Doskočil 2006: 272–348). Neo-Stalinist 'normalisation' could begin and would not be thrown off-course by the social unrest that marked the first anniversary of the invasion.

Is there a relationship between the communism of February 1948 and the reform communism of spring 1968? In the view of anti-communists, the two were not fundamentally different: both conceived of the state as an agent endowed with absolute power to do good and that good was defined by the communist ideology. The difference between the two communisms was simply the instruments used to put the ideology into practice. By contrast, those on the political left – both the Czech reformist, non-Stalinist left and many on the left in the West – soon started to create a myth out of the Prague Spring, the myth of a possible path to a just, equitable socialist society. Indeed, the context for the Prague events was provided by the dramas of 1968 in Western Europe. For this group the adjectives *social* and *just* largely defined the nature of *democracy.*

3.4.3. The 1970s and the era of 'real socialism'

In the early 1970s the KSČ was restored to a position of power as a result of three waves of purges. In the first wave the main representatives of the so-called right wing and opportunists were expelled from the party. In the second wave, members of the legislature, public administration, army and police, universities (Urbášek 2008: 48–75), mass organisations and the media were subjected to background checks. This wave was accompanied by a clampdown on magazines, the dissolution of editorial boards, and the abolition or transformation of many institutions and organisations.[38] During the third wave, 70,000 committees screened Communist Party members in what was called a 'party card exchange'; about 500,000 were expelled from the party,[39] the criterion being not so much their behaviour in 1968 as their willingness to

---

38 For example, in the November 1971 elections to the National Assembly only 60 deputies were re-elected (Cigánek 1993: 58-59).
39 That is less than one-third of the membership. The leadership gradually allowed the new intake. For KSČ cadre policy in early 1970s, see Hradecká (1998).

support the new course taken by Husák. This course eschewed repression and large trials[40] and largely depoliticised Czechoslovak society. Proof that KSČ's internal unity and hegemony were restored came in December 1970 with the adoption of *Lessons from the crisis period within the party and society after the 13th Congress of the KSČ* – in effect, a new official history of the party. At the 14th Congress in May 1971 the KSČ declared its emphasis on deepening ideological unity within the party and reinforcing its links with progressive workers' movements around the world. The KSČ strengthened and reinforced the party apparatus and state bureaucracy. This gave it control over all spheres of society, as in the 1950s, but now without the same ideological content. It now used the instruments of technocracy, such as the strict application of a rigorously dual, yet superficial, model of Czechoslovak federalism and an emphasis on a balance of the numbers of Czechs and Slovaks occupying offices of the party and the state as well as the media.[41] The elections to the Federal Assembly in January 1971 confirmed this hegemony. Turnout was 99.4 % of those registered in the electoral rolls and 99.8 % voted for the candidate list of the National Front. Thus, throughout the 1970s and 1980s, the KSČ was, alongside the Socialist Unity Party of East Germany, the Soviet Union's most reliable partner in Central Europe.

From the mid-1970s, the attractiveness of the communist regime rested on a social contract. In exchange for popular consent to the political status quo, the KSČ guaranteed the population a decent standard of living, increased leisure time and entertainment, and regular ritual festivals (such as May Day parades, lantern parades, and Spartakiads). A network of mass interest and social organisations and the largely loyal community of Czech artists facilitated the regime's 'pastoral oversight' of society, producing a wide range of entertainment, with television dominating. Indeed, this 'real socialism' involved the foregrounding of mediocrity, loyalty, lethargy and indifference to politics as the key virtues of a socialist citizen. This contract between the KSČ and society was valid as long as the KSČ was able to supply material goods to

---

40 The trials in 1970–1972 of rebels such as Jaroslav Šabata, formerly employed at the Regional Committee of the KSČ in South Moravia, or Milan Hübl, former rector of the party's Political University, are nevertheless interesting, as they document the fates of some formerly prominent KSČ members. For more details, see Otáhal (1993: 11–33).

41 The consequences were sometimes absurd, for instance, in sports where there were attempts to achieve a balance of Czechs and Slovaks in Czechoslovak national teams. The situation created latent nationalist tensions which would eventually materialise into a real political conflict between Czechs and Slovaks after 1989.

those categories of the population dependent on the regime and to confirm their scepticism towards potential change (Možný 1991).

For these reasons, the hegemonic position of the KSČ was not threatened by the publication of Charter 77 in January 1977 by its first signatories, Václav Havel, Václav Hájek, and Jan Patočka. The Charter was an intellectually remarkable moral appeal and proclamation of ideas. It was neither contained within the structures of the party and state nor was it a political step to found an oppositional platform. As a result, the Charter was not entirely intelligible even to people opposed to the communist regime – if indeed they found out about it at all. The effects of the Chartist movement and other formations that sought an alternative to the regime (especially the independent cultural scene, itself consciously apolitical) could be observed only many years later.[42]

The Czechoslovakia of the 1970s and 1980s is not difficult to classify. A number of authors (Dvořáková and Kunc 1994: 127–143) have already challenged the use of the term *totalitarianism* to describe this period, preferring the designation *authoritarian post-totalitarianism*. Many of totalitarianism's attributes disappeared during this period, not only in Czechoslovakia but in the whole Soviet bloc: (1) the regime ceased to be able and willing to interfere with social life in its entirety; (2) ideology waned or disappeared and was replaced by the technology of power; (3) due to events such as the year 1968 in Czechoslovakia, 1956 in Hungary, and the late 1970s and early 1980s in Poland, the regime was no longer able to appeal to the 'symbolism of its birth'. Still, to the very last moment, the communist regime in Czechoslovakia cleaved to the absolute dominance of the state in the economy. The KSČ's political monopoly also survived until the end, as there were no alternative political projects. This does not mean that autonomous social structures, such as the Catholic Church or the nascent environmental movement, were absent; what was lacking was the understanding that regime change depends upon the willingness to act politically. It was not home-grown opposition that accelerated the approaching demise of communist rule, but international developments and conflicts within the KSČ itself. And these were spurred by socio-economic rather than political issues.

---

42 Various leftist groups (Trotskyites and others) were more eager to pick up the task of formulating political alternatives. For a broader view of opposition in Czechoslovakia see Otáhal (2011).

4. The Velvet Revolution: the causes and process of the decline of communist power[1]

Stanislav Balík

Signs of the approaching collapse of communist rule could be observed from the mid-1980s onwards. In July 1985, a large Catholic pilgrimage was organised in Velehrad, a place linked with the beginnings of Czech and Moravian Christianity. Although the communist establishment sought to prevent the pilgrimage or at least impose severe restrictions on it, they found they no longer had enough power and authority. The pilgrimage became the largest anti-regime gathering of the communist era, with nearly 200,000 people participating, almost two-thirds of them young. The presence of young people was particularly painful for the regime, as it flew in the face of communist descriptions of the Catholic Church as a concern only of a few old people (Cuhra 2001: 168–174, Halas 2004: 625–626).

Less than a year later, in April 1986, the dysfunction of the channels of power and information was made evident in the regime's inadequate response to the disaster at the nuclear power plant in Chernobyl. For ideological reasons, the KSČ absurdly refused to inform the public about the possible dangers, as by doing so it would admit that Soviet nuclear technology was imperfect. The party preferred to put Czechoslovak citizens at risk.

At the same time in the Soviet Union, the *perestroika* reform movement, linked with the elevation of Mikhail Sergeyevich Gorbachev to the post of general secretary of the Communist Party of the Soviet Union in March 1985, was becoming increasingly vocal. Among other changes, perestroika reduced the pressure exerted on dissident circles. As a consequence, expressions of opposition, first cultural and later civic, became more common. The transformation of the communist bloc that was linked with the phenomena of *perestroika* and *glasnost* complicated rather than eased things for the KSČ. At its 17th Congress in March 1986 the party mostly ignored *perestroika* and sought to preserve the status quo. The KSČ leadership found itself in a blind alley. The party was led by many of the same people who had initiated the 'normalisation' nearly two decades before and for whom unconditional obedience to Moscow was the main component of their identity. To carry out

---

[1] Parts of this chapter are revised from Balík 2015 and Balík, Holzer and Kopeček 2008.

perestroika and *glasnost* now (following the Moscow model) would mean renouncing their own policies (for the discussions and developments in the highest echelons of the KSČ, see Štefek 2014: 71–142). Thus, the 1985-1989 period was marked by careful manoeuvring – in effect, a show of disrespect towards Moscow, even though obeisance to the Moscow line had hitherto been the very essence of Czech communism. Within the structures of the KSČ, this widened the gap between the leadership (the 'old guard'), who felt threatened by the reform vision, and the younger, technocratic generation of party officials whose interest was in finding a way forward that would allow them to preserve their individual positions, even if the party as a whole were to lose its monopoly on power.

Until November 1989, the latent conflict within the party between a pragmatic wing willing to admit some reform (for instance in the economy) and an ideologically orthodox wing that rejected such an option as it might unleash processes that could gradually dismantle the KSČ's monopoly, did not develop into an open clash. Some of the steps taken, such as the replacement of Gustáv Husák in the post of general secretary of the ÚV KSČ with Miloš Jakeš, the resignation of the ideologist Vasiľ Bilak from the ÚV KSČ, and the amendment of the act on elections to the Federal Assembly that allowed multiple candidates to contest a seat, cannot be described as an adequate response to the evolving situation. Rather, they indicate that the majority of the party elite lagged behind developments and desperately sought to preserve at least some power. Thus, in the second half of the 1980s the party showed numerous signs of decay. As their patron, the Soviet Union, ceased to exercise strict oversight over them, the KSČ leaders found themselves in a new, historically unprecedented situation. The waning of the KSČ's political monopoly in the late 1980s was accompanied by deep disillusion within the party and a merciless reality check for its leaders.

What emerged in Czechoslovakia was the situation often seen at the end of a totalitarian regime: the party-state was divided into two wings – a reform wing and a conservative wing – and an unofficial opposition, including both dissident circles (Palouš 1993) and wider strata of society, which was becoming more active. Czechoslovakia nonetheless differed from most Eastern European countries in that the reform communist wing was of insufficient strength and, more importantly, lacked strong personalities in its leadership (Vykoukal, Litera and Tejchman 2000: 592–593). Furthermore, unlike in Poland and Hungary, the Czechoslovak opposition was small – though increasingly active, its numbers were very low. The broader public had only a faint knowledge of the opposition leaders, including Václav Havel.

As far as the relationship between society and politics was concerned, the social contract (see Chapter 3) was being eroded during the late 1980s, primarily due to the inappropriate structure of the country's economy. The regime ceased to be able to satisfy the growing consumerist expectations of its population. These expectations – which the regime had been able to fulfil sufficiently throughout the 1970s – were raised by the visibly improving standards of living in Western Europe, and Czechoslovak citizens were particularly sensitive to the comparisons they were inevitably making with their neighbours, Austria and West Germany.[2]

From 1988 onwards, the nature of the opposition movements and their strategies gradually changed. New organisations were created, mostly by the young generation. In comparison with their predecessors, they preserved the emphasis on the defence of human and civic rights, but for the first time political arguments *sensu stricto* appeared with regime change as their aim.

Petitions became a symbol of the last years of communist rule. In the largest petition ever, supported by more than half a million people in late 1987, the Moravian Catholic Augustin Navrátil demanded religious freedom. In June 1989 the petition 'A Few Sentences' *(Několik vět)*, written by Charter 77, demanded that political prisoners be released and independent movements, trade unions, and associations be allowed (it was signed by about 40,000 people, but this was still marginal support; see Balík and Hanuš 2007: 60; Otáhal 1999). Despite all this, until November 1989 the growing expressions of opposition lacked a common organisational and political platform and a coherent strategy (Měchýř 1999: 60–63; Suk 1997a: 9–11).

The course of events and change of atmosphere in society were ultimately precipitated by events abroad: the quick disintegration of communist regimes in Poland (Dudek 2002: 32–80), Hungary, and the German Democratic Republic (Vykoukal, Litera and Tejchman 2000: 706–708). Crucial was the massive wave of East Germans who fled into West Germany, which affected

---

2 This can be supported by contemporary opinion polls. According to one, more than half of KSČ members and officials mistrusted the leadership of the party and state (Vaněk 1994: 22–24).

Czechoslovakia when they headed for the West German embassy in Prague (Tůma 1999: 163).[3]

4.1. The events of November 1989

Within Central Europe, Czechoslovakia is distinctive in that the two phases of transition to democracy – liberalisation and democratisation – occurred concurrently.[4] In other words, regime change was not preceded by a period of intentional liberalisation. Rather, the parallel unfolding of the twin processes was a sign of the old regime losing its strength. Czechoslovakia nonetheless did successfully transition to a democracy with guarantees. How did the whole process evolve?

Very broadly speaking, it was sudden and quick. Whereas in mid-November 1989 Czechoslovakia was an isolated, unreformed, communist oasis in Central Europe, within a few weeks its domestic communist regime collapsed and relinquished power. The swiftness of its capitulation and the speed with which society emancipated itself, was redolent of falling dominoes.

The trigger was provided by the police suppression of an authorised student demonstration, held in Prague on 17 November 1989 to commemorate the 50th anniversary of the death of the student Jan Opletal, a victim of Nazi persecution. It was not the first time the police had taken such harsh measures against demonstrators: it beat many of them in August 1988 and in January 1989. Perhaps the crucial difference that led to the mass mobilisation of the public was the rumour that a student had been killed. Although disproved by the regime two days later, the psychological impact of the accusation was nevertheless extraordinary.[5] Outraged by the police action, students called a

---

3 For the disintegration of the communist bloc, see Durman 1998; for the realities of Czechoslovak power, see Suk 2004: 22–27 and Vaněk 2006: 324–327.

4 Liberalisation is the initial stage of transition, consisting of such processes as opening, reformulation, or *perestroika,* which open the hitherto closed political system. Successful liberalisation is followed by the second stage of transition, democratisation, during which democratic institutions are constructed and democratic rules of the game established. See Przeworski 1992, Dvořáková and Kunc 1994: 90.

5 A range of questions and conjectures have quickly surrounded the events of 17 November, some of which will probably never be answered with any degree of certainty. Among the most discussed was the question of who ordered the brutal measures taken against the demonstrators on Prague's Národní třída and whether this was an attempt to discredit certain Communist

protest strike and were soon joined by actors from Prague's theatres. Riding the wave of spontaneous mass protest, the Civic Forum (OF) emerged on 19 November 1989 with Václav Havel as a central figure. Existing opposition initiatives along with many people outside the circles of dissent quickly joined the Forum. OF was strongly decentralised – local Civic Forums were created in small municipalities, factories, and offices, but their links with the OF centre in Prague were minimal. In Slovakia, the Public Against Violence (VPN) movement, a 'sister' movement to the Forum, was founded at practically the same time. Demonstrations in which hundreds of thousands participated began first in Prague before spreading to other large cities. They culminated in a successful two-hour general strike on 27 November 1989, confirming that the Forum commanded broad public support (for more details, see Suk 2003: 73–92).

The November demonstrations had something of a carnival atmosphere (Kenney 2003) and were led by an alliance between, on the one hand, students and intellectuals and, on the other, actors and artists. These two social groups had enjoyed a privileged position in Czech national life ever since its revival during the nineteenth century. This instance was the first of many interesting reflections of the Czech nation's past during what was called the Velvet Revolution. It was not, however, an exclusive alliance. OF also appealed to workers, and important roles in creating this appeal were played in the Forum by Petr Miller (a blacksmith) and Valtr Komárek (a well-known and respected economic forecaster), who later became ministers.

4.2. Fall of the executive

When in its founding proclamation of 19 November 1989 OF called for the resignation of eight particularly compromised communist leaders, there was only one member of the government among them (Suk 1997a: 1). At that moment the Civic Forum was not seeking to assume executive power. The first phase focused not on altering the government, but on provoking unspecified

---

Party officials. According to one interpretation, it was an attempt to depose the existing KSČ leadership and replace it with another that would be clearly in favour of *perestroika*. The Gorbachev leadership or the Soviet secret police (KGB) supposedly connived in the operation. None of these conspiracy theories has ever been plausibly proven (Bartuška 1990: 241–248).

changes within the KSČ. Lacking strategies for how to proceed, the Czechoslovak opposition was entirely unprepared to take power.

Dialogue became its chief strategy, but the dialogue was between an ill-defined 'state' and a similarly vaguely defined 'opposition'. The terms of this dialogue were not clearly established in advance. The Forum spoke for the opposition, and after some delay the federal Prime Minister Ladislav Adamec, a reformist within the KSČ, emerged as the representative of those in power. He did so, however, as a representative of the state, rather than the party, after it became clear that the *de facto* holder of power – the leadership of the KSČ – was unable to act and unwilling to engage in dialogue. That the party had lost its 'will to power' was evident as soon as its attempt to use force through its paramilitary units in the People's Militia ended in fiasco.[6] At the same time, the mass media – state-controlled TV, radio and newspapers – also refused to obey the ruling forces, facilitating the spread of protests beyond Prague. The National Front, the body 'unifying' all the parties and those mass organisations that were permitted, equally began to disintegrate (*Poslední hurá* 1992: 70, Otáhal 1994: 110, Cysařová 1999: 297–307). The short interlude in which the KSČ replaced its general secretary with the unknown and unremarkable Karel Urbánek did not help the party.

As Adamec took the initiative, the once-proclaimed and long-respected leading role of the KSČ in state and society came to an abrupt and decisive end. Further developments led directly to a constitutional and democratic political system.

The aforementioned successful general strike, in which 75 % of citizens participated, was a powerfully symbolic event (Suk 1997b: 84). It marked the transition from the mass demonstrations to the start of negotiations. In subsequent talks with Adamec, the Forum focussed on its vision of controlling, rather than exercising, power. This gave Adamec a free hand to form a new administration, and on 3 December 1989 he unveiled what became known as the '15+5' government, consisting of 15 communists and five non-communists. Although this proposal was based on an agreement with OF, spontaneous demonstrations began again in earnest, and the public rejected the 15+5 government, prompting OF to alter its strategy and resolve to participate directly in government. The support of economists from the Prognostics

---

[6] Units were called from regions to Prague where they were supposed to help the police to pacify the situation. Some of the militias never left for Prague, however, and two days later Jakeš brought the whole operation to a halt.

Institute of the Czechoslovak Academy of Sciences, in particular Václav Klaus, were instrumental in this change. The economists were pragmatic and understood that by taking up posts in the executive they would be able to influence the flow of events more efficiently than they could by merely exerting external control. In response to this, Adamec resigned (Suk 2003: 58) with a haste that was extraordinary when compared with the situation abroad. Timothy Garton Ash aptly commented that what took 10 years in Poland, 10 months in Hungary and 10 weeks in East Germany, took 10 days in Czechoslovakia (Garton Ash 1993).

Negotiations between Adamec, who had already announced his resignation, and the Civic Forum resulted in the nomination of a new federal prime minister, Marián Čalfa, a KSČ member who had been the minister for legislation until November 1989. As recently as mid-1989 Čalfa had been responsible for drafting a more repressive press law. His government, appointed on 10 December 1989, had as its chief task to lead the country to free elections. The Forum obtained a strong position within the Čalfa government. In particular, it held the main ministries concerned with the economy, but non-communists also occupied the posts of first deputy prime minister, foreign minister, and minister for labour and social affairs. In terms of party affiliations, the allocation of posts in the government did not secure dominance for the Forum: ten members of the government were communists, two were from the Czechoslovak Socialist Party, two from the Czechoslovak People's Party, and seven were non-partisans nominated by OF and VPN (Fiala, Holzer, Mareš and Pšeja 1999: 95). However, for some of the communists, party affiliation was merely a residue of the past and in practice they no longer represented the party. In any case, this was the first government since May 1946 in which the communists did not have a notional or actual majority.

In terms of choosing people to occupy posts in the 'power' ministries of defence and interior, which, given that regime change was not yet achieved, were of cardinal importance, the Forum leaders displayed political naïveté. The appointment of the communist General Miroslav Vacek as defence minister apparently yielded no ill effects for the country's security.[7] The Ministry of the Interior proved a much more serious problem. Until the end of December 1989, it was administered collectively. The portfolio was then given to Richard

---

[7] Vacek was previously the chief of the general staff of the Czechoslovak People's Army. At Havel's unexplained request, Vacek remained in office even after the 1990 elections and was removed only in October 1990.

Sacher, who was Havel's choice for the post. The period of collective administration and Sacher's tenure were a time of anarchy at the ministry, which was exploited in particular by the secret police, who shredded a vast number of documents, including 'live' dossiers that included details of the work of secret agents (Suk 2003: 356–360).

Another fundamentally naïve step was taken before the appointment of Čalfa's government. Inspired by the Polish experience, round-table talks were initiated by the KSČ with the participation of the parties incorporated in the National Front and OF and VPN. Though the talks had minimal impact on the make-up of the new government, they helped to legitimise the KSČ as a serious actor (Hanzel 1990: 295–380) and effectively precluded a future ban on the Communist Party, something that was seriously considered at the time. Be that as it may, the Czechoslovak 'round table' was in no way an analogy of such talks in Poland and Hungary.

The figure of Prime Minister Čalfa is an interesting one. Until Čalfa's appointment, Adamec believed that he, Adamec, would preserve some influence over the executive through Čalfa. For its part, the Forum believed that Čalfa was only a short-term solution. Ultimately, it was Václav Havel who derived the greatest benefit from Čalfa. Havel established a close alliance with this technologist of power before his first election as the country's president, and their alliance survived the first free elections in 1990. Čalfa thus led the government until the 1992 elections. Indeed, Čalfa symbolised the notion of legal continuity, a key component in OF's strategy. By maintaining legal continuity with the communist regime, the transition of power to the new regime could be smooth, but another consequence was that the overwhelming majority of communist crimes could not be prosecuted, as their perpetrators acted largely within the limits of so-called 'socialist legality'. That is to say, they had acted in accordance with the legal provisions valid at the time, even though these laws were considered illegitimate by the new regime. Still, the rejection of large-scale punishments – one of the very reasons for the descriptor 'Velvet Revolution' – was an important characteristic of the regime change.

4.3. President

The year 1989 illustrates interesting connections between older and recent Czech history. Many authors have already pointed out the extraordinary position enjoyed by the president in the Czechoslovak and Czech political systems (Šimíček 2008, Novák and Brunclík 2008). Since the foundation of the republic in 1918, the president was never the chief of the executive and did not hold political power in the true sense of the word, though he always commanded significant political influence, far surpassing his constitutional powers.

It is interesting to investigate the origins of this situation. Usually a simple reference is made to Tomáš Garrigue Masaryk, the first Czechoslovak president ('President-Liberator', as he was called; in office 1918–1935) who imbued his office with a particular *esprit*. Nevertheless, even the extraordinary figure of Masaryk cannot fully explain the deeply ingrained acceptance of the importance of the presidential office. Indeed, Masaryk only picked up the threads of something that ran deeper – the desire of the Czech nation for a just and good king, a desire once expressed for Emperor and King Franz Josef I. But Franz Josef I painfully disappointed the hopes the Czechs had placed in him: he did not fulfil their dreams to have him crowned King of Bohemia, and he did not grant them the self-government they wanted. In reference to the tradition of the independent Principality and Kingdom of Bohemia, T. G. Masaryk took as his headquarters Prague Castle, the ancient seat of Bohemian princes and kings. In the century since the foundation of the republic in 1918, Prague Castle has been the official residence of Czechoslovak and Czech presidents. The Czech Republic is one of six in Europe where the president is based in a former royal residence,[8] and Prague Castle is the oldest continuous seat of a head of state in the world.

The importance attached to the presidency by Czechoslovak society is also apparent from the fact that Czechoslovakia was the only communist country in Central and Eastern Europe in which this post was never abolished or even suspended. Indeed, the most powerful men of the regime – the successive heads of the Communist Party's Central Committee – have usually felt the need to legitimise their position by having themselves elected as presidents of the Republic.

With respect to the events of 1989, another aspect of Prague Castle's history comes to the fore. Throughout Czech history, every takeover of power was incomplete until the challenger had captured the Castle and sat within its walls. Sitting on a stone seat was the practice until the thirteenth century. Later kings were crowned in St Vitus Cathedral, a few hundred meters from the stone

---

8 Austria, the Czech Republic, Italy, Portugal, Romania, and Russia.

seat. Even the communist takeover in June 1948 was completed only when the chairman of the KSČ, Klement Gottwald, was elected president at the Castle and took part in the ceremonial Te Deum in St Vitus Cathedral. 1989 was no different.

This explains why the Velvet Revolution culminated and the transition to democracy was confirmed in the election of a new president and not a new parliament (as in Poland and Hungary). The last communist president resigned on 10 December 1989, several hours after he had appointed a new government. At that time, it was unclear who his successor would be. The communists promoted a direct method of election in which the chances of the former prime minister Adamec would have been great, as shown by a December 1989 opinion poll (Suk 2003: 200). However, direct election was not adopted. Instead, the desire to have a new president before the beginning of a new year prevailed (this violated the constitution then in force), which left the task of electing the country's president in the hands of parliament. At that point the 'problem of parliament' had to be resolved: the body that was to elect the new (potentially non-communist) president was made up of KSČ members and supporters (formally non-partisans or members of the non-communist satellite parties) elected in 1986. This was the birth of the so-called Čalfa phenomenon: the new prime minister convinced MPs to vote for the leading figure of anti-communist resistance, the dissident Václav Havel, as the new president of the country. The close alliance between Havel and Čalfa, which continued even after the 1990 parliamentary election, dated to this time.

On 29 December 1989, Havel was unanimously elected president in an open parliamentary vote (Fiala, Holzer, Mareš and Pšeja 1999: 99). At this symbolic moment, the fall of the communist regime was complete: the man who only seven months before had been a political prisoner was now president. It was also a symbolic humiliation of the Communist Party, as every one of its MPs voted for Havel in a live TV broadcast. Havel then greeted his supporters in the courtyard of the Castle, where the stone seat once stood, and attended the liturgy of Te Deum in St Vitus Cathedral. The circle of history was closed, the change complete.

4.4. Representative bodies

It is part of the Czechoslovak/Czech political tradition that parliament is ignored at points of crisis. So it was in 1938, 1945, 1948, 1968 and 1989 as well. Parliament came into the spotlight to some extent at the point of the presidential election, and more so afterwards. In late 1989, an act was adopted that allowed the co-option of new MPs into parliament to replace those MPs who had resigned their seats. In January 1990, a constitutional act was adopted permitting the removal of MPs and the co-optation of others into the vacant seats, but this could not take place until March 1990. The term of the parliament elected in 1986 was also shortened and the MPs' mandate was changed from imperative to free. Therefore, empty seats were filled not on the basis of elections, but on the basis of proposals by political forces (including the KSČ) (Suk 2003: 283–290). This was one of the fundamental elements of the early part of the transition. The question of elections was pushed into the background, and indeed elections to parliament took place only in June 1990, more than half a year after the November 1989 events, and nearly six months after Havel's election as president. For that reason, the elections were not so much a fundamental break as a retroactive ratification of the break.

Half of the MPs were newly co-opted. The co-option method, necessary but problematic in itself and defensible only for a brief period, was therefore used to create a legislature which adopted the first fundamental acts transforming the non-democratic substance of the Czechoslovak political regime (Gerloch 1999: 41–43).

The aforementioned constitutional act on co-option was also used to make personnel changes in local authorities, the national committees which were the organs of public administration in municipalities and regions. Using this act, the most compromised deputies were removed from office and representatives of the non-communist opposition co-opted in their stead. This only happened on a substantial scale in larger cities. A fundamental change in personnel only took place after the November 1990 local elections, which restored democratic local self-governance. This also meant that for the entire year following the November 1989 regime change, municipalities and towns remained under the rule of the former exponents of communist power (Balík 2009: 57–58).

4.5. A Velvet Revolution?

The character of the Czechoslovak communist regime's demise was influenced by a number of circumstances. There was no distinctive, cohesive group within the Party waiting for its opportunity to replace the old guard. Nor was there an opposition group ready to take over. The absence of the former was the reason the KSČ subsequently evolved differently from other Central European communist parties, ultimately ending up on the left fringe of the political spectrum and never participating in post-communist governments. The small number of opposition activists was the reason the new democratic regime desperately lacked experts able to participate in the exercise of power. Therefore, for the most part it had to rely not only on often unprepared people from the grey zone,[9] but also on former communist cadres.

If the communist regime lost its legitimacy in the eyes of the public, it was neither because it failed to deliver social justice and equality, nor because of the repression of the communist secret police (StB). Its demise was a consequence of economic underperformance (Turek 1995: 47). This also explains why the secret police, its transformation, and the preservation of its archives, were not a priority for the new rulers. Although the public originally wished for StB officials to be punished in some way, Havel and the other newly-powerful leaders around him did not create the conditions under which such retribution could take place.

This explains why steps to redress old injustices were not an immediate priority. And it is also an explanation for the initially-lauded and later much criticised 'velvet' character of the revolution. A society removing its political regime because of oppression and universal terror or injustice behaves differently from one that mainly wants to change the functioning of its economy.

When the change of regime and ultimately of the whole social arrangement failed to fulfil the expectations of many in the populace, a sense of disillusion set in that may be said to remain to this day. According to recent opinion polls, the post-November 1989 developments have failed to fulfil the expectations of more than half of the public (see e.g., ČTK 2014).

---

9 A term coined by sociologist Jiřina Šiklová to describe the silent majority in society, who were neither communists nor dissenters.

4.6. Conclusion

The fall of the communist regime in Czechoslovakia and the country's transition to democracy should not be taken as confirming the illusion that communism was a mere derailment, a random paradox, or a temporary deviation from Czech society's natural position in the West. In recent years a number of works in the social sciences have focussed on the functioning, features, and characteristics of Czech communism and its place in historical memory (Mayer 2009). However, a debate about its emergence, rise to power, and success has largely been lacking (Balík and Holzer 2005; Holzer 2009). The significant role of the communist movement in twentieth-century Czech politics was not a historical anomaly. It was, by contrast, one of its most characteristic traits.

In analysing this phenomenon, one cannot but respect the potential of the Czech left, which has historically been the dominant and most dynamic mover of Czech politics (consider the substantial support for the left in the first elections held under universal male suffrage in 1907 and 1911, the Austro-Hungarian era). However, this analysis entails a certain view of politics itself. In the Czech environment, a 'procedural' understanding of politics as a sphere where freely expressed opinions clash and compromises are sought has never established itself. Far more common has been a view of politics as a campaign for justice.

During the nineteenth century the Czech nation fought the Habsburgs; in the first half of the twentieth century Czechoslovak democracy fought the Germans; and throughout the twentieth century the Czech proletariat fought the bourgeoisie. The Czech left has, on the one hand, repeatedly shown a remarkable confidence in the progressive vision of a political future as best represented in Western political thought by Marxism; on the other hand, it has also occasionally shown an ability for critical self-reflection, having obtained practical experience with the methods of implementing such a vision (Reiman 2000). After World War II, Czech communists certainly did not have to struggle for power – the left had already had power for a long time. This is also the reason why the 1960s were mythologised, especially in the cultural discourse, where that period is thought of as a true golden age. The contribution of the artistic community to the process of forming modern Czech national life and the building of an independent state is undeniable, perhaps even determinative, throughout all the stages of its genesis (Kusák 1998). The true conscience of the Czech nation is not a statesman, not a military leader or a man of wealth, but a writer.

The idea even suggests itself that the famous 'meaning' of Czech history, sought by Czech intellectuals since the second half of the nineteenth century, was realised during the communist era. Not only in the forty-year long attempt to implement the communist ideal of a classless society; but also in the sense that even the anti-communist movement which emerged from that period of lack of freedom conceived of politics not as a clash of interests, but, again, as a struggle of good with evil, a clash that had an evident moral dimension. The tenor of the times naturally required distinctive arguments, instruments, and personalities. The Charter 77 movement (or at least an important part of it), symbolised by the figure of Václav Havel, had all of this in abundance. The problem was that their total moral commitment – resulting from the extreme situation in which Czech dissidents found themselves – their 'non-political politics' had to lose its legitimacy after the fall of communism. Their dreams and desires were, paradoxically, aimed at the achievement of a situation where they would lose their power and appeal. This is also a reason why some in Czech society today are still disappointed by November 1989 and feel that the Velvet Revolution has been 'stolen', a feeling that survives despite all the positive change November 1989 has brought: unprecedented freedom, strong economic growth, and substantial environmental improvements.

The authenticity of Czech communism mentioned above explains the disappointment with the 'results of November 1989' felt by another segment of Czech society. This is the only way to explain why in June 1990, in a situation of almost 100 % voter turnout, the Communist Party polled 14 % of the vote. Such strong support cannot be explained by protest voting, the harsh consequences of the economic reform, rising prices, the devaluation of savings or unemployment, as none of these factors were present in Czechoslovakia at that moment. By contrast, the failures of central planning, Czechoslovakia's lagging behind Austria and Germany, countries with which it had once boldly compared itself, and serious environmental damage, were all acutely felt. Despite all this, the Communist Party, though almost completely lacking dynamism and credible leadership, was the chosen alternative for one seventh of the populace. In November 1989, that party lost its opportunity to govern and shape society according to its ideological tenets. Since then it has represented a nostalgic memory rather than a real alternative.

5. The Velvet Divorce: the end of Czechoslovakia

Lubomír Kopeček

At the stroke of midnight on 31 December 1992, a mere three years after the Velvet Revolution, Czechoslovakia ceased to exist and two new independent states were created in its stead. In the memories of most Czechs and Slovaks, the main instigators, or in the view of some, the 'guilty parties' in this velvet divorce were Václav Klaus and Vladimír Mečiar, the leaders respectively of the two victorious parties in the June 1992 elections, the Civic Democratic Party (ODS) and the Movement for Democratic Slovakia (HZDS). From the perspective of those who are nostalgic for Czechoslovakia – they tend to be of more advanced age today – it was an arbitrary decision on the part of these two politicians, one that did not respect the will of the majority of Czechs and Slovaks to preserve Czechoslovakia. Indeed, contemporary opinion polls showed continued support in both nations for the union as well as good mutual relations.[1] Yet such a view distorts the deeper roots and genesis of the Czecho-Slovak breakup.

5.1. Legacies of the past and Slovak nation- and state building

Past legacies played an important role in the breakup of Czechoslovakia, the most important of which was, from 1918 onwards, the Slovak question. The core concerns were the completion of the nation-building process and the position of Slovakia within the common state. Although both the Czech lands and Slovakia had been part of Austria-Hungary, their political cultures, methods of governance, and levels of modernisation were very different, which stemmed from the dissimilarities between the Austrian and Hungarian parts of the Empire. The Czech lands ranked among the most economically developed

---

1 For reasons of space this chapter is necessarily selective, leaving out of consideration some interesting but less essential issues such as the attitudes of the Hungarian minority towards Czechoslovakia and the influence of exile Slovak organisations in the process of Czechoslovakia's division.

parts of the Empire with an almost 100 % literacy rate and a mature civic culture as well as a rich assortment of associations and political parties. The Czech nation–building process was successfully completed during the nineteenth century, not least thanks to the democratisation of Austria in the last decades of the Empire's existence.

By contrast, Slovakia was at the end of the Empire a largely agricultural and traditional country with a high rate of illiteracy. Its politics was negatively marked by the dominance of Hungary, which put severe restrictions on the political rights of Slovaks, and created a parochial political culture, all of which tended to delay nation-building (Almond and Verba 1965, Hroch 1999).

Over the decades of their coexistence in one state, the social, economic, cultural, and religious differences between the Czechs and Slovaks decreased, but never disappeared entirely. Jiří Musil, for instance, has asserted that after 1989 Slovak society was more solidary and more communal (*gemeinschaftlich*), while Czech society was more associative (*gesellschaftlich*) (Musil 1995: 87).

Between 1918 and 1938 the natural Slovak tendencies towards emancipation and autonomy clashed with the notion of 'Czechoslovakism', the idea of a united Czechoslovak political nation, and the centralist conception of the state (Kováč 1997, Lipták 1998, Bakke 2004). Unlike most Czechs who perceived Czechoslovakia as 'their state', Slovaks had more varied feelings ranging from identification with Czechoslovakia to separatism. These attitudes were influenced by political, social, and religious factors as well as the external context. It suffices to recall that the main champion of autonomy and the later founder of the Hitler-allied Slovak State was the conservative Catholic Hlinka's Slovak People's Party, which mobilised its adherents using protests against the 'centralist, Hussite and atheist' Czechs.

The unfortunate events of Munich, the successful push for Slovakia's autonomy in autumn 1938, and the establishment of the Slovak Republic shortly afterwards firmly embedded themselves in the Czech national consciousness and were to contribute in the future to Czech misgivings about handing more powers to Slovak national institutions. This was demonstrated during the era of the Third Czechoslovak Republic and after 1948 when the centralist system was reinstated, albeit without the official doctrine of Czechoslovakism (see Chapters 2 and 3 for more details).

The Slovak question, however, was merely dormant for a time, only to be brought back to life towards the end of the 1960s in connection with the liberalisation of the communist regime. The result was a federal arrangement influenced by the Soviet model. Federalism was a means to 'recognize and coopt the Slovak nation and thereby limit the political and economic dominance of the Czech lands' (Bunce 2004: 427). From the viewpoint of Slovak nationalism, it was only a partial success, as thanks to the regime of 'normalisation' and the KSČ's political monopoly, the new arrangement remained strongly centralist over the next two decades. The powers of the government of the Slovak Republic and its parliament were very limited. The bicameral federal parliament operated merely as a lever of power for the communist regime and the federal government was effectively subordinate to the KSČ's Central Committee.

Even if the federation was merely a facade, it did fundamentally strengthen Slovak self-confidence and accelerate the nation-building process. Valerie Bunce as well as other scholars such as Juan Linz and Alfred Stepan have argued convincingly that the late 1960s ethnofederal line dividing Czechoslovakia into two formally equal republics and the new constitutional arrangement acted subversively vis-à-vis Czechoslovakia, laying the seeds of its future disintegration (Bunce 1999, 2004, Linz and Stepan 1996). It also mattered that there was no third balancing entity with a similar degree of autonomy and similar institutional foundations. Neither the populous Hungarian minority in the south of Slovakia, nor Moravia – a historically and culturally distinct region in the eastern part of the Czech lands – were awarded such status. Paradoxically, the political monopoly of KSČ had cemented Czechoslovakia and when it disappeared in 1989, the system of republic- and federal-level institutions became an important instrument for Slovak politicians, one they could use to push their political agenda (Leff 2000).

5.2. The pitfalls of democratic transition, or was communism pure evil?

In the early 1990s the perception of the communist regime in Slovakia was less negative than in the Czech lands. Significantly contributing to this perception was not only the above-mentioned federalisation of the state, but also the modernisation and, in particular, industrialisation and urbanisation of Slovakia, which radically transformed traditional Slovak society, after 1948. These efforts were often accompanied by social engineering, yet the worst instances of this occurred in the 1950s, and the methods employed during the subsequent decades were much milder.

Also worth mentioning in this connection is the different character of the 'normalisation' regime in Slovakia. Already in the early days of normalisation, the purging of KSČ of reformists was less extensive in Slovakia than it was in the Czech lands, and the steps taken against those affected were likewise less harsh (Maňák 1997). Similarly, censorship of the arts was less strict in Slovakia. What could not get past the censors in Prague could, at least occasionally, be published in Bratislava. The considerable continuity of the Slovak communist elites, from the period preceding the Soviet occupation of 1968 through normalisation, was a strong factor in these gentler policies (Marušiak 2008).

Given the centralism of the communist regime, this mitigation of the normalisation process in Slovakia must not be overestimated. Yet the 'softer' form of Slovak communism exerted an influence, making the local elites more consensual, and this consensus was based on their shared ethnic origin. The funeral in 1991 of Gustáv Husák, the last communist president and the main symbol of the normalisation, provides a telling ex-post-facto proof, and a gesture entirely unimaginable in the Czech lands: it was attended by the Slovak Prime Minister Ján Čarnogurský and the speaker of the parliament František Mikloško, both of whom were leading Catholic dissidents before November 1989.

The proportion of the population which after 1989 had a positive view of the social and economic changes associated with the communist regime was greater in Slovakia than in the Czech lands. Only a few Slovaks considered the communist era to be without value, a feeling much more prevalent among Czechs (Příhoda 1995, Marušiak 2008). This difference between the two parts of Czechoslovakia was further evidenced during the radical economic reforms of the 1990s, when the unemployment rate increased sharply in Slovakia, but not in the Czech lands. This was not only a direct consequence of economic reform. Industrialisation in Slovakia had been influenced by the Soviet model and heavy industries dominated. With the end of the Cold War and the disintegration of the Eastern bloc, many arms factories in Slovakia simply lost their customers.

In response, Slovak society was much less welcoming to the privatisation of state property, fearing the return of 'heartless capitalism'. This provided the perfect space for social demagoguery and an interpretation of the economic transformation as a plot by Prague to exploit and impoverish Slovakia (Bútora and Bútorová 2003: 80). Among the Czechs, in turn, this gave rise to concerns that Slovakia would become a hindrance to economic transformation, an argument exploited to good effect by many right-wing politicians and journalists.

Meanwhile, there was an intellectual environment in Slovakia that was sharply opposed to the concept of centrally administered economic reform as promoted by Václav Klaus at the federal ministry of finance (for Klaus's notion of reform, see Chapters 6 and 9). In early 1990 a group of former Slovak reform communists associated with the 'Obroda' group published their own economic proposal. Under this scheme, a significant proportion of state ownership would be preserved, the process of economic change would have to respect the specific situation of Slovakia, and the implementation of reform would be fully under the authority of Slovak national bodies. Overall, it was a statist manifesto, one that led towards separation (Šútovec 1999, Rychlík 2002). Before the 1990 elections most of the politicians and economists associated with it – for example, Augustin Marián Húska and Hvezdon Kočtúch – were key members of the main driver of the Velvet Revolution in Slovakia, the VPN, and when that movement disintegrated, they helped to found Mečiar's HZDS.

Looking at the origins of the post-November 1989 elites one does well to remember that former communists were much more strongly represented among the Slovaks than among the Czechs. Tellingly, the most popular Slovak politician immediately after November 1989 was the leading figure of the reform-communist experiment of the Prague Spring, Alexander Dubček. However, it was not only people connected with the Prague Spring, but also some highly-positioned communists of the normalisation era who managed to rise politically in the new Slovakia, and they did so without being dependent on democratic politicians. (An example of such dependency at the level of the federation was Marián Čalfa, fully loyal to President Václav Havel.) The persistence of these 'transition communists', as Soňa Szomolányi described them, is what permitted VPN to adopt the approach it did in late 1989 (Szomolányi 1999). At that time, VPN showed no intention of assuming key state offices in Slovakia and long held onto its strategy of serving as an 'external check' on government – one that the Czech OF quickly abandoned. Thus, highly positioned communists of the pre-1989 era, Milan Čič and Rudolf Schuster, became respectively the prime minister of the Slovak government of 'national understanding' and the speaker of the Slovak parliament during the Velvet Revolution. They deftly placed their bet on a rhetorical defence of Slovak interests against 'Pragocentrism', a stratagem that secured their political survival and a sharp rise in their popularity (Šútovec 1999, Szomolányi 1999, Suk 2003).

Adoption of a more or less radical nationalist line became a general trend in Slovak politics, which soon became apparent in other successful political parties, whether the Christian Democratic Movement, whose roots could be traced to the erstwhile Hlinka's Slovak People's Party, or the Slovak National Party. Indeed, the latter party was the first to espouse Slovak independence after the 1990 elections. The emphasis on a nationalist line was also characteristic of the Communist Party of Slovakia, which began not only to abandon its Marxist-Leninist identity, but also to loosen its relationship with the Czech communists, ultimately winding down the Czechoslovak Communist Party at the end of 1991. Even some of VPN's liberal founders, specifically, the leader of the Velvet Revolution in Slovakia Ján Budaj, were calling in the spring of 1990 for a 'second revolution, a national revolution' (Suk 2003: 438).

Soon after November 1989, and despite their political differences, the majority of the Slovak elite took as their objective the building of a Slovak state, which they took to be the best way of guaranteeing their nation (Rokkan 1999b). This did not rule out the preservation of Czechoslovakia, albeit it only allowed a very loose form of association. However, such notions collided with very different thinking on the part of the majority of the Czech elite and general public alike, who, as Carol Skalnik Leff has put it succinctly, 'had never found a value of their own in decentralization and national self-assertion, a perspective that would have given both sides a common starting point for a durable bargain' (Leff 2000: 45). This lack of understanding between the Czechs and Slovaks, or perhaps their indifference to each other's priorities, became fully apparent as early as 1990, first during the so-called Hyphen War, which was essentially symbolic, and later in the conflict over the purview of authorities, where political power was at stake.

5.3. The Hyphen War and the battle over powers

It was Václav Havel who unwittingly initiated the Hyphen War, when he asked MPs at a session of the federal parliament in late January 1990 to change the name of the state. Havel thought that the adjective 'socialist', being a residue of the communist past, should disappear from the official name *Českos-*

lovenská socialistická republika to form the new name Czechoslovak Republic. The federal parliament, however, postponed its decision on the issue, thus creating a space in which nationalist conflict could be ignited. Whereas the Czechs largely accepted Havel's proposal without objection, in Slovakia there was much resistance, as the name was redolent of the 'Czechoslovakist' First Republic. The Slovaks proposed the hyphenated version *Česko–Slovensko*, which was sharply rejected by the Czechs as it reminded them of the negatively-coloured designation of the post-Munich republic of the years 1938–1939 (see Chapter 3). A new national emblem proposed by Havel was also controversial, but of secondary importance in the ensuing discussion.

The emotional dispute over the hyphen continued throughout spring 1990 in parliamentary forums, in the media, and in city squares. The solution eventually adopted was Schweikian in its absurdity: an ungrammatical expression, *Česká a Slovenská Federativní Republika*. The unofficial short name *Československo* was to be written as one word in Czech, but with a hyphen in Slovak (Rychlík 2002: 123). All in all, it was an unsatisfactory compromise.

The Hyphen War accelerated Slovakia's progress to nationalism (described above), but it also had an important impact in the Czech lands, where the historical analogy with the year 1938 renewed concerns about Slovak demands. The first call to separate from Slovakia appeared at the time, but it was still politically marginal. The idea and the slogan 'Let them [that is, the Slovaks] go' (*ať si [Slováci] jdou*) entered the Czech lexicon. It was expressed using literary hyperbole in May 1990 by the writer Ludvík Vaculík: 'The younger Slovak brother has grown up, he wants his own bed, and the older Czech brother should give it to him. But as we know the younger brother, he'll want the bed next to the window in the summer and the one next to the heater in the winter. No bed for you, brother; have a house of your own' (Měchýř 1999: 307). The feelings of alienation were mutual and subsequently reinforced by the fatigue that set in as negotiations concerning the future character of the state dragged on. The discussion about federal budgetary transfers from the Czech lands to Slovakia also intensified. These transfers helped to balance the economic differences between the two parts of the federation and, in the context of other Slovak demands, met with increasing disapproval on the part of many Czechs.

Another dispute that was important for political elites was that over the new division of powers between the federation and the two republics. Discussions about the proposals, intended to remove the communist legacy of centralism, lasted for most of 1990 and were accompanied by steps verging on political blackmail. During his visit to Prague, the Slovak Prime Minister Vladimír Mečiar (then the leader of VPN) had a surprise announcement to make to his Czech counterpart, Petr Pithart: the Slovak parliament, Mečiar alleged, was ready to declare that its acts were sovereign over acts passed by the federal parliament if Mečiar's proposed act on powers was not adopted. Such a declaration would constitute a *de facto* end of the federation. Mečiar, however, was not telling the truth and his strategy only increased the mistrust present in Czech-Slovak relations (Wolf 1998, Rychlík 2000 and 2002).

The act eventually adopted in December 1990 significantly curtailed the powers of the federal authorities and strengthened those of the republics, but was not without issues. It did not clearly delineate the boundary between the authority of the federal and republic institutions, thus opening space for disputes over powers. In terms of the functionality of the new arrangement, a particularly large question mark hung over the fact that in some areas such as economic reform and transport, legislative power remained with the federation, but the implementation of legislation was in the hands of the republic-level authorities (Stein 1997). In consequence, some politicians of the emerging Czech right harshly criticised Prime Minister Pithart for being too soft during negotiations. The dispute over powers weakened the position of moderates in Czech politics and the result achieved was evidently only a temporary compromise.

5.4. Deadlocked negotiations and nearly incompatible constitutional ideals

After an agreement was reached over powers, there followed protracted and ultimately only partially successful negotiations on the new constitutional foundations of the state. These negotiations included, variously, representatives of the Czech, Slovak, and federal governments, leaders of the national parliaments and the federal parliament, and sometimes also representatives of individual parliamentary parties as well as President Havel. In what was considered a crisis of Czechoslovakia, Havel sought to find mechanisms to help to resolve the situation. He was instrumental in the establishment of the Constitutional Court, which was to resolve the emerging conflicts over the scope of federal and republic powers. However, the Court could not be a panacea for what was an evident lack of political consensus (Stein 1997).

Similarly stillborn was the idea of enshrining in the constitution the possibility of calling a referendum. Havel, who was the chief champion of the idea, hoped that a referendum would demonstrate support for preserving Czechoslovakia. However, the problem was that a general question: 'Are you in favour of a common state?' would solve nothing under the circumstances, as the answer would certainly be in the affirmative in both republics. Yet the general public in the two parts of the federation had dramatically different notions of what 'a common state' entailed. Opinion polls showed that, whereas in the Czech lands most people were in favour of a unitary state or a federation, in Slovakia the majority preferred a much looser arrangement and there was a sizeable group advocating independence (IVVM 1991). Quite expectedly, the federal parliament was unable to come to an agreement on the wording of the referendum.

Moreover, there was the issue of the inconsistency of opinions or impossible couplings, as pointed out by some surveys, mainly in Slovakia. For instance, almost a third of those in Slovakia who supported a federation also demanded the primacy of Slovak laws over federal laws, a demand inconsistent with federation (Aktuálne problémy slovenskej spoločnosti 1992). Politicians responded to this situation: Mečiar's HZDS, which won the 1992 elections in Slovakia, took ambiguous positions, preferring a confederation while not entirely ruling out a federation. By contrast, in the Czech lands, ODS had outlined its goals clearly ahead of the elections: either a 'functional' federation, by which was meant a strong centre of state, or a division into two states.

Václav Havel's attempt to save the common state by mobilising citizens also ended in failure. The president, a capable playwright by profession, dramatically chose the date of the second anniversary of the Velvet Revolution for a televised speech outlining his idea of large-scale constitutional reform in Czechoslovakia (Havel 1992a). This would involve a substantial strengthening of the president's powers, including the option of calling a referendum, dissolving the federal parliament and issuing decrees until new parliamentary elections were held, as well as a far-reaching reform of the federal parliament including its electoral system. Havel's appeal brought thousands of people out to the squares of several large Czech cities, but in Slovakia, where his authority had much declined in the meantime, it failed to elicit a significant response. The federal parliament subsequently rejected all of the constitutional reforms proposed by Havel. The strategy of mobilising the masses, so successful in November 1989, faced a radically different situation two years later.

Havel's decreasing popularity in Slovakia reflected a more general local trend of fading trust in federal institutions and politicians, especially members of government, even though they were often Slovaks themselves. The expressions 'federal Slovak' or 'Prague Slovak' were pejorative in Slovakia, suggesting that the person described was not sufficiently defending Slovak interests, serving rather as an ally to Czech politicians. This understandably had negative consequences for the popularity of those so designated. The (Slovak) federal Prime Minister Marián Čalfa (1989–1992) provided the best example: his considerable popular support in Slovakia melted away over time. The negative perception of 'Prague Slovaks' had older analogies which reached back to the communist era and even further to the First Republic; it was also partly grounded in reality (Leff 2000). During negotiations over the constitutional arrangements after 1989, federal politicians usually had opinions closer to those of Czech (republic-level) politicians. But rather than being a 'betrayal' of their national interests by Slovak federal politicians, this situation reflected the logic of their position at the centre of the state and their concern with keeping this centre strong.

These times were not without interesting paradoxes. For instance, the federal minister of finance, chair of ODS and soon to be one of the two 'fathers' of the division of the state, Václav Klaus, was interested not only in carrying through radical economic reform and in having a strong centre of the federation, but also in keeping the Slovak economy afloat, i.e., preventing an economic collapse. During negotiations in late 1991 about the new federal budget, Klaus successfully pushed for a compromise that preserved some of the financial transfers from the Czech lands to Slovakia for the next year, despite opposition from Pithart's Czech government and Klaus's own party (Stein 1997, Kopeček 2012a).

The final attempt to negotiate a new arrangement for the common state was made in February 1992 in Milovy – a remote village with difficult access for journalists. In this relative isolation a compromise was reached in which both sides made significant concessions, but the agreement was subsequently rejected by the Slovak parliament, with not only the opposition but also some representatives of government parties against it (Stein 1997). The failure of the Milovy agreement had a significant impact on the atmosphere before the elections and radicalised moods. Symptomatically, in early 1992 the group of those wanting Czech independence was marginal, yet at the time of the elections in June, opinion polls showed that 13 % of respondents supported independence (IVVM 1992).

Even if the Milovy agreement were in force, it would not have secured stability and peace in Czech-Slovak relations because Slovak politicians did not consider it a lasting solution – not even those who negotiated it. The attitude of a leading Slovak negotiator, the chair of the Christian Democratic Movement and Slovak Prime Minister Ján Čarnogurský, is telling.[2] Before the Milovy agreement was concluded, Čarnogurský spoke about his vision in which Slovakia would have its own star on the European Union flag and said that his 'ultimate goal was the independent membership of Slovakia in European integration structures and international organisations' (Čarnogurský 1997: 238). Čarnogurský later confirmed that he envisaged the Milovy agreement remaining in effect, at most, until the accession of Czecho/Slovakia to the European Communities (Rychlík 2002). To sum up, on the eve of the 1992 elections the Czechs and the Slovaks – both elites and masses – had very different ideas about their preferred constitutional arrangement.

5.5. Institutional blockage

The ethnofederal model proved destructive to Czechoslovakia, and it is worth illustrating in more detail some of the specific issues impeding its functioning in the early 1990s. The federal parliament in particular merits attention. Its lower chamber, the Chamber of the People, reflected the actual distribution of the populace in the country, whereas the upper chamber, the Chamber of Nations, was divided into two halves, Czech and Slovak. In order to become laws, a substantial range of bills had to be passed by a majority of all MPs in the Chamber of the People as well as majorities in both sections of the Chamber of Nations. In some cases, such as constitutional acts, a three-fifths majority was needed (Constitutional Law 1968). Thus, a relatively small group of MPs in one of the two sections of the Chamber of Nations could block the passing of any law. A proposed constitutional act, for instance, could be blocked by 31 MPs out of the total of 300 MPs in the federal parliament (Stein 1997).

---

2 In spring 1991 Vladimír Mečiar was removed from the post of prime minister. He then successfully reinvented himself as the main martyr of the 'struggle for Slovakia' and became the principal leader of the opposition

This issue became manifest in the very first months of the democratic era, when what previously had been one of KSČ's levers of power was transformed into a genuine legislative body. The quick disintegration of OF and VPN after the 1990 elections and the continued fragmentation of other parties turned the legislative process into the Achilles heel of the political system. By then it was too late to change the absurdly complex mechanism – such change might have been possible in the revolutionary atmosphere of 1989, but not in the competitive atmosphere that followed, as it went against too many interests, especially those connected with Slovak national aspirations. For Slovak politicians the option of easily blocking a decision constituted an achievement that they were unwilling to renounce (Linz and Stepan 1996, Stein 1997, Wolchik 2000, Kopecký 2000, Suk 2003).

It is important to note that the 1992 elections created in the two parts of Czechoslovakia two entirely separate party systems, thus paralysing the parliament for the future. Nevertheless, the process which separated the Czech and Slovak party systems did not start with the 1992 elections, but during the establishment of the democratic regime (Fiala 2001). OF and VPN had emerged as two independent 'national engines' of democratic transition. Though originally connected by informal links between their founding elites (most of whom were former dissidents), the two organisations diverged in terms of institution-building and personnel. Linz and Stepan have pointed out the disintegrative tendencies inherent in Václav Havel's decision not to attempt to establish a country-wide party in 1989, a decision they explained by reference to Havel's anti-political and anti-institutional thinking, which was also characteristic of most of his advisers (Linz and Stepan 1996: 331).

Here it must be added that the emergence of two distinct formations, OF and VPN, was in no small part due to the differences in the nature of the dissident movement in the two republics. Slovak dissidents tended to be Christian, while Czech dissidence was mostly 'civic' in character. Perhaps even more important were the limited contacts between Czech and Slovak dissidents – a consequence of the repression in communist Czechoslovakia – and the much smaller number of Slovak dissidents overall, decreasing their importance in VPN relative to OF. In any case, Havel's attempt at pro-Czechoslovak citizen mobilisation, described above, lacked the support of political parties, and his influence on the political successors to OF and VPN had also waned by then.

Also important for the separation of the two party systems were the failures of other attempts at common, or at least cooperating, Czech-Slovak parties, including the already-mentioned (ex-)Communists, but also the Christian Democrats, the Greens, and the Social Democrats. Towards the end of its existence, Czechoslovakia faced an institutional blockage, to which the mutual isolation of its two national party systems contributed significantly.

5.6. Dismantlement

The experience of the first years after November 1989 fundamentally influenced the actions of the two parties victorious in the 1992 elections, ODS and HZDS. The key role was played by the chair of ODS, Václav Klaus, who proved to be an effective crisis manager. Having established that HZDS would not accept a federation with a strong centre, Klaus together with other ODS politicians pushed HZDS to accept the division of Czechoslovakia in early summer 1992, although this was only confirmed two months later when a timetable for the separation was agreed. The two independent republics were scheduled to come into existence on 1 January 1993. The new federal government headed by Jan Stráský, appointed in July 1992, had as its task to prepare for the division. That its mandate was temporary was signalled by its comprising only ten members, allocated on the basis of national parity: four members from ODS (plus one Czech Christian Democrat) and five members from HZDS. Klaus and Mečiar preferred to become prime ministers of their respective republics. When in mid-July the Slovak parliament adopted a declaration of Slovak sovereignty, Havel resigned the presidential office, saying that he did not want to be 'a hindrance to historical development [...] or a lame-duck president sitting out the few weeks before ultimately leaving his office.' (Havel 1992a: 198) Havel's bid to be re-elected by the federal parliament failed shortly before that, chiefly due to resistance from HZDS. The federal parliament did not manage to elect Havel's successor. In early September the Slovak parliament adopted a new constitution; the Czechs only passed theirs in mid-December 1992.

The dismantlement of Czechoslovakia in the second half of 1992 was not entirely smooth, chiefly due to vacillation on the part of HZDS politicians who mostly perceived 'full' independence as a risky leap in the dark. Vladimír Mečiar even attempted to resuscitate the idea of an economic and defence commonwealth. Due to these hesitations the bill dissolving the federation was not at first passed by the federal parliament. It was rejected not only by most of the Czech and Slovak opposition parties, but also by some HZDS MPs (Stein 1997, Rychlík 2002). Still, there was no mutually acceptable alternative on the table. Klaus's party refused to negotiate a looser political arrangement under the heading of Czechoslovakia.

In early October 1992 ODS and HZDS issued a joint proclamation confirming the validity of the agreement on separation. Mečiar took on the role of the 'father' of independence, which was to become an important source of his political legitimacy in independent Slovakia. In late November the federal parliament accepted, in its second attempt, the division of the state. By that time, a significant part of the Czech opposition, consisting mostly of the left and the centre-left, had acquiesced in the separation. This confirms Carol Skalnik Leff's more general observation that 'Czechoslovakia was a state that everyone wanted, but no one wanted enough' (Leff 2000: 45).

The last months of 1992 were filled with negotiations over a series of agreements on a large number of issues from border traffic and citizenship to duty-free trade. Also concluded was an agreement on the property of the state being dissolved: real estate was to pass to that successor state wherein it was located, whereas movable assets and those located abroad were divided in a 2:1 ratio to the benefit of the Czechs (this ratio reflected the size of the populations of the successor states). However, not all the agreements lasted and not everything was resolved satisfactorily. The joint currency was divided in spring 1993, even though originally there was to be a monetary union between the two states. Yet given the differences in the economies of the two countries this was a necessary step. There were several items concerning the division of property where no satisfactory solution was found, and these were only resolved definitively in the late 1990s. Nonetheless, it was a quiet and civilised separation overall, and one that was in strong contrast to the bloody disintegration of Yugoslavia and the chaos that marked the end of the Soviet Union.

5.7. Ex-post considerations

The discussion about what could have saved Czechoslovakia continues to this day. Some authors consider the possibility of a consociational arrangement, for which Czechoslovakia had certain precedents in place. However, they add that such a solution would have required a different tradition and a mutual willingness to compromise among elites. This solution would need to have been cultivated over the long term in order to keep together two national societies who were growing distant from each other (Rychlík 2000, Kopecký 2000). After the 1992 elections it was already too late for a consociation. Institutionally, Czechoslovakia was close to collapse, and trends were toward an increasing and potentially dangerous national polarisation. Today the quick and 'velvet' divorce therefore still seems to have been a rational solution.

One of the positive aspects of the velvet divorce was the good mutual relationship between the Czechs and Slovaks it created for the future. Irrespective of their party affiliation, the political elites of both countries continually emphasise the superior quality of their relationship. Although it is not always clear what its real political content is, personal contacts between the two nations continue to be excellent as is cooperation in a number of policy domains. The Czechs consider the Slovaks their closest ally, which in the words of one sociological survey 'is not actually understood as very alien' (CVVM 2010). The Slovak view of the Czechs is similar. Current views of the division of Czechoslovakia are more positive than was the norm at the time. Many of those who disagreed then have re-evaluated their opinion over time (CVVM 2012). Czechoslovakia was a state in which several generations lived their lives, yet its demise was not a turning point with fatal consequences.

6. Czech political institutions and the problems of parliamentary democracy

Lubomír Kopeček

Since 1993 the Czech Republic has undergone changes which have tested the functionality of its institutions. This chapter first describes how the Czech constitution was adopted and then analyses the key elements and mechanisms of the country's political regime, considering both formal institutions and political practice. The intention is not to overwhelm the reader with exhaustive lists of powers granted to the individual authorities. Rather it is to provide an intelligible overview introducing the basic institutions and their mutual relations along with an analysis of the problems of contemporary Czech democracy.

6.1. The adoption of the Czech constitution: Circumstances, influences, and controversies

The dismantlement of Czechoslovakia required the urgent establishment of the institutions of the new Czech state and the adoption of a constitution was a crucial part of this process. Although the 1968 constitutional act on the Czechoslovak federation envisaged a separate Czech constitution, none was adopted and attempts to create one after 1989 were hampered by unresolved issues in the Czech-Slovak relationship (Stein 1997). After the 1992 elections, two commissions were created to prepare the constitution, one in the government and the other attached to the Czech National Council (the Czech parliament). Whereas the personnel of the governmental commission reflected the make-up of the centre-right coalition government led by Václav Klaus (ODS), the parliamentary commission included representatives of all parliamentary party groups, including the opposition (Filip 2002). Nonetheless, the conviction soon prevailed that it was best to entrust such an ambitious document solely to the governmental commission, which consisted of politicians and constitutional experts, the latter mostly academics and civil servants. It was largely the constitutional experts who wrote the constitution, yet the roles of several politicians cannot be ignored, as they naturally sought to include their own particular preferences in the constitution. Worth mentioning especially is the chair of the governmental commission, Prime Minister Klaus, whose vision was close to a majoritarian democracy inspired by the British model, that is, a strong executive which faces few obstacles in realising its programme.

Although Klaus dominated politics at the time, he was only able to implement his vision to a limited extent. Not only was he busy dismantling Czechoslovakia, but the opposition retained significant influence over the creation of the constitution and was interested in constitutionally limiting executive power. The Czechoslovak constitution stipulated that three-fifths of all deputies in the Czech National Council must vote in favour of a new constitution. The government did not command such a majority and thus needed the votes of at least some opposition deputies. This forced the government to make concessions, perhaps best demonstrated by the failure of Klaus's proposal that constitutional acts be adopted by an absolute majority of deputies and senators. This would have made changes to the constitution relatively easy to adopt. The opposition, however, was able to enforce a greater, three-fifths, majority (Stein 1997, Kopeček 2010a).

This and other controversial points were discussed over several days in the first half of December 1992, during a session of the Czech parliament's constitution committee, which worked out the complete text of the constitution. Its adoption by the Czech parliament – by a majority much larger than necessary – on 16 December 1992, two weeks before the new state came into being, was relatively smooth. The only parties not to support it in the final voting were the extreme right Republicans and the Moravians, whose proposed administrative division of the state was not adopted.

The introduction of majoritarian elements into the constitution was hindered not just by the opposition, but also by the initial conception of the constitution as chosen by the governmental commission in summer 1992. This conception was inspired by the Czechoslovak constitution of 1920 and reflected the contemporary view that Masaryk's republic was the best model of democracy. The governmental commission refused to draw on communist constitutions, as the commission – quite naturally – sought to distance itself from a communist legacy that was perceived negatively (Němeček 2010). Several well-known constitutional theoreticians who had political leanings to the left were not invited to participate in the governmental commission. This reflected the centre-right profile of Klaus's government and probably also influenced the decision to use the 1920 constitution as a model. The problem with this was that the 1920 constitution relied heavily on the constitution of the

Third French Republic (1870–1940), which had often been criticised for an excessive dominance of the legislature over the executive. Despite the differences, such as the somewhat stronger position of the prime minister in the Czech constitution, traces of this inspiration remained visible.

The historical distance from interwar Czechoslovakia is evident in the constitution's preamble, which for understandable reasons contained no mention of the 'Czechoslovak nation' – as in the 1920 constitution. The preamble of the 1992 constitution opened with the words 'We, the citizens of the Czech Republic', and referenced the 'time of the reconstitution of an independent Czech State', 'inalienable values of human dignity and freedom', 'respect for human rights', 'civil society', the Czech Republic as 'a member of the family of democracies in Europe and around the world', and the principles of the rule of law.

Human rights were not just mentioned in the preamble, but also firmly anchored in the constitutional system. Instrumental in this was the pre-Velvet Revolution tradition of dissent, for which human rights were the key issue. In 1991, the federal parliament had adopted a special constitutional act, the Charter of Fundamental Rights and Freedoms, which included a large number of political, economic, social, minority, and other rights. However, the Charter became one of the most contentious points during the adoption of the constitution. The opposition deputies insisted that it be included in the constitution. Prime Minister Klaus refused, arguing that this would be 'an infestation of the constitution with what are often merely nominal and unenforceable rights' and pushed for a much narrower definition of human rights (Lidové noviny 1992). The dispute was eventually resolved by the invention of the concept of *ústavní pořádek* (a constitutional order), which included the constitution, the Charter and other constitutional acts, each of equal importance.[1] Thus, the Charter did not become a formal part of the text of the constitution narrowly understood, but the opposition essentially obtained what it wanted (Výborný 2003).

The opposition was less successful with its demand to include in the constitution the option of calling referendums. Although the constitution did mention direct democracy, the implementation of a referendum was conditional upon the adoption of a special constitutional act. Although several

---

1 The constitutional system also includes international treaties on human rights and fundamental freedoms. This is based on a somewhat controversial interpretation put forward by the Constitutional Court (Filip 2010).

attempts have been made since the adoption of the constitution to pass such an act, to date all but one was unsuccessful. The only national referendum in the era of the independent Czech Republic, and indeed in the whole of Czech history, was the referendum on the country's accession to the EU in 2003. A one-off constitutional act was adopted for this vote. By contrast, referendums are often used at the local level, but they can only be concerned with affairs that fall within the purview of the municipality. Since 2010 regional referenda can also be held, but so far this option has not been utilized.

Besides the government and opposition, a number of other actors were material to the birth of the constitution, of which the most remarkable was Václav Havel. Having resigned the presidential office of Czechoslovakia as it was about to disappear, Havel quickly set his sights on the presidency of the new, smaller Czech state. Given his international reputation and high popularity at home, he was a natural candidate. Havel's interest in constitutional matters is evidenced by his consultations with some of those who were preparing the constitution – at that time he was a private citizen rather than an office holder – and especially in his own concept of the constitution. Particularly worthy of note are Havel's pleading for the direct election of the head of state and 'a president who is strong or at least stronger than before' and with 'at least such powers as would allow him independent political action' (Havel 1992b). Havel's vision of a strong president was evidently influenced by his experience in the first years after the Velvet Revolution when the head of state wielded enormous political influence as well as by the traditionally high prestige of the presidential office.

However, Havel's vision clashed with the prevailing balance of power, that is the domination by Klaus and ODS, who pushed hard to minimise the president's powers and under no circumstance would have allowed direct presidential elections. Klaus's attitude was influenced by the history of his conflictual relationship with Havel. Though Klaus was willing to support Havel's candidacy, he was definitely not interested in creating a competing locus of power at Prague Castle, one that could rely on the legitimacy provided by a direct presidential election. By contrast, the idea of a stronger president was welcomed by the opposition as well as by some politicians in minor government parties, who viewed Havel as their natural ally. The result was a compromise. Ultimately, the scope of presidential powers enshrined in the constitution was narrower than Havel would have liked, but the head of state also did not become a figurehead. Thus in the executive were sown the seeds of political dualism, which was to have significant consequences for the functioning of the political regime. There is some historical irony in the fact that in 2003 Klaus became Havel's successor as the country's president.

It was not just Václav Havel who was trying to influence the shape of the constitution. Others were fighting for the survival of their institutions. The chair of the Czechoslovak Supreme Court Otakar Motejl provides an illustrative example: he managed to convince the governmental committee preparing the constitution that – unlike most federal institutions – his should not be abolished, but continue as the Supreme Court of the new state (Jiránek and Pečinka 2000, Kopeček 2010a). The existing Czech Supreme Court was transformed into two high courts, and existing regional and district courts were likewise preserved. Thus a complex four-level judicial system came into being and resisted later attempts to simplify it. Paradoxically, it was Motejl as minister of justice, who in the late 1990s spearheaded these attempts, arguing that the four-level system 'gives rise to questions of jurisdiction' and a three-level one 'would be more effective' (Motejl 1999).

Despite the haste with which it was adopted, the constitution did provide a solid basis for the functioning of the new state. Some unresolved issues and problems that arose over time should have been easy to fix, but the necessary broader consensus and political will were sometimes lacking. The introduction of direct presidential elections in 2012 proved to be riskier, as it introduced into the political regime a strong destabilising element, as described below.

6.2. The parliament and fragile cabinets

The constitution set out a parliamentary regime for the Czech state. This is clearly stated in its article 68, according to which the government is accountable to the Chamber of Deputies, the 200-member lower chamber of parliament (the Chamber was created in 1993 by transforming the existing Czech National Council). The Chamber of Deputies is the key arena where the government clashes with the opposition. The constitution also features other typical traits of a parliamentary regime such as the opportunity for deputies to table oral or written questions to the government, and the possibility of simultaneously serving as a member of government and parliament.

Of essential importance is the investiture vote, taken by the Chamber after the president has appointed the government. The government needs to win an absolute majority of votes of the deputies present. As governments lacking a parliamentary majority are relatively common (see Table 6.1), winning the investiture vote is sometimes tricky. As early as 1996 the existing government coalition lost its majority support. It won confidence thanks to an agreement with the opposition, the Czech Social Democratic Party (ČSSD), whose deputies left the Chamber when the motion of confidence was made, thus lowering the number of votes needed to win confidence. The situation reoccurred in 1998, with a different constellation of forces, when ODS decided to tolerate ČSSD's minority government. Thanks to this arrangement, dubbed the Opposition Agreement, the ČSSD government remained in office for the entire electoral term (see Chapter 8 for more detail).

During the first decade and a half of the twenty-first century, there were moments when the will was lacking to come to an agreement that would protect a government without a majority in the Chamber. The experience of the Opposition Agreement, which elicited a very negative public response and lost ODS the 2002 election, played an important role here. After the 2006 election the situation became extreme, as for more than six months no government could win the Chamber's confidence, since the left and the non-left parliamentary camps each controlled exactly half of the deputies. In order to win confidence, the centre-right coalition government of Mirek Topolánek persuaded two deputies from the opposition to support his government. These 'political turncoats' also supported the government when it was pushing through its legislative agenda. This and other similar cases were controversial and were accompanied by allegations of corruption and other misdeeds. Such incidents are unhealthy signs and highlight the country's problematic political culture.

The government can also ask for a confidence vote during the electoral term. The vote is decided in the same way as the investiture vote; the government has to be supported by an absolute majority of the deputies present. Such a vote of confidence is usually linked with the passing of an act of particular importance for the government. The government might also be seeking to confirm that it commands sufficient support in the Chamber. In spring 2012, for example, Petr Nečas's government called and won a vote of confidence after another member of the coalition, the Public Affairs party, was pushed out.

For a vote of no confidence to succeed, there is a stricter requirement than for a vote of confidence: an absolute majority of all deputies, whether present in the Chamber or not, must vote against the government. A motion of no confidence needs 50 votes to be tabled, a requirement which is a hindrance to the opposition, but not an insuperable one. The first motion of no confidence took place in 2003, and since then the opposition has frequently tabled such motions, though only one has succeeded. The successful vote brought about the demise of Mirek Topolánek's cabinet in 2009, the fifth attempt on the part of the opposition to overthrow that government. When a government commands a significant majority in the Chamber, the aim of the opposition is not so much to remove the government as to attract media attention.

The prime minister organises the work of the government, chairs its meetings and acts in its name (Article 77 of the constitution). According to the constitution, he or she does not enjoy a privileged position in governmental decision-making, and when votes are taken in the cabinet, his vote is of equal weight to those of any other government member (Just 2012). However, the position of the prime minister within the executive is strengthened by the fact that some decisions made by the president have to be countersigned by the prime minister (or another authorised government member). Importantly, it is usually the chair of the party that won the election who becomes prime minister and, according to an established interpretation of the constitution, his resignation means the end of the government. Furthermore, the prime minister has a strong say (at least according to the constitution) in appointing and removing ministers, as that is done by the president acting on the basis of the prime minister's recommendation. In reality, however, the prime minister decides only about the portfolios held by his own party. The constitution does not allow the president to remove a prime minister who enjoys the confidence of the Chamber, and neither is the president allowed to circumvent the prime minister in appointing or removing ministers or to act independently of him. Despite this, the head of state has substantial space to manoeuvre, and may complicate the prime minister's position, as described below.

Czech prime ministers also face other limits, which diminish or even threaten their position and also weaken the effectiveness of the government. The most serious among these is government instability, which has been chronic during several electoral terms. For instance, the 2002–2006 term saw three different cabinets even though formally the government coalition remained intact. The next electoral term, 2006–2010, also featured three cabinets (see Table 6.1). The average duration of a cabinet since 1992 has been less than two years. The Czech Republic thus exhibits significantly lower government stability than is the norm in Western Europe. Yet in the context of the 'new' democracies of Central and Eastern Europe, this is not exceptional as short-lived governments are a relatively common phenomenon in the region

(Müller and Strøm 2000, Havlík 2011b, Grotz and Weber 2012, Döring and Hellström 2013).

One consequence of the instability of Czech governments is the occurrence of technocratic or, as the case may be, 'semi-political' cabinets, which are used as an expedient to overcome political crises (Hloušek and Kopeček 2013). Analogies to this solution can be found in interwar Czechoslovakia as well as in other European countries such as Italy and Greece. However, in a parliamentary democracy based on elections, frequent recourse to governments of unelected technocrats is a problematic practice, even though a technocratic government must be approved by a vote of confidence in the Chamber.

The main causes of government instability are weak backing from the Chamber and, above all, the heterogeneity of government coalitions, which are often made up of parties that are ideologically diverse. This complicates their ability to communicate, to agree on a common programme, and to implement their policies. The fact that, as a rule, government coalitions are made up of three parties, does not make it easy to coordinate government activities. The coalition of the left-wing Social Democrats, centre-right Christian Democrats, and liberal Freedom Union, in office from 2002 to 2006, provides a telling example: it was plagued by constant dissension, mainly due to the parties' dissatisfaction with the implementation of their respective programmes. Towards the close of the electoral term the largest party in government, the Social Democrats, actually pushed through some of its agenda with the help of the opposition Communists (Cabada 2006, Čaloud, Foltýn and Havlík 2006). Furthermore, factions sometimes appear within parties that are in government, and this can be very destructive. For instance, the already-mentioned government of Mirek Topolánek, in office from 2007 to 2009, consisted of the Civic Democrats, the Greens, and the Christian Democrats. These parties were rather remote from each other in terms of their programmes; this caused much intra-party frustration, giving rise to factionalism and disloyalty on the part of some deputies and providing the opposition with an opportunity to table a successful motion of no confidence.

Factionalism and the substantial decentralisation of parties have weakened the prime minister's position. It is not just the heterogeneity of coalitions, but prime ministerial weakness which has commonly caused government crises. For example, in 2004 the Social Democratic Prime Minister Vladimír Špidla resigned after the failure of his party in European elections provoked a wave of intra-party dissent. Prime ministers' main role in Czech politics is to moderate conflicts and interests within government coalitions, and their ability to do so varies significantly. Only rarely can a prime minister be described as the indisputable leader of the government. Thus, the position of a Czech PM is very different from that of a British PM or a German chancellor (Hloušek 2015).

The position of the government is weak in part because the constitution has not endowed it with instruments that would allow it to influence the agenda of the Chamber, the rate at which individual items are debated or the manner in which the Chamber deals with government bills. There is no need to seek the government's approval of amendments made to bills, and the government has no power to close a parliamentary debate. The mechanisms that govern the functioning of the Chamber are not interlinked with those of the government. This fact, combined with the recurring fragility of governments, substantially bolsters the political autonomy of the Chamber (Kysela 2013).

Many features of Czech parliamentarianism are similar to what Giovanni Sartori calls 'assembly government' (Sartori 1994), in which the domination of parliament over government is typical. Czech coalition cabinets are not very stable, they are often not able to act and speak with a single, clear voice, and they have difficulty pushing through their legislative agenda. Prime ministers cannot act quickly and decisively. Governments are afforded little protection from the Chamber of Deputies, which can easily threaten a government's existence. Due to significant government instability, political responsibility for the exercise of governmental power is often unclear (Novák 2004, Kubát 2013). Both the constitutional design (including the proportional electoral system) and the party system play a key role here and are reflected in the character and make-up of parliament and government. Nor can one ignore the political culture and the sometimes very questionable behaviour of political actors. The culture of the Chamber of Deputies is symptomatic in this respect, as there appears to be an unwillingness to create firm rules and a tendency to circumvent rules already in place (Wintr 2010). This phenomenon, furthermore, is not limited to the Chamber, but constitutes a general trait of Czech politics and society.

However, the Czech situation is better in some respects than Sartori's example of a typical assembly government, the French Third Republic. The constitutional protection given to the government against parliament is somewhat stronger. Also positive is the fact that party discipline in the Chamber of Deputies is relatively high, giving some cohesion to parties and preventing the atomisation of power. Rule by parties, though viewed by the

Czech general public with much disdain, in fact prevents the country from becoming an unmanageable 'republic of deputies'.

Table 6.1: Governments in the Czech Republic since 1992

Government term	Prime minister and party affiliation	Parties in government	Support in the Chamber of Deputies (number of deputies of governmental parties at the formation of the government)	Type of government
July 1992–July 1996	Václav Klaus I (ODS)	ODS, KDU-ČSL, ODA, KDS	105	Minimal winning coalition*
July 1996–January 1998	Václav Klaus II (ODS)	ODS, KDU-ČSL, ODA	99	Minority coalition
January 1998–July 1998	Josef Tošovský (non-partisan)	KDU-ČSL, US, ODA, non-partisans	61	Semi-political government
July 1998–July 2002	Miloš Zeman (ČSSD)	ČSSD	74	Single-party minority government dependent on agreement with ODS
July 2002–August 2004	Vladimír Špidla (ČSSD)	ČSSD, KDU-ČSL, US-DEU	101	Minimal winning coalition
August 2004–April 2005	Stanislav Gross (ČSSD)	ČSSD, KDU-ČSL, US-DEU	101	Minimal winning coalition
April 2005–August 2006	Jiří Paroubek (ČSSD)	ČSSD, KDU-ČSL, US-DEU	101	Minimal winning coalition

September 2006–January 2007	Mirek Topolánek I (ODS)	ODS	81	Minority government, which did not win confidence of the Chamber
January 2007–May 2009	Mirek Topolánek II (ODS)	ODS, KDU-ČSL, SZ	100	Minority coalition**
May 2009–July 2010	Jan Fischer (non-partisan)	-	-	Technocratic government
July 2010–July 2013	Petr Nečas (ODS)	ODS, TOP 09, VV (LIDEM, which split off from VV, replaced VV in government)***	118	Minimal winning coalition
July 2013–January 2014	Jiří Rusnok (non-partisan)	-	-	Technocratic government, which did not win confidence of the Chamber
January 2014–	Bohuslav Sobotka (ČSSD)	ČSSD, ANO, KDU-ČSL	111	Minimal winning coalition

Source: Havlík and Kopeček 2008, updated.

Note:
* The term minimal winning coalition means that no party is superfluous.
** Not strictly a minority, as the government had exactly half the number of deputies in the Chamber.
*** Following the schism in VV and the emergence of the new party LIDEM in spring 2012, Nečas's government could be considered a new government, i.e., Nečas II, as the make-up of the government coalition changed, and its support in the Chamber diminished. However, the whole period 2010-2013 may be considered one government term: VV was the smallest party in government and played a minor role. Furthermore, there was no change in the perception of Nečas's government among the public or media.

6.3. The Senate's image as an unnecessary institution

One of the serious disputes at the time of the constitution's writing was over the establishment of parliament's upper chamber, the Senate. It was not just the opposition who rejected the Senate; many politicians in government and constitutional experts who prepared the constitution had their doubts as well. In the end, a Senate comprising 81 members was included in the constitution chiefly thanks to the efforts of the politicians of the Civic Democratic Alliance (ODA). The main arguments put forward by the supporters of the Senate were that there had been a second chamber in the First Republic and that many other European countries had one. What these arguments failed to consider was that most of these countries were federations, or were ethnically or otherwise heterogeneous. Unlike interwar Czechoslovakia, the Czech Republic was and is a relatively homogeneous country. Another proposal was for a sort of division of labour between the two chambers of parliament, with one dedicated to private law and the other to public law, but this suggestion was unrealistic. Similarly, the idea that the Senate would become a 'house of sages', where party affiliations would be unimportant, was not pursued (Němeček 2010). Today most senators are elected on a party ticket, though their party affiliation is often weaker than is the case with deputies.

One consideration that aided the inclusion of the Senate in the constitution was the idea that initially it would be filled with the Czech deputies from the federal parliament who would be losing their jobs. This vision of a smooth transition into the new institution and of obtaining attractive new positions contributed to the painless end of Czechoslovakia. In practice the Senate was not filled with federal deputies. Paradoxically, this was due to resistance mounted by ODA, the party that had pushed for the establishment of the chamber in the first place. ODA was the only party in Klaus's government coalition not to have had representation in the federal parliament. The Senate came into existence only after a delay in late 1996. In the interim period the Chamber of Deputies exercised the powers of the Senate. This delayed creation of the Senate strengthened the tendency to question its meaningfulness (Kysela 2004, Just 2012). Characteristically, the opposition Social Democrats and the far-right Republicans sought to have the Senate removed from the constitution, but were unsuccessful.

The first elections to the Senate meant that new political offices were created, reconciling previously doubtful politicians to its existence. But a sceptical public still saw the Senate as unnecessary and largely continues to see it that way. Voter turnout for Senate elections has traditionally been much lower than for the Chamber of Deputies, despite the fact that the Senate uses a majority electoral system, which works to personalise the elections (for more details see Chapter 7). When, as is usual, the first round of Senate elections is held on the same day as regional or local elections voter turnout tends to improve, but it declines rapidly in the second round (Lebeda, Malcová and Lacina 2009). For instance, in 2014 turnout for the first round was 38 %, but in the second round only 17 %. At the time of Czechoslovakia's demise, fears that it would sow the seeds of future secessions militated against the logical principle of a Senate representing the country's individual regions (Kysela 2004, Dvořáková and Kunc 1999). The law for Senate elections defined single-member constituencies, however, for the most part these are not homogeneous entities and lack a clear connection with the regions, which were established only later. This too contributes to the low public interest in the upper chamber.

The constitution sets a senator's term at six years, compared with four years for a deputy. The Senate is renewed gradually, with a third of the seats contested every two years. Shifts in voters' electoral preferences thus affect the composition of the Senate less than they do the Chamber of Deputies. In addition, unlike the Chamber of Deputies, the Senate cannot be dissolved. Some constitutional experts and senators argue that this makes the Senate a stabilising element within the political system, ensuring its political continuity (Pithart 1999, Kysela 2004, Bahýľová 2010). This stability, however, cannot address the Senate's essential weakness: it has few powers, which is a consequence of the fact that it has never been much in demand.

This weakness is most conspicuous in the law-making process. According to the constitution, the government, deputies, senators, and regional assemblies can initiate legislation.[2] However, senators (and regions) rarely do so, and they account for only a small percentage of bills. Governments have traditionally been the most active, introducing slightly more than half the total number of bills. They are followed by deputies, who introduce about 30 to 40 % of bills (Syllová 2013).[3] In order to pass a bill in the Chamber, a majority of deputies

---

[2] The text of the constitution stipulates that only the Senate as a whole may initiate legislation. However, since 2004 parliamentary procedure allows even a single senator to introduce a bill as long as the Senate passes the proposal.

[3] The only exception was the period of instability from 1996 to 1998, when deputies introduced almost half of the bills.

present have to vote in its favour. When the Chamber has passed a bill, it is referred to the Senate, which has several options: it can pass the bill, resolve not to consider it, reject it, or amend it. In the first two cases the bill is approved. If the Senate rejects the bill, the Chamber of Deputies can override this decision relatively easily with an absolute majority of all deputies. A majority of deputies present is needed to accept the amendments. In order to reject amendments, the same conditions apply as when the Chamber votes on a bill rejected by the Senate, that is, an absolute majority of all deputies.

The changes the Senate makes to the bills coming from the Chamber of Deputies are often minor. This reflects its role as an "inspector" of legislation, and there is a relatively high chance that the Chamber will accept such amendments. Yet at certain times the Senate shows a more pronounced tendency to act as a political corrective. This is connected with the preponderance (or lack thereof) of opposition in the Senate. The opposition is naturally hostile to the legislative agenda of the government. To illustrate, one may compare two electoral terms, 2006–2010 and 2010–2013. The number of bills referred from the Chamber to the Senate was about the same in both, and a government led by ODS was in power most of the time. In the first term 2006–2010, when there was a majority of parties in support of the government in the upper chamber, the Senate defeated only nine bills and returned 46 with amendments. In the second term 2010–2013, when the opposition prevailed in the Senate, it defeated 37 bills and returned 80 with amendments. Thus, the upper chamber shifted from relative acquiescence and passivity to noticeable activity (Syllová 2013).

As it is relatively easy for the Chamber to override a Senate vote, the opposition can rarely make use of the upper chamber as a veto on governmental proposals (Tsebelis 2002). This can be illustrated by the fact that, out of the above-mentioned 37 bills defeated by the Senate in 2010–2013, the Chamber was able to override all except 9 (Syllová 2013). However, the chances of a Senate victory increase if the governmental parties do not have a strong majority in the Chamber.

The Senate is not the parliamentary opposition's only weapon. It can also ask the Constitutional Court for judicial review of legislation. The Court can annul all or part of an act if it contravenes the constitution. Judicial review can be initiated by a fifth of deputies or senators. During the first two decades of the Czech Republic's existence, more than 100 such motions were tabled, and about a third were partially or fully successful. Opposition members of parliament initiated three-fifths of these motions, and senators have been very active during some electoral terms (Kopeček and Petrov 2016).

When the Chamber is dissolved, the Senate assumes the power to adopt legal measures proposed by the government. However, such measures must subsequently be approved by the newly-elected Chamber. In practice this power was first employed in 2013, more than 20 years after the adoption of the constitution, and was accompanied by debate concerning its necessity. Hence the question remains open as to whether it will become a common practice.

Exceptions, where the Senate is a strong veto player, are the passing of constitutional and electoral acts and international treaties. In these cases the approval of the upper chamber is necessary. A three-fifths majority of all deputies and of voting senators is required to pass constitutional acts and some international treaties. A simple majority in both chambers is sufficient to change the electoral laws (and some international treaties as well). In practice, these situations are rare but not negligible. They were most conspicuous during the era of the Opposition Agreement (1998–2002), when the Senate was able to block attempts made by ODS and ČSSD to change the constitution.

Another of the Senate's important powers is that it confirms the president's nominees for the Constitutional Court. The smoothness of this process depends on the occupants of these institutions. In the early years of Václav Klaus's presidency, the Senate was largely hostile to the president and rejected his nominees. This partially paralysed the Constitutional Court, as several positions remained vacant (Kühn and Kysela 2006). To a lesser extent, the problem reappeared at the end of Klaus's presidency.

There have been repeated attempts to give more powers to the upper chamber. They have all foundered. On the contrary, with the introduction of direct presidential elections in 2012, senators lost their power to elect the president alongside the deputies, and the televised elections were one of the few moments that reminded the general public of the Senate's existence.

The Czech parliament is asymmetrically bicameral. The upper chamber is so weak that it rarely influences politics in important ways, and this fact affects public perceptions. As a result, an image has emerged of the Senate as an unnecessary institution. The public knows little about it and believes it lacks a purpose. Senate elections are thus often thought to be pointless.

6.4. Regional arrangements: a complicated genesis and a problematic result

One important issue remained unresolved when the constitution was adopted: the territorial division of the state. This was connected with the Moravian movement. Their fundamental demand was that the eastern part of the country, the historic land of Moravia, be made a coherent entity and be given significant powers (Mareš and Strmiska 2005, Springerová 2010). The right-wing parties who won the 1992 elections, however, were worried about the implications of granting autonomy to Moravia. What they wanted to avoid, in the wake of the division of Czechoslovakia, was to encourage another secession. Furthermore, it was unclear how the western part of the state, Bohemia, would be administratively divided. Although other opposition parties and the governmental KDU-ČSL supported a territorial arrangement based on the principle of historical lands, the issue was of fundamental importance only to the Moravians.

After 1993 several attempts were made to find a workable solution to this issue, but they quickly foundered over incompatible views and the Civic Democrats' unwillingness to support swift decentralisation. Led by Václav Klaus, the party feared that the new territorial units might become bastions of the opposition and hinder the centre's control over economic reforms. Only in autumn 1997 after the Moravians were politically marginalised was a compromise found concerning the character and boundaries of the new regions, yet their actual establishment was postponed until 2000. Various ideas and interests influenced the character of the 14 regions that were created. Politicians in different parts of the country had different ideas about the shape of their region, ideas that crossed party lines. This led to significant differences between the regions in terms of their areas and populations.[4] Even more importantly, the new regions, with a few exceptions, were mostly artificial creations, often lacking homogeneity and the loyalty of their residents (Šimíček 2001, Balík 2005). The building of regional loyalties proved to be a long process with varying degrees of success. It was necessary to harmonise the structures of public authorities with the new regions, a protracted and expensive business that in some cases still remains unfinished. For example,

---

[4] Most of the regions were relatively small and paradoxically it soon became necessary to combine two or three regions into larger units (the so-called NUTS II) for the purpose of obtaining EU funding.

the jurisdiction of regional courts and public prosecutors does not correspond to the boundaries of the self-governing regions. Another controversial point was the decision not to respect the historical border between Bohemia and Moravia. The motivation was to prevent any recurrence of Moravian regionalism.

The regions today enjoy several independent powers, typically in managing their own property and establishing their own legal entities. They also exercise some powers delegated to them by the state in areas such as land use planning, education, welfare, health, and transport (Hledíková, Janák and Dobeš 2005). However, the contents of these policies is sometimes determined by the central government and the scope of regional authority is limited to more technical matters, for instance, repairs to less important roads. There is thus less space for political decision-making at the regional level than at the national level. A consequence of this is that in campaigns for the regional assemblies, the differences between parties' programmes tend to be slight, and national rather than regional issues tend to be key for winning these elections (Eibl et al. 2009, Eibl, Gregor and Macková 2013).

The introduction of regions has had other effects. The very first regional elections were held in the middle of the national electoral cycle. They proved a debacle for the ruling Social Democrats, as many voters used the regional elections to express their dissatisfaction. This 'retribution' by voters against governmental parties is a frequent feature of Czech regional elections. For example, in 2008 some media pundits tellingly dubbed the regional elections an 'orange tsunami' because the oppositional Social Democrats, whose colour is orange, triumphed, whereas the parties in government – the Civic Democrats, the People's Party, and the Greens – came to grief. Thus, although regional elections are 'second-order elections', they can disrupt the cohesion of coalition governments. Furthermore, regional elections lead to competition between the parties in national government. It is true that other instances of second-order elections, namely those to the Senate, European Parliament, and local elections, have similar effects. Yet regional elections have proven particularly dangerous to governments.

The political make-up of the national government is often different from that of regional councils (the executive branch of regional government), and this sometimes causes friction. Situations where the regional councils and their governors come into sharp conflict with the central government can ultimately lead to attempts to block national policies. For example, the centre-right government led by Mirek Topolánek introduced co-payments for medical care.

After the victory of the Social Democrats in regional elections on a platform of opposition to these payments, several regions decided to pay these fees for the patients, which created political and legal problems.

Another consequence of the establishment of regions is the regionalisation of party elites. The new regional platform offered alternative new options in terms of power and resources, which have encouraged not only inter-party but also intra-party competition. The importance of regional party officials has risen sharply, with some obtaining tremendous influence over their parties' decision making. Some parties suffered serious divisions. ODS, for instance, could be better described as a confederation of regional organisations than a unified party. This had a significant impact on ODS's loss of favour among voters after 2009.

Regional government came into being as the result of a political compromise. As time passes and the regions establish themselves, citizens have become reconciled with their existence, yet the system is far from optimal.

6.5. The president's aura and constitutional inviolability

Although the constitution does not make the president the head of the executive, his or her position and powers are not negligible. The constitution builds on a specific historical and political tradition, which begins with the first Czechoslovak president, Tomáš G. Masaryk. Not only did he found the Czechoslovak state in 1918, he also made the presidential office one of the regime's principal pillars. It is only a slight hyperbole to say that Masaryk was a monarch on a republican throne. Like Austrian emperors, Masaryk was endowed with some powers that had a distinctly monarchist tinge: the power to grant pardons and declare amnesty. The present constitution still gives these powers to Czech presidents.

Václav Havel, the president of Czechoslovakia after November 1989, imbued the office with an ethos strongly based on morality and the tradition of anti-communist dissent. He transferred these characteristics to the new Czech state, which he headed for a full decade from 1993 onwards. By contrast, what faded was Havel's position as a key political actor. As new democratic institutions were being created, Havel not only 'ruled', he also 'governed' (Kysela 2006). As time passed, this was no longer the case. Nonetheless, the long continuity of Havel's Czechoslovak and Czech presidencies has attached an informal charisma to the presidential office, or perhaps better, a semi-religious aura surrounding the head of state (Kopeček and Mlejnek 2013). Almost by default, the president is expected to ensure good governance and resolve social problems (Kysela 2008, Mlejnek 2011, Brunclík 2013). This aura has granted much credibility to Havel and his successors, Václav Klaus (2003–2013) and Miloš Zeman (2013–). Further, it has provided them with opportunities to influence politics and informally strengthen their position. All three presidents have been activists at certain times and in certain domains.

The exceptional position of the president according to the constitution is apparent from the fact that he represents the state internationally, cannot be held responsible for official actions and cannot be removed. He is elected for a five-year term and can hold the office twice in succession.[5] The only exception to the irremovability of the president is a complicated impeachment process, presided over by the Constitutional Court.[6] The president is therefore considered to represent the identity and integrity of the Czech state, and to act as a guarantor of the constitutional order (Gerloch, Hřebejk and Zoubek 1999, Wintr 2008, Klíma 2008). The scope of his authority is not limited to the executive, but includes relations with the central bank and parliament which are described below. The president's practically inviolable position gives him an obvious advantage over the much more vulnerable prime minister. The president has almost always been more popular than the prime minister. This is due not only to the symbolic importance of the former's office, but also the fact that he is unencumbered with the problems of day-to-day governance and political infighting.

With the introduction of a direct election in 2012, the president now has a mandate directly from the voters. Yet his powers have remained practically unchanged. He still cannot be held responsible for his official actions, though in this respect, at the very least, a change would have been patently desirable

---

5 When compared to other presidents' terms of office, the formulation in the Czech constitution is atypical: no one may be elected president more than twice 'in succession'. This has opened discussion on whether someone might become a president for a third non-consecutive term. Though theoretically possible, this scenario is unlikely.

6 This procedure has only been used once, against President Klaus in 2013, and was unsuccessful. Since the direct election of the president was introduced, the procedure has been changed: in addition to high treason, the president can now be impeached for gross violation of the constitution. In order to begin the proceedings, the motion now has to be supported not only by a three-fifths majority of senators present, but also by a three-fifths majority of all deputies, making the procedure extraordinarily difficult.

(Kysela 2008). The first president so elected, Miloš Zeman, has used the argument of his having a direct mandate from voters to defend a number of steps he has taken, steps that have increased his political importance.

In the public perception of the Czech president, the illusion or myth of non-partisanship plays a role and is linked with his semi-religious aura. According this perception, the president represents the entire nation and is not linked with a particular party or parties. The ideal of the head of state as 'above parties' was even mentioned in some older legal commentaries on the constitution (e.g., Pavlíček and Hřebejk 1998). The roots of the myth can be traced back to Masaryk, yet even then it did not correspond to Masaryk's actions. The myth doggedly persisted in the public consciousness and in the 1990s was revived by the moralising style of the Havel presidency and his scepticism towards political parties. Again, the myth did not reflect political reality. Havel was closer to some parties (or its factions) and distant from others. His relationship with ODS, for instance, was openly hostile from the late 1990s onwards, and these feelings were mutual.[7]

The idea of a president 'above parties' might have been compatible with a person who would accept a largely ceremonial role. Such a role, however, was incompatible with the strong personalities of Havel and his successor Klaus. The chances that a truly non-partisan president might take office were further diminished with the introduction of direct presidential elections. The struggle to win the electorate's votes naturally pushes candidates to offer politically distinctive programmes. Ahead of the first presidential election in 2013, Miloš Zeman, the candidate who ultimately won, presented himself as an indignant tribune of the people, fighting against the unpopular cabinet led by Petr Nečas (ODS) under the banner of 'Stop this government'. The idea that by a wave of a magic want all of this would disappear after the election and the head of state would become a sagacious and unbiased figure beloved by all was unrealistic.

---

[7] Havel plumbed the depths of their mutual antagonism in his famous speech at the Rudolfinum in 1997. It included a harsh critique of the transformation era and especially of the 'father' of the economic reform, Václav Klaus.

6.6. Presidents, prime ministers, and the dangers of political dualism

This section presents an overview of some of the president's powers and the influence they may exert over politics. The president may dissolve the Chamber of Deputies, but only under circumstances strictly prescribed by the constitution; his space for manoeuvre is limited. He can also veto legislation without a countersignature by the government. An absolute majority of all deputies may override the president's veto, hence these vetoes are rarely successful. Even governments lacking a parliamentary majority usually find enough votes in the Chamber to overturn the veto. An exception is vetoes at the end of the parliamentary term when deputies are no longer in session and can no longer overturn the veto. This is similar to a pocket veto in the USA.

The president can initiate a judicial review of legislation, which can function like a veto. Thus, he can employ the same weapon that is available to deputies and senators. Havel did so frequently and successfully, whereas Klaus was reticent due to his antipathy towards the Constitutional Court and higher courts generally. He even spoke pejoratively of 'juristocracy' (*soudcokracie*), or the domination of the courts over politics (Klaus and Loužek 2006, Smekal and Pospíšil 2013). Although Zeman made some use of judicial reviews, all in all, the head of state, like the Senate, has proved to be a rather weak veto player.

Appointment powers are more important than vetoes to the presidential office. Particularly noteworthy is the president's relationship with the Czech National Bank, which, while independent of government, is an important influence on monetary policy. The appointment of the Bank's board, governor, and vice-governors is entirely in the hands of the president, and no other authority may challenge his choice. By contrast, the president is much more limited when appointing justices to the Constitutional Court. The president therefore holds a strong, albeit indirect, instrument with which to influence the country's economy.

Havel was fully aware of this. Characteristically, his second term (from 1998) was marked by disputes, especially with Zeman and Klaus, the leaders of the two main parliamentary parties. Both pressured the president to consult with other constitutional bodies before making his nominations. There was even an unsuccessful attempt to limit the president's influence over the central bank.

Paradoxically, after later become presidents themselves, both of Havel's critics made full use of the power of appointment. In choosing their particular appointees, they followed their particular preferences: Klaus, monetarist and Zeman, Keynesian. The gusto with which they each staffed the bank board according to their own vision was strengthened by their experience as prime ministers in dealing with the central bank.

The constitution offers the president significant foreign policy powers, particularly in representing the state internationally (Article 63 of the constitution). The president's important decisions in this area are subject to countersignature by the government. Constitutional theorists emphasise that the president is not authorised to create his own foreign policy and that the main role should be played by government in cooperation with the president (Vyhnánek 2010). Despite that, the president's political visions have often been at variance with those of governments, irrespective of the requirement for a countersignature.

For Havel, support for human rights and a strong Euro-Atlantic orientation were essential. In 1999, he harshly criticised Miloš Zeman's government when it vacillated over supporting NATO's aerial bombing of Serbia. According to the president, it was necessary to support the Czech Republic's allies. He described the military action as a humanitarian act whose purpose was to prevent the expulsion of Albanians from Kosovo. The common thread running through Klaus's presidency was his opposition to deepening EU integration. This sometimes seemed like an anti-EU campaign and included his attempts to block the European constitution and the Lisbon Treaty. Prime ministers responded by criticising the president for overstepping his powers. Prime Minister Jiří Paroubek even threatened to limit the president's foreign travel and put forward the idea that the president would have to follow the government's instructions (Kysela 2006, Brunclík 2008a, Kopeček 2012a). During the crisis in the Ukraine in 2014, President Miloš Zeman opposed sanctions imposed by the EU against Russia and so came into conflict with the position taken by Bohuslav Sobotka's government.

To date the conflicts between presidents and governments over foreign and European policies have never led to an outright clash. The ability of presidents to take an independent line in foreign policy has been much limited by their lack of organisational capacity. Still, because of these conflicts, the country occasionally speaks in different voices internationally, which has undesirable consequences in foreign affairs.

Though manifest in the representation of the country abroad, the dualist tendency in the executive is even more pronounced in the process of government formation and the resolution of government crises. The constitution is based on a principle that the president should play a moderating and facilitating role in negotiations between political actors. In reality this has mostly been the case, but the boundary between moderating and undue activism on the part of the head of state is unclear. In appointing and removing prime ministers and government members, presidents have exploited the fact that the relevant clauses in the constitution are brief and abstract. This has given them significant space to manoeuvre. The constitution says that 'the Prime Minister shall be appointed by the President of the Republic' and that the president 'shall appoint and recall on the proposal of the Prime Minister the other members of the Government' (Article 68). It does not stipulate within what period of time the prime minister should be appointed or other ministers recalled. Havel and later Klaus took advantage of this clause to entrust individuals with forming a government without concurrently appointing them prime minister. Given how regularly this mechanism is used, it has become a constitutional convention (Šimíček 2003).

Neither does the constitution specify the manner of, or criteria for, choosing the prime minister. There is only the constitutional corrective that, should the president twice appoint a government that fails to win the Chamber's confidence, it is the speaker of the Chamber who nominates the third candidate for prime minister (Article 68 of the constitution). This provision ought to force the president to carefully consider the chances of his designated prime minister winning the confidence of the Chamber (Kysela 2008, Molek 2010). However, the president loses the option of nominating the prime minister only on his third attempt, and historically this has not yet occurred. Generally it is true that if party leaders have a clear plan for a majority government, there is little space for the president to play a role. But, in a politically complex situation, the president's space for manoeuvre is much greater, and so is his ability to push through a solution that suits him or block one that does not.

President Havel pushed through his own vision most conspicuously in late 1997. When the existing centre-right government disintegrated, the president entrusted Josef Lux, the chair of a smaller coalition party, with holding talks to form a new government. Lux's informal mission duly helped to form a government led by Josef Tošovský, previously head of the central bank. The prime minister and several other ministers were non-partisans, which suited

Havel's ambivalent views of parties. It is worth recalling here Havel's original vision of the constitution, alluded to above. It afforded the president the option of creating a technocratic, non-partisan government, one that would not need to win a vote of confidence, should the parliament find itself unable to agree on a 'political' government (Havel 1992b: 381). The idea of technocratic governments was not included in the Czech constitution; yet its influence on the Tošovský government was evident. However, this government was not purely technocratic; rather, it was semi-political, with several politicians from parties hitherto in government (ODS was represented in the new government by one of its factions, which later created a new party, the Freedom Union – see Table 6.1). The Tošovský government had to win the Chamber's confidence, which it did by promising to limit its term and agenda.

President Klaus increased his space for manoeuvre by introducing specific conditions not stipulated in the constitution. This can be demonstrated by the situation that arose in 2004, when the Social Democratic Prime Minister Vladimír Špidla resigned, and the president tasked his successor in the party leadership, Stanislav Gross, with forming a new government. Klaus stipulated that Gross form a majority government that would not rely on the communists during the vote of confidence. This reflected Klaus's efforts to limit the influence of the communists, a view that was strongly supported by the public. Gross managed to fulfil these conditions – proof of which included signatures of a majority of non-communist MPs – and the president duly appointed his government.

Gross's government quickly fell apart over the murky financing of his apartment purchase and the business activities of his wife. The ministers of one of the minor parties in the coalition, KDU-ČSL, resigned, re-opening the possibility of a minority government relying on communist support. Klaus responded by not accepting their resignation and chose to delay, while exerting informal pressure on the prime minister. In doing so Klaus was aided by the fact that the constitution did not stipulate a deadline for recalling the resigning ministers. Gross's intra-party support foundered and he ultimately resigned as prime minister. Formally, the existing coalition was preserved and a new government formed, led by a different social democratic prime minister (Brunclík 2008b, Kopeček 2012a).

Miloš Zeman went the furthest in imposing his conception of the cabinet. When the centre-right Petr Nečas government fell in mid-2013, the president responded by appointing a non-partisan prime minister, Jiří Rusnok, who put together a caretaker government. Zeman's approach was novel in that the appointment of Rusnok and the formation of his government were undertaken with no prior agreement with any of the parliamentary parties. The president presented party politicians with a *fait accompli*. For the first time in the history of the Czech Republic, a government was created that could unreservedly be described as presidential. Yet, Rusnok's government failed to win the confidence of the Chamber of Deputies, who subsequently agreed to dissolve itself and call early elections. This limited not only its mandate but also that of the Rusnok government. Rusnok's government, however, ruled for the next six months without a parliamentary mandate, a problematic situation, given that the Czech Republic is ostensibly a parliamentary regime.

The early election took place in autumn 2013. The pro-presidential party, bearing Zeman's name and including some of the ministers in the Rusnok government, failed to win any seats. Soon after the election, the president's faction within the Social Democrat Party lost their intra-party struggle. Hence the structural preconditions for any future government connected with the president disappeared. Zeman, it is true, delayed the formation of the new government and sought to veto some of its ministers, but ultimately a classic coalition government accountable to the Chamber of Deputies took power. The shift from parliamentarianism to a semi-presidential regime was, therefore, only temporary. It confirmed that the president's influence can be substantial, even decisive at times; yet the president lacks an institutional basis that would allow him to govern and wield real executive power.

6.7. The constitutional court and the political consequences of judicial decisions

While parliament and government institutions have deep roots in Czech history, the constitutional judiciary developed fully only after 1989. The Constitutional Court was part of the institutional design of the First Republic, but its influence was limited. Under the communist regime the court did not function, even though a constitutional amendment adopted in the late 1960s provided for a court. Only in 1991, after the birth of the democratic regime, was a court instituted, but its life was cut short when Czechoslovakia ceased to exist. However, the Czech Constitutional Court began working in 1993 (Schwartz 2000, Přibáň 2002, Balík et al. 2003).

The Czech Republic adopted the European model of constitutional judiciary with a special constitutional court which is not part of the ordinary judicial system. As in other emerging democracies of Central Europe, the aim was to create an instrument that would help to consolidate constitutional democracy and to protect the country from a return to authoritarianism. Also influential was the growing importance of constitutional courts globally, since the mid-twentieth century. The Czechs and their neighbours in Central Europe were particularly inspired by the German constitutional judiciary (Vallinder 1995, Sadurski 2010, Stone Sweet 2012).

The purpose of the constitutional judiciary – that is, to facilitate the consolidation of democracy – is reflected in Article 83 of the Czech constitution, where the Constitutional Court is described as 'a judicial body charged with the protection of constitutional rule'. Its tasks include both the abstract review of constitutionality, determining whether legal norms are compatible with the constitutional system, and the concrete review of constitutionality, deciding upon constitutional petitions filled by individuals.[8] The Court consists of 15 justices appointed by the president for a ten-year term. Justices can be reappointed for one additional term, a practice which is not exceptional. Reappointments do, however, lead to discussion as to whether this is good for justices' independence, as they might be influenced by the opinions of the authorities that appoint and confirm them, i.e., the president and the Senate respectively.

In politically important affairs, such as impeachment proceedings against the president, the review of the constitutionality of acts, or the compatibility of an international treaty with the constitution, the Constitutional Court decides as a plenum. However, even decisions that might at first sight seem banal and are decided by panels of only three judges can have enormous political consequences. For example, in 2000 the Constitutional Court ruled that ČSSD was the owner of the People's House (*Lidový dům*) in Prague, a large and profitable piece of real estate in the centre of the city. In doing so it overturned the decisions made by other courts and helped to put the party on a secure financial footing (Šimíček 2013).

In addition to the constitutional judiciary, an administrative judiciary, headed by the Supreme Administrative Court, is also well developed. The administrative courts often make decisions affecting politics, as their jurisdiction includes parties, elections, and local referendums. For example,

---

[8] Naturally, even in these cases, what matters is whether or not the constitutional system has been contravened.

the Supreme Administrative Court's dissolution of the far-right Workers' Party in 2010 set a precedent for bans on political parties and established the boundaries of acceptable behaviour. Criminal justice affects politics in a similarly important way, for example, in ruling on offences committed by deputies. To illustrate, in 2012 the leader of the Public Affairs party Vít Bárta was convicted of bribing another deputy. This contributed to a rift within the party, which was subsequently ejected from the government.

Nonetheless, the most important judicial body for politics is, without a doubt, the Constitutional Court. This is not only because it is the court of last instance, but especially because it is precisely the Constitutional Court who decides on what has been termed 'mega-politics', that is, the key disputes that define the political system (Hirschl 2008). An example of such a dispute was the court's review of the Lisbon Treaty, initiated in 2008 by Eurosceptic senators and president Klaus, who sought to block the Treaty. However, the Constitutional Court ruled that the Treaty did not contravene the constitutional system. Another example of mega-politics were the impeachment proceedings launched by senators against president Klaus for high treason, filed only a few days before Klaus's term expired in 2013. The main charge against Klaus was his controversial use of the presidential amnesty. However, the Constitutional Court refused to hear the case, pointing out that the president's term had expired in the meantime.

'Mega-politics' disputes most often arise in connection with the judicial review of legal regulations and especially of acts. These cases are decided by the plenum of the Constitutional Court. In these instances the Court undertakes an abstract review of constitutionality. This is ex post review, i.e., the court examines legislation passed by parliament. The court cannot engage in a priori review of bills. Judicial review can be initiated by the president, groups of deputies or senators, and under certain circumstances other actors, including ordinary courts and citizens. During the first decade of the Czech Republic's existence, the most famous case of mega-politics involved the annulment in 2001 of several key clauses in the electoral law. These clauses might have seriously changed the structure of the party system (see Chapter 7). It is telling that petitions to have these clauses abolished were submitted by both President Havel and a group of senators.

Another case of a 'mega-politics' dispute *par excellence* occurred in 2009, and has been the Constitutional Court's most controversial entry into politics in the history of the Czech Republic. This case was not initiated by a proposal to have a law annulled. Rather, a deputy initiated a constitutional petition. His grievances were two-fold: he opposed a one-off constitutional act, passed by parliament, which shortened the term of the Chamber of Deputies, and, at the same time, criticised the president's decision to call an early election. These, the deputy alleged, contravened his right to exercise his mandate as a deputy. The Constitutional Court annulled the constitutional act and the planned early election, arguing that, due to its one-off nature and retroactivity, the constitutional act in question interfered with the essential characteristics of a democratic state that respects the rule of law (Article 9 of the constitution) (Nález Ústavního soudu ze dne 10.9. 2009).

In making this decision, the plenum of the Constitutional Court was not unanimous. Two judges dissented. Criticism of the decision was fierce. Some critics argued that the Constitutional Court was not authorised to evaluate the constitutionality of a constitutional act (Fiala 2010, Balík 2010). Other critics admitted that, under extraordinary circumstances, the Constitutional Court may annul a constitutional act, but questioned whether the decision to end an electoral term early – a decision passed by a constitutional majority – was truly unconstitutional. The situation would have been different, one critic argued, had the parliament extended its term (Šimíček 2009). It has also been pointed out that one-off constitutional acts are commonly used in the Czech legal system (Kühn 2009). The strongest argument, expressed in various ways by most of those who opposed the Court's decision, was that the Court had both overstepped its authority and failed to consider the consequences of its annulment of the election, which was political chaos.

Although this intervention by the Constitutional Court was problematic, it had one positive effect in that a general (as opposed to one-off) change was made to the constitution. In addition to the existing options for the dissolution of the Chamber of Deputies, which are very difficult to enact in practice, the Chamber can now also dissolve itself if at least three-fifths of all deputies adopt a resolution to this effect. Given frequent government instability, this is a reasonable option, and one that was used to dissolve the Chamber in 2013.

The Constitutional Court's entries into the political arena are sometimes problematic. Yet in comparison with other Central European and Western European states, the Czech Constitutional Court is not an extreme case of judicial activism (Stone Sweet 1992, Stone Sweet 2000, Sadurski 2009). The Czech Republic is simply part of a more general trend of the judicialisation of politics in contemporary democracies. As a rule, constitutional justices, and judges generally, do not enter the political space on their own initiative, but are drawn into it by politicians. It is worth quoting here an insight of Wojciech

Sadurski (2010: 105), which fits the Czech situation well: 'the greater the tensions between political forces, the greater the possibility that [...] adversaries will turn to the constitutional court to contest the policy choices of political opponents'. The position of judges is different from that of politicians, or more precisely, politics looks different from the courtroom than from the parliamentary arena. Yet it is worth remembering that judges have opinions and values as well and these influence their interpretation of legal norms and their willingness to push for what they consider to be right. Therefore, courts are among the actors who have an important influence on politics, even though they are not elected themselves.

6.8. Conclusion: malfunctioning institutions and the need for reforms

Giovanni Sartori considers government stability to be a necessary, though not sufficient, condition of effective governance (Sartori 1994). The Czech Republic does not fulfil this condition. Its coalition governments are politically heterogeneous and their backing in the Chamber of Deputies tends to be weak. Both of these facts have an impact on government durability, which is mostly short. The government expends much of its energy on conflict resolution within the coalition and on finding tricky political compromises concerning the government agenda. The situation is made worse by the fragile position the government has vis-à-vis the Chamber of Deputies, as demonstrated by frequent votes of no confidence. Though the opposition rarely deploys this weapon with any success, these attempts still constantly vex and occupy the government, which lacks serious instruments to influence the working of the Chamber. The prime minister is usually not a strong government leader, and his position, even within his own party, is often precarious. He has competitors within the government coalition – the leaders of other governmental parties – as well as outside the cabinet, in the person of the president. Thus, the Czech Republic is close to the model of assembly government with excessive domination of the Chamber of Deputies over the cabinet.

Several veto players also influence Czech governance: the Senate, the president, and the Constitutional Court. Their ability to block the government agenda is conditional. For the Senate to be effective, the opposition needs a majority in the upper chamber and the government needs to lack strong backing in the Chamber of Deputies. The president needs to be unhelpful, if not openly hostile, to the government. Still, these veto players can occasionally have a serious impact on the political process.

The constitution does not make the president the leader of the executive, but he has several significant powers and his position is almost inviolable. The brevity of some articles of the constitution and their ambiguity provide the head of state with the ability to influence politics at key moments such as government formation and crises. The weight of the president is further increased by the informal aura attached to his office.

The introduction of direct presidential elections in 2012 increased the dualism between the prime minister and the head of state, providing a stronger foundation for the president's activism. Although the Czech Republic remains a parliamentary regime, the direct election has introduced another potentially destabilising element. Government parties may hinder the president's activism as long as they are capable of basic cohesion and enjoy the backing of the Chamber of Deputies. Important for presidential activism is the temperament of the office holder, and whether or not he has allies among the relevant parties.

The political heterogeneity of governments combined with their short durability and frequent changes of ministers do not allow for effective governance. One consequence of this is the public mistrust of politics and politicians. Politicians are held in low esteem. According to surveys, the profession of politician is among the least respected (CVVM 2013). This sends a clear signal to governments.

Czech political institutions need reforms. It is hard to disagree with those authors who consider it desirable to rationalise the parliamentary regime, which means strengthening the position of the cabinet and weakening the power of the Chamber of Deputies (Novák 2008, Kysela 2013, Kubát 2009 and 2013). The Chamber should support the government rather than vie with it for power. The means to achieve this rationalisation include, first of all, a change in the government formation procedure, such as the introduction of time limits, strengthening the powers of the prime minister, and the introduction of a constructive vote of no confidence (Kubát 2013).[9] This should be accompanied by a reduction in and clarification of the president's powers, limiting his options of actively influencing politics and acting as a serious power player. Also desirable would be a reform of the proportional electoral system used for

---

9 A constructive vote of no confidence means that the opposition must approve a new government at the same moment that it votes no confidence in the old government.

the lower chamber of parliament. This would lead to a consolidation of the party system and reduce the number of parties in government, thus easing government formation and governance.

Some less important political institutions such as the Senate also need reform. The present manner by which senators are elected is evidently unattractive to voters and fails to establish clear links between Senators and their constituencies. It would make more sense to transition to an indirect election, involving regional or perhaps even local assemblies. The abandonment of the direct election of a political institution does not signify that democracy has been defeated; on the contrary, it might well do it a service.

7. Electoral systems and an obsession with elections

Stanislav Balík

One notable feature of the political developments after the creation of the independent Czech Republic was the increasing number of bodies elected directly by citizens. To the lower chamber of parliament and local assemblies were added: in 1996 the Senate (a third of which is elected every two years); in 2000 the regional assemblies; in 2004 the European Parliament; and in 2013 the president. Thus, the Czech Republic became the promised land of elections, the country of constant elections.

For instance, in the space of less than five and a half years, between June 2009 and October 2014, Czechs have voted in 11 elections. If the lower chamber of parliament and the president serve expected terms, 2015 will be the last non-election year for the next 12 years – the next scheduled non-election year is 2027.

The Czech political cycle has long ceased to be ideal, divided between a time for policy making and a time for elections. Indeed, Czech politics now finds itself in a permanent election campaign. The government of Bohuslav Sobotka, appointed in early 2014, faced its first electoral test – albeit a second order one, that of the European Parliament – a mere 114 days after taking office. The time when, under normal circumstances, the government should have been at its most active, implementing difficult and unpopular measures, was instead marked by attempts not to alienate voters. Furthermore, shortly after these elections, campaigning began again, this time for the local and Senate elections in October 2014.

Occupied with constant elections, the parties in government do not rule; rather, they administer. This does not suit the mood of the electorate, who do not consider the administration of the country a sufficient achievement. Repeatedly disappointed by governments, they are increasingly opting for radical alternatives. Connected with this is a paradox: although voters are constantly electing politicians, this does not translate into closer links between the represented and their representatives. On the contrary, there is an increasing feeling that political elites are remote from voters, that those 'above' do what they want to do, and that politicians are unaware of the problems of 'ordinary people' (Linek 2010).[1]

The problem seems to be the identification of the mechanism by which rulers are chosen (democracy) with other issues – constitutionality, protection of rights and freedoms, rule of law, separation of powers, good governance, and functional policing. Problems in the political system are then described as deficiencies of democracy. And the best cure for democratic deficiencies, it is argued, is more democracy (Zakaria 2005: 302–308). It is then not enough to elect deputies and senators directly. It is alleged that to improve democracy, one must also directly elect the president, mayors, and regional governors.

Figure 7.1: Evolution of voter turnout in the Czech Republic, 1990–2014

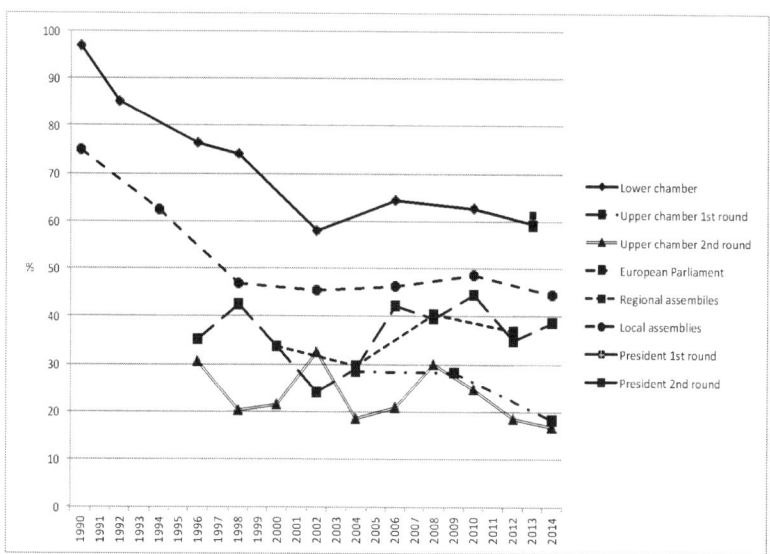

Source of data: Volby.cz

---

[1] As far as decreasing voter turnout is concerned, the matter is a complex one. In addition to the number of elections one must also consider the European a decreasing voter turnout is a widespread issue, particularly in the post-communist world. For what is perhaps the most comprehensive view of the matter see Linek 2013.

Yet, as Figure 7.1 shows, the increasing number of elections is inversely related to voter turnout. A simple comparison of voter turnout 1990 and 2013/2014 shows that there has been a drop to about three-fifths of the original values: from 96.8 % to 59.5 % in the case of the lower chamber of parliament and from 74.8 % to 44.5 % for local assemblies. Turnout in the decisive second round of Senate elections decreased from 30.6 % in 1996 to 16.7 % in 2014. Voter turnout for elections to regional assemblies ranged from 30 to 40 %. For the elections to the European Parliament it was already low in 2004 and 2009 at about 28 %, and in 2014 it dropped by a further ten percentage points to 18.2 %, the second lowest value in the EU. However, the trends in voter turnout have not been straightforward. Until 2004, turnout monotonically decreased for all types of elections. In the second half of the 2000s, there was a slight increase in voter turnout, only for the trend to reverse again after 2010. The lowest-ever turnout in local elections was recorded in 2014.

Declining voter turnout is in itself is not necessarily a warning sign. The problem is with those representative bodies which have been elected by only a third, a fifth, or even a sixth of those eligible to vote and whose democratic legitimacy is thus called into question. This includes the Senate, regional assemblies and the European Parliament. It is probably not accidental that these bodies are deemed non-essential by democratic theory. One can envisage, and indeed practical examples can be found of, democratic countries which have a single-chamber parliament, single-level territorial self-governance, and no equivalent of the European Parliament. Thus it is problematic to claim that the cure for deficiencies of democracy is more democracy, at least in the sense of directly electing more bodies.

A proportional electoral system is used to elect Czech representative bodies at all levels of governance (municipalities, regions, the lower chamber of parliament, and the European Parliament) with the exception of the Senate, which is elected using a majority system. Until 2013 only the collective representative bodies, not executive bodies, were elected directly (mayors and regional governors are elected indirectly by their respective assemblies). Since 2013 the president has been elected directly and political discussions about the desirability of electing mayors and governors directly have been ongoing for more than a decade. Although the commitment to introduce direct elections for mayors has been included in a coalition agreement and a government policy statement, the majority necessary to put this into practice has not yet been found.

7.1. The electoral system for the Chamber of Deputies

Since the early 1990s, the lower chamber of parliament, the Chamber of Deputies, has been elected by a proportional electoral system with open party lists. The main parameters of the system have remained unchanged since 1990, but there have been some small amendments, most recently in 2001. The chamber is elected for a four-year term, however, there have been two early elections (in 1998 and 2013) and in 2009 an early election was effectively prevented by the Constitutional Court (see Chapter 6 for more details).

The proportional electoral system that was in force in the early days of the independent Czech Republic was adopted in 1990 more as a result of historical accident than a well thought-out plan. Although figures such as Václav Havel pushed for a majority system, a proportional system was adopted in part due to the historical tradition of the mythologised First Czechoslovak Republic and in part due to fears that political pluralism would be suppressed in a majority system (Kopeček 2010a: 43–44). Eligibility to vote and stand for office is limited to Czech citizens. One needs to be 18 years of age to vote and 21 years to be elected. From the outset the Chamber of Deputies had 200 seats divided between eight constituencies using the Hare quota. Seats were allocated proportionally to parties in two rounds using the Hagenbach-Bischoff quota. For the first round a countrywide threshold of five percent applied. For the second round, parties compiled special lists of candidates not elected in the first round.

Since 1992 there has been a threshold for coalitions: seven percent for coalitions of two parties, nine percent for coalitions of three parties, and 11 percent for coalitions of four or more parties. Voters could cast up to four preferential votes on their chosen party list, and those candidates who won the support of at least three percent of all voters who voted for that candidate list in the constituency moved to the top of the list.[2]

This system was used for the elections to the Chamber of Deputies in 1992, 1996, and 1998. It was criticised for its high proportionality which, in connection with the fact that parts of the political spectrum were occupied by anti-system parties, led to a situation where ruling coalitions had very small

---

2 In 1990 preferential voting was more complicated: a voter could assign up to four votes which, however, only counted if at least a tenth of those who voted for the party used their preferential votes. A specific candidate had to win an absolute majority of these votes in order to be placed on the top of their candidate list.

majorities. Sometimes no ideologically coherent majority coalition existed at all. In the context of President Havel's calling into question the importance of elections for the character of government, a serious attempt to change the electoral system was made in the late 1990s.

The ambition to change the electoral system in order to strengthen large parties and weaken small ones was the foundation of the 'opposition agreement' and later the 'toleration patent'. The reform was fundamentally limited by the fact that the Czech constitution stipulates proportional representation for the lower chamber of parliament and majority representation for the upper. As the two parties to the opposition agreement soon lost their constitutional majority in the upper chamber, they had to construct their electoral reform within the limits of the constitution. Their aim was to change the electoral system in such a way that, while formally remaining proportional, it would lead to ideologically coherent majority coalitions composed of just one large and one small party. Thus in 2000 a new electoral law was adopted which significantly increased the number of constituencies from eight to 35, thereby substantially decreasing the number of seats allocated (still by the Hare quota) in constituencies to five or six. There was, however, the stipulation that the number of seats in a constituency must not fall below four. Following much discussion about electoral formulas, where ODS preferred less proportional formulas than ČSSD, the modified d'Hondt formula was adopted.[3] The electoral threshold was also changed: the five percent countrywide threshold was multiplied for coalitions, hence reaching ten percent for a coalition of two parties, 15 percent for a coalition of three, and 20 percent for a coalition of four or more parties. Preferential voting was also amended: two preferential votes could now be cast on the chosen party list (previously four), and candidates needed to win only seven (previously ten) percent of the vote for their particular list in order to win seats.[4]

This electoral reform was never put into practice, however, as President Havel challenged it at the Constitutional Court for contradicting the required principle of proportional representation. In one of the most significant rulings of the first decade of its existence, the Constitutional Court annulled the law, even though there was no uniform scholarly opinion about the effects of the

---

3 The modification consisted of changing the first divisor from one to the square root of two, i.e., 1.42, and was intended to make it more difficult for small parties to obtain their first seat.
4 However, these changes need to be understood in the context of the substantial reduction of candidate lists to about six candidates.

proposed reform. In contrast to the opinion of the Constitutional Court, some political scientists claimed that the adopted electoral system was still within the limits of proportional systems. Others argued that it was false to talk about a proportional or a majority system and that one ought to speak instead of systems with a proportional or majority effect (for one proponent of such views, see Kubát 2004).

The Constitutional Court having annulled all the essential parts of the law in 2001, there was a risk that there would not be a valid law in force for the upcoming elections. In the parliamentary debates that ensued, a compromise electoral system was constructed that essentially remains in effect today. Its fundamental characteristics correspond to the system in force until 2000, but many of its details are different. Today the country is divided into 14 constituencies and the d'Hondt divisor is used to convert votes into seats within the individual constituencies. The countrywide party threshold is five percent, increasing for coalitions as described above. This is in fact the only significant serious change that has been preserved from the 2000 electoral reform (Chytilek, Šedo, Lebeda and Čaloud 2009: 292–314).

Since the amended electoral law of 2001, there has been change in only one aspect of the electoral system: preferential voting. Whereas the 2001 amendment allowed only two (previously four) preferential votes per candidate list and a candidate had to collect seven (previously ten) percent of the votes cast for their list in order to be moved to the top, further changes were made in 2006. The number of possible preferential votes was again increased to four, and the threshold was further decreased, to five percent. This gave voters considerably more control over the identity of their representatives. Whereas in 2002, 12 candidates placed in unelectable positions on the lists were elected thanks to preference votes and in 2006 only six, by 2010 there were 46 (and one sixth of regional party leaders failed to win seats due to preferential voting), and in 2013 29 (Kneblová 2010: 172, Kneblová 2013: 248).

A significant disadvantage of the present electoral system – part of the already-mentioned compromise – is the unequal size of constituencies, which correspond to the self-governing regions, even though this is not necessary. The number of seats allocated in a constituency depends on voter turnout, which is relatively uniform across the country. In 2013 25 seats were allocated in the largest constituency, whereas in the smallest there were only five. Thus, in order to win a seat in a small constituency, a party had to obtain about 20 percent of the vote. The distortion induced by this system – a disproportionality caused by the existence of small constituencies – became manifest in 2006

(Trávníček 2012: 30–31). Two small parties obtained a similar number of votes, but a very different number of seats: KDU-ČSL received 7.2 % of votes and 13 seats as compared to the Greens (SZ) who received a similar percentage of votes (6.3 %) but less than half as many seats (only 6). The reason was differences in the distribution of their electoral support: whereas KDU-ČSL's support was concentrated in medium-sized and large constituencies, SZ's was spread much more uniformly across the country. Hence the system as it stands today is an unreasonable compromise, with a single electoral system acting differently in different constituencies: in the smallest its effects are closer to a block vote system, whereas in large ones it is proportional.

Despite the change adopted in 2001, the electoral system has a tendency to produce a chamber that is highly representative but not very functional (Novák 1996). Thus far, no ideologically coherent coalition of less than three parties could have been created in any electoral term, and in some terms no coherent majority coalition could have been formed. The last seriously minded attempt to change the system was made after the election stalemate of 2006 where the right and the left each obtained exactly half the number of seats.[5] The reformers were aimed not so much at strengthening the large and weakening the small parties as at giving the winning party a majority bonus of some sort. Although the government submitted a bill containing the electoral reform, the Chamber of Deputies rejected it after the fall of Topolánek's second government (Trávníček 2012).

The arguments about the necessity of reforming the electoral system continue, and are usually put on the table after elections when difficulties with forming a government coalition reappear. In 2012 an initiative called the Direct Election of Deputies (*Přímá volba poslanců*) appeared. Though its title was misleading, it promoted a more personalised electoral system whose effects would in fact be majoritarian. More recently, Andrej Babiš, leader of the ANO party and supporter of a majority system, put the issue back on the agenda after the 2013 election. ODS has long held a similar view. ČSSD and small parties, by contrast, are traditional supporters of a proportional system.

---

5 The stalemate itself could have been resolved by a simple amendment to the constitution, changing the even number of deputies (200) to an odd one (199 or 201).

7.2. The electoral system for the Senate

The Czech Senate is elected by a two-round majority system. The system has remained unchanged since the first Senate elections in 1996. Citizens need to be 18 years of age to vote and 40 to be elected for a six-year term. The country is divided into 81 single-member constituencies and every two years a third of the Senate is up for election. The first elections in 1996 were held in all constituencies with senate seats randomly assigned to initial two-, four- or six-year terms. Representatives of political parties and movements as well as independent candidates can stand for election. In order to be elected in the first round, a candidate must win an absolute majority. If no candidate wins greater than 50 % of the vote, a second round is held for the two most successful candidates from the first round one week later. Whichever of them wins more votes wins the seat. Ties are decided by lot (Chytilek, Šedo, Lebeda and Čaloud 2009: 304–309). The Senate's electoral system was designed to be as different as possible from that of the Chamber of Deputies. While the lower house system leads to party voting and hence to a partisan Chamber, the Senate was conceived as a chamber made up of independent figures or personalities with local political links (Schorm 1999: 54).

Voter turnout for Senate elections tends to be low. It is usually higher in the first round, which is almost always held concurrently with regional or local elections. It is rare for candidates to win their seats in the first round. Between 1996 and 2014 this only happened nine times out of 334 races. Since the founding elections in 1996 when four candidates were elected in the first round, no more than a single candidate was elected in the first round in any subsequent election. When first-round victories do occur, they tend to be connected with a dominant current in national politics. Not coincidentally, the last such victory was recorded in 2008 when ČSSD was very strong. Since then there has been a much more even balance between political forces with no one party dominating. Senate majorities have changed with these swings. There have already been overall victories for right-wing, left-wing and centrist parties. In the first term, ODS was the strongest party and it also controlled the upper chamber in 2004–2008. The era of the opposition agreement saw a significant rise in support for the parties associated with the Coalition of Four; their two parliamentary party groups gradually came to dominate the Senate in 2000–2002. During 2008–2014, ČSSD enjoyed an absolute majority in the Senate after years of being a minority force (in the 2004 elections, for instance, it failed to win a single seat out of the 27 contested). Since 2014 power has been more balanced in both chambers. In 1996, 1998 and 2014 Senate elections were held at nearly the same time as elections to the lower chamber, yet that did not necessarily spell an advantage for parties in government and a disadvantage for the opposition.

The electoral system for the Czech Senate can be considered problematic. A procedure in which only two candidates pass to the second round is quite unusual for democratic legislatures and is most frequently used for the election of a president. The centripetal effect of the Czech system should, in theory, lead to the election of a consensual candidate, yet that is not necessarily the case. A system, which aims to establish consensus not through negotiations, but through vote choices may not be suitable for a legislative body, which is intended to represent the plurality of interests in society. Though inspired by the French National Assembly, which allows more than two candidates to advance into the second round. The Czech system, by contrast, is not conducive to the creation of political alliances between the first and the second round (Chytilek, Šedo, Lebeda and Čaloud 2009: 147–151).

7.3. The presidential electoral system

Until 2013 the president was elected indirectly at a joint session of the two parliamentary chambers. Groups of at least ten deputies or senators could propose candidates. In order to be elected in the first round, a candidate had to win the absolute majority of all members of each chamber. Failing that, a second round would be held where an absolute majority of the members present in each chamber was sufficient. A third round followed where candidates would need an absolute majority of those present in both chambers together. Starting with Václav Havel's second term in 1998, this procedure proved problematic, especially so in both of Václav Klaus's elections, as Klaus was elected only in the ninth round of voting in 2003 and the sixth in 2008.

The successful introduction of direct presidential elections was preceded by a long debate and a number of failed attempts. The main impetus was provided by the peculiar circumstances of Václav Klaus's second election in 2008 (Musilová and Šedo 2013: 16). In the end most parliamentary parties supported the idea of direct election (or at least claimed to support it in their programmes) as did most voters. By contrast, political scientists and constitutional lawyers warned, in scholarly and popular works alike, against the intended and unintended consequences of the change. Media pressure was fundamental in pushing through the change.

Since the constitution was amended in 2012, the president is elected by secret ballot on the basis of universal, equal and direct suffrage, according to the absolute majority formula. The age requirement for candidates is the same as for those contesting Senate seats – candidates must be at least 40 years old. Any Czech citizen of full legal age may propose a candidate and proposals must be supported by a petition signed by at least 50,000 eligible voters. The right of MPs to propose candidates was preserved: a group of at least 20 deputies or 10 senators may do so without a petition.

Whoever obtains an absolute majority of valid votes cast in the first round is elected. If no one obtains such a majority a second round is held two weeks later between the two most successful candidates from the first round. Whoever obtains the larger number of valid votes cast in the second round is elected.

The former Social Democratic Prime Minister Miloš Zeman, who was nominated by citizens, not his own party, won the first direct election. Since his assumption of office a discussion has been underway about a potential regime shift towards semi-presidentialism (see Chapter 6).

7.4. The regional electoral system

Regional assemblies are elected by a proportional system. Only citizens with permanent residency in the region who are aged 18 or over can vote or stand for election. The assembly's term is four years. The whole region is one constituency in which 45, 55 or 65 representatives are elected.

There is a five percent threshold for political parties and movements as well as coalitions. Votes are converted into seats using a modified d'Hondt formula where the first divisor equals 1.42. This electoral system is the product of the era of the opposition agreement, characterised by its strong efforts to prevent small parties from entering into representative bodies. However, in this case the modification of the d'Hondt formula does not have the desired effect because of the large district magnitudes.

Party lists are open. Voters can cast up to four preferential votes, and those candidates who win at least 10 % of the total votes cast for their list are moved to the top of the list. Only registered political parties and movements can stand for election (Chytilek, Šedo, Lebeda and Čaloud 2009: 317). In practice this limitation is circumvented by nominally 'independent' parties standing for election. Voter turnout is a relatively low 30–40 % of those eligible to vote.

National political parties continue to dominate the regional assemblies. ODS won in 2004 and ČSSD four years later, each taking more than two-fifths of the seats available. The results of the first elections in 2000 and the most recent elections in 2012 were more balanced. Regional elections offer substantial and growing opportunities for independent groups. However, so far, they have taken a distinct minority of seats. Regional elections to date have always taken place roughly in the middle of the electoral cycle of the Chamber of Deputies and have confirmed the predictions of the second-order elections theory: low voter turnout, protest voting against the government, the dominance of national political issues, and greater chances for small and new parties (Reif and Schmitt 1980).

7.5. The local electoral system

Local assemblies are elected by the most complex system of all. When local self-government was reinstated in the early 1990s, a proportional electoral system with free lists was adopted for local elections. In 1994 it was modified to a proportional system with open lists advantaging small parties (Šaradín and Outlý 2004: 38–39). In 2001 a five percent threshold was introduced and the electoral formula was changed. Only citizens with permanent residency in the municipality and aged 18 or over can vote and be elected.

Czech local self-governance is very fragmented. Within Europe, only France is comparable. The 10.5 million inhabitants of the Czech Republic are divided into 6,253 self-governing municipalities, 78 % of which have fewer than 1,000 inhabitants (in fact, a full quarter of municipalities have fewer than 200 inhabitants). This fact, however, is not reflected in the electoral system: the Czech Republic is one of the few countries which uses the same electoral system in all municipalities from the smallest village to the largest cities. This system is open list PR. Voters can choose candidates from multiple party lists (a practice known as *panachage*) but cannot cast more than one vote for a candidate whom they highly favour (there is no cumulation). The classic d'Hondt divisor and a five percent threshold are used to convert votes into seats (Chytilek, Šedo, Lebeda and Čaloud 2009: 315–317). The impact of *panachage* is limited by the fact that only those candidates who win at least 10 % more preferential votes than the average on their list are moved to the top of the list.

Although a municipality's territory can be divided into wards, in practice this option is not employed (in 2014 there were only three such cases) and the municipality's area is usually one large constituency where five to 70 seats are distributed, depending on the size of the municipality and the discretion of the local assembly.[6] Registered political parties and movements as well as independent candidates and associations can stand for election. Independent candidates and associations have to produce the signatures of seven percent of voters. This high number of required signatures poses a particular obstacle in large cities. Hence it is easier to found a national political party or movement, and indeed, more than ten national entities with 'independent identities' have emerged over the last two decades. They run under names such as the Association of Independents, Independents, Independent Choice, and Non-Partisans. The objective of these 'independent parties' is merely to provide service to local independent candidates.

In 2001, there was a change of electoral formula from the Saint Laguë to the d'Hondt method (ODS was the biggest proponent of the change). Whereas the Saint Laguë divisor advantages small parties to the detriment of large ones, the d'Hondt formula does the opposite as long as the assembly size is small. Voter turnout in these elections tends to be about half of eligible voters, making it the third highest after elections to the lower chamber of parliament and presidential elections.

The most controversial aspect of this system is its hidden effects. Although to voters it pretends – especially due to the option of *panachage* – to be a personalised system in which voters directly choose candidates, the system behaves differently when votes are counted. On the basis of the sum of preferential votes, the formula first assigns seats to parties and only subsequently decides how these seats are allocated within the party to candidates. By voting for a particular candidate a voter might inadvertently help a different candidate to be elected. Hypothetically, it is even possible for a candidate who received no preferential votes at all to be elected, while candidates from the same list, who have received hundreds or even thousands

---

6 The option of dividing a municipality into wards attracted much attention in 2010, when it was exercised (and not for the first time) in the capital, Prague. This division eliminated small parties (those polling less than about 10 % of the vote) from Prague's municipal assembly.

of preferential votes, do not win a seat (Balík 2009: 104–106). It may be only professional psephologists who understand how this unique electoral system functions. It is difficult to say who benefits from these rules, which are a compromise between preserving the position of those who compile the candidate lists and allowing citizens to influence election results.

The system also has major (and mostly devastating) consequences for local party systems. For example, in the town of Sobotín, 11 seats were contested by eight parties and associations, seven of which won a seat. This example – which is not atypical – points to the deficiencies of the electoral system, which favours a weak candidate at the top of a weak list over a much stronger candidate in the middle of a more successful list. In theory this could be an equivalent candidate. A candidate who obtains 300 votes as the eighth-placed candidate of the party *Let's make our town beautiful*, which wins four seats, would not be elected. If the same candidate were instead to stand as the leader of the list *Let's make our town clean*, which wins only one seat, the very same person would get elected, even if he only received, let's say, 100 votes. It is no wonder that local party systems fragment (Balík 2012: 39–51). This can create a situation where in order to form a majority in the 15-member local assembly more parties are needed than there are places in the five-member local council (the executive body of the municipality elected by the assembly). This is an unfortunate situation that limits executive turnover and thus is at variance with the fundamental idea of democratic elections.

The local level of Czech government is inextricably linked with the phenomenon of independence; candidates distance themselves from parties. Groupings brandishing their independence usually aggregate and articulate the interests of social groups in the same way as (if not more than) any political party, but many voters automatically award bonus points to the independents. In the smallest municipalities, political parties have been practically non-existent since 1994. Over the past two decades they have been retreating in larger municipalities as well (see Balík, Gongala, and Gregor 2015 for more details).

7.6. The electoral system for the European Parliament

Czech MEPs are elected through a proportional electoral system with open lists and preferential voting. Citizens need to be 18 to vote and 21 to be elected for a five-year term. The entire country forms a single constituency and the d'Hondt divisor is used to convert votes into seats. A five percent threshold applies to both parties and coalitions. In 2014 the threshold was the subject of a constitutional complaint. The Supreme Administrative Court recommended that the Constitutional Court annul the threshold as unconstitutional, but the latter Court rejected the proposal (Directive No. 176/2015 Coll.).

A voter may cast up to two preferential votes on their chosen list. In order to be placed at the top, a candidate has to capture at least five percent of the preferential votes cast for the given list (Chytilek, Šedo, Lebeda and Čaloud 2009: 317).

The number of seats distributed in the Czech Republic has changed with EU enlargements: in 2004 there were 24 seats, five years later 22, and in 2014 only 21. The first two elections brought significant victories for the Eurosceptic ODS (which polled more than a third of the vote). The third elections produced balanced results for the top three parties, where two percentage points separated the winner from the party that placed third, with the winner obtaining only about 16 % of votes (see Volby.cz). The top three parties all became members of Eurofederalist parliamentary party groups (EPP, S&D, and ALDE respectively).

7.7. Conclusion

Since the turn of the twentieth and twenty-first centuries, the Czech Republic has become a promised land of elections. The electorate, however, has responded with lukewarm interest, apparent in declining voter turnout. A retrospective glance also demonstrates that the country is a laboratory for electoral systems both proportional and majoritarian. The operation of some of these systems is non-problematic (the European Parliament, regional assemblies); others are unsuitable for the purpose (the Senate); and still others are defective (local assemblies). Due to the not entirely successful reform of the system used for electing the lower chamber of parliament, one may observe the different effects of a single electoral system in variously sized constituencies with various degrees of proportionality.

8. Reshuffling the party system: from non-politics to anti-politics

Pavel Pšeja

In just two months at the end of 1989 the communist regime in Czechoslovakia collapsed suddenly and, for most citizens and external observers, unexpectedly – introducing a discontinuity into the nature and logic of the party politics of Czechoslovak (or more relevantly for our case, Czech) society.[1] In neighbouring countries such as Poland and Hungary a significant and increasingly institutionalised opposition had developed over time, gradually producing new political parties that offered alternatives to the dominant party-state. Czechoslovakia had no such a parallel structure.[2] When communism fell, the country lacked clearly articulated political forces that had distinct ideological profiles, could establish basic relationships, and were able to formulate programmatic agendas.[3] It cannot be claimed that there are no connections between party politics before and after the Velvet Revolution. It is nevertheless remarkable that only a few political parties provide such links. The post-communist party system in the Czech Republic featured traits that strongly differentiated it from its predecessors not only in the way it worked, but also in the principles on which it was based.[4]

When communism collapsed, the party system itself and public attitudes about parties began to form in an environment where experience of political participation and civic activism had been lacking for two decades. This led to divergent ideas about how political representation was to function and whether political parties were adequate for mediating the political will of citizens at all. This essentially normative dispute was further complicated by the need to establish a democratic party system in relatively short order and in an

---

[1] In order to understand how the Czech party system works, one would obviously have to examine the evolution of the party system and individual parties, the main cleavages, and changes in patterns of electoral support. Such an extensive analysis is beyond the scope of this chapter. For a more detailed interrogation of some of these aspects, see Hloušek and Kopeček 2008, Linek 2014, and Pšeja 2005.
[2] The literature examining the various aspects of these issues is extensive. Linz and Stepan 1996 provide a good example.
[3] This includes civic groups such as Charter 77 or the Committee for the Defence of the Unjustly Prosecuted (VONS), whose agenda went beyond purely political activities.
[4] For the issue of discontinuity see Fiala and Strmiska 2001.

environment where the very notion of political partisanship was negatively coloured by Czech historical experience. This naturally influenced the formation of the party system, its consolidation and the public's perception of political parties. This chapter describes the main trends in these areas since November 1989 and the factors that contributed to each stage of the Czech party system's development.

8.1. Party system formation and the dispute about the nature of political partisanship

The Czech party system began to form early in the regime change process. The first political parties emerged in late 1989, and a formal framework for the functioning of the party system was put in place in January 1990 with the adoption of the 'Act on Political Parties', which legally allowed a multi-party system to operate. The main driver of these changes, particularly in the first weeks and months after the fall of the communist regime, was the Civic Forum (OF), a broadly-conceived pro-democracy movement, which represented the majority of the general public.[5]

Views of political partisanship split the public into two groups. The first considered the construction of a standard party system and political parties to be a necessary and logical component of a functional democratic system. This component had been denied to Czech society by the previous non-democratic regime, but under the new conditions, it offered the opportunity for various interests in society to clearly establish themselves. In this view, standard political parties were the best mediators of these interests when they located themselves on a traditional left-to-right axis.

The second section of public opinion, by contrast, based its view on the communist era. They rejected partisanship as a discredited tool of political participation. Indeed, under the communist regime, the very term 'party' was largely synonymous with the Communist Party of Czechoslovakia, which loaded the term with strongly negative connotations. Thus, political partisanship came to be viewed as the promotion of the narrow interests of a specific 'elite', which in no way corresponded to the needs of the ordinary citizen.

---

5 Symptomatic of future development was the fact that the Civic Forum operated only within the Czech Republic. Its counterpart in Slovakia was Public Against Violence (VPN). See Chapter 5 for more details.

Symptomatic of this attitude was the Civic Forum's slogan: 'Parties are for partisans, Civic Forum is for everybody.' However, it needs to be emphasised that the negative Czech perception of political partisanship had deeper roots,[6] and that the era of single-party rule only strengthened rather than created this tendency. A specific manifestation of this attitude was the notion of 'non-political politics'. This concept not only played a key role at the inception of the democratic party system in the Czech Republic, but over the last 25 years has repeatedly materialised in political initiatives that have defined themselves in opposition to traditional party politics. What gives this notion a unique dimension is that it has been strongly linked with a specific view of morality and ethics, where these are explicitly understood as the opposites of politics and ideology.[7] The concept is strongly legitimised by its connection with the figure of Václav Havel, although his position on the issue of parties and partisanship was not as clear-cut as it is often thought to be.[8] In any case, the conviction that non-partisanship or trans-partisanship (the latter if we adopt the interpretation of 'non-political politics' as a viewpoint that is not limited by party interests and hence standing above parties in terms of its ability to represent citizens' interests) should play an important role is one of the factors that has long formed, at least implicitly, the stances of a substantial part of Czech elites and the general public.

This normative dispute, the roots of which can be traced to the period before the 1990 elections,[9] has fundamentally contributed to the formation of the new party system and the distribution of electoral support. Virtually all of the parties that emerged as part of this process found themselves in an uneasy

---

[6] One of the causes was the cartel approach to the allocation of political power, which has earned interwar Czechoslovakia the epithet of 'partitocracy'. For a more detailed characterisation of the roles and behaviour of political parties at the time, see Chapter 2, or such works as Balík et al. (2011: 68–71) and Harna 2004.

[7] There exists in the Czech Republic a long and extensive discourse about 'other', non-political, or anti-political politics. See, for example, Bělohradský 2000, Havelka 1998, Loewenstein 1995 or Otáhal 1998. It is somewhat paradoxical that in this context the term 'anti-political politics' is sometimes presented as synonymous with non-political politics, at other times as an alternative to it. Yet Václav Havel himself, who is often mentioned in this connection given his impact on Czech attitudes towards partisanship after 1989, employed it very infrequently. Jan Holzer, who has identified specific 'traditions of Czech politics', offers a different point of view – see Chapter 2 or Holzer 2006: 272.

[8] See Martin Fendrych's and Tomáš Němeček's interview with Václav Havel (Fendrych and Němeček 1998).

[9] For a detailed analysis, see Suk 2003.

position: in short order and practically from scratch, they not only had to form themselves, create intra-party structures and decision-making mechanisms, but also define their electorates and delineate their programmes. The turbulent developments between November 1989 and June 1990 thus logically resulted in the emergence of various political currents, some of which attempted to draw upon the traditions of the First Republic to at least some degree.[10]

At that time, the Civic Forum was not just the dominant political force, it was also a very specific kind of actor. It brought under one roof a varied mixture of individuals, who had as their goal a political and economic transformation that would result in the establishment of a democratic political system and a (social-) market economy. Yet the Forum never was – and in the view of many of its leading figures, was never intended to be – a classical political party with a hierarchical structure and exclusive membership. This did not prevent the swift development of standard political parties, but they operated largely outside the framework of the Forum, which disintegrated in February 1991.

Among those parties were, in particular, the traditional ones, which in various forms continued their pre-1989 existence (in fact, their traditions were even longer, dating back to the First Republic or earlier). Most important were KSČ,[11] the Czechoslovak Socialist Party (ČSS), ČSL[12] and ČSSD.[13] With the exception of the last, these parties were incorporated within the so-called National Front prior to 1989 (see Chapter 3). Their fates and developments differed dramatically, however. The Communist Party – which, unlike the overwhelming majority of post-communist parties of the region, never seriously transformed itself – has continuously managed to preserve a relevant position in the political party system. By contrast, ČSS failed in the 1990 parliamentary elections and did not become a relevant player. Like the communists, the People's Party succeeded, but unlike the former, its success

---

10 Given the substantial change in the stratification of Czech society, these tendencies did not have a great chance of success. For an analysis of the attempts to draw on the parties representing the interests of the countryside, which had been very successful during the interwar Czechoslovakia, see Mareš and Pšeja (2008).

11 As early as March 1990, the Communist Party of Bohemia and Moravia (KSČM) was created as the Czech Republic's organisation within the federal KSČ; from autumn 1990 KSČM pursued an independent policy line, thus effectively replacing KSČ.

12 The present name of the party, Christian and Democratic Union – Czechoslovak People's Party, dates to March 1992.

13 Operating since February 1993 as the Czech Social Democratic Party.

was dependent on its ability to undergo large-scale internal transformation, during which it cut itself off from its pre-1989 alliance with the communists. It established itself as a modern Christian-democratic party. The evolution of the Social Democrats was somewhat different: like the ČSS, it failed in the 1990 election, but unlike the ČSS, it managed to gradually strengthen its position, winning parliamentary representation and eventually becoming one of the two major parties.

Whereas all of these traditional parties had clearly-established political profiles, the last party to become a relevant component of the Czech party system was a nationalist one though, paradoxically, its nationalism was Moravian rather than Czech. The formation of the Movement for Autonomous Democracy – Society for Moravia and Silesia (HSD-SMS) in April 1990, only two months before the general election, was surprising in itself, the support it immediately garnered even more so.[14] The particularity of Moravian nationalism and its political manifestations is particularly evident when considered in light of the absence since 1989 of any relevant party promoting ethnically-defined Czech nationalism.[15]

Another factor was fundamental for the early days of Czech partisanship after November 1989: the Czech party system established itself as a 'national' one. A few exceptions aside, political parties in Czechoslovakia did not seek to create organisations that covered the whole of the federation and thus attempt to win votes across the country. Rather they were formed in either the Czech or Slovak Republic (see Fiala 2001 or Pšeja 2005: 33). This resulted in the development of two distinct party systems with weak connections. The attempts by the Social Democrats and later (especially in the first half of 1992) by ODS to create functional federal parties were failures and the genuinely federal parties remained entirely marginal.

---

14 It must be added that the party was mainly autonomist and almost never assumed secessionist stances. For details, see Pernes 1996 or Springerová 2010.

15 Some manifestations of nationalism were recorded among the far-right Republicans (see below), yet they were not dominant in the party's agenda, where traits such as populism, anti-communism, and xenophobia prevailed.

8.2. On the road to traditional partisanship: 1990–1998

Whereas the first half-year of the Czech democratic party system was mainly characterised by discussions about the meaning of political partisanship, accompanied by parties' attempts to establish themselves as institutions, define their ideologies and gain meaningful support, the first parliamentary elections provided a clear direction. Table 8.1 shows the results of these elections. After the elections, the key factor that fundamentally affected both the formation of the party system and public opinion about party politics was the disintegration of the Civic Forum and the gradual delineation of the main actors within the party system and their mutual relations. As Fiala and Hloušek have argued, 'the convincing [...] victory of the Civic Forum [...] sent out a clear signal that the era of the first cleavage in the country's transformation – the dispute between the Communist Party and the forces of reform – was practically over. [...] Crucial for the completion of the structure of relevant cleavages was the period 1991–1992, during which the socio-economic cleavage of the transformation was evidently strengthened. [...] The importance of the other [...] cleavages declined gradually' (Fiala and Hloušek 2003).

Spurred by the disintegration of the Civic Forum, the Czech party system regrouped very quickly and sorted itself along a standard left-to-right political axis. As early as the summer of 1990, two main factions became apparent within the Forum. One promoted the original vision of the Forum as a trans-partisan entity that would eliminate the role of traditional political parties and allow civil society to become the dominant force shaping Czech politics. Another defended the irreplaceable role of parties and suggested that the Forum should itself gradually transform into a standard party. This dispute came to a head during the autumn of 1990, when it was increasingly apparent that the 'non-political' vision of the Forum and politics were generally becoming marginalised. At the turn of 1990/1991, it was already evident that the Forum could not survive in its existing form. Given the incompatibility of both the normative ideas and the practical politics of the two factions, the Forum eventually fell apart in February 1991, enabling a natural polarisation of the party spectrum and the emergence of standard political parties.[16]

The main successors to the Civic Forum were as follows. Those within the Forum who preferred traditional parties and established themselves as liberal

---

16 For a detailed analysis of the causes and progress of the Civic Forum's demise, see Pšeja 2005, Pšeja 2004a, Kopeček 2010b, and Honajzer 1996.

conservatives promoting the quick implementation of market reform formed the Civic Democratic Party (ODS)[17] and the smaller Civic Democratic Alliance (ODA). Meanwhile, a large part of the Civic Forum's elite formed the Civic Movement (OH), which to some extent continued with the project of 'non-political politics', though it also featured a degree of left-liberal ideology. The demise of the Forum did not spell a clear victory for either of the two competing conceptions of politics. Until the second parliamentary elections in 1992, it was unclear which of the two would eventually win, though opinion polls indicated ODS was more popular than OH. ODS was also much more successful in appealing to the electorate outside Prague.[18]

The results of the 1992 elections (presented in Table 8.2) gave a clear direction to political partisanship in the Czech Republic, signalling a victory of traditional partisanship over endeavours to create a new non-partisan, or perhaps even better, trans-partisan way of mediating the political will of citizens. The electoral term 1992–1996 was characterised by a general acceptance that the economic transformation of the country was a success, the Czech Republic being the 'poster child' of post-communist transformation in Central Europe. Classical parties were understood as the principal agents of this development.[19] This period confirmed the consolidation of the political right. Those parties that had already established their profiles at the time of Civic Forum's demise, in particular ODS and ODA, were to remain stable in these years. The only exception to this was the establishment of the Association for the Republic – Republican Party of Czechoslovakia (SPR-RSČ), a populist far-right party characterised by anti-establishment and sometimes xenophobic rhetoric and an emphasis on 'a tough approach to domestic security, the ethnicisation of social issues and crime […] and a resistance to […] some postmodern values' (Mareš 2005: 1596). Although the SPR-RSČ was able to

---

17 Led by Václav Klaus, who symbolised the 1990s Czech transformation, including its negative aspects. For a detailed interrogation of Klaus's role within the Civic Forum, see in particular Kopeček 2010a and Pšeja 2004b.

18 The advantage of ODS over OH was substantial, with about 20 % of the electorate expressing in opinion polls its support for the former and about five percent for the latter. Yet it was not inconceivable that the OH would eventually profit from Václav Havel's support. An additional advantage for ODS was that it quickly built up local party organisations and led a much more aggressive campaign.

19 As noted by Lubomír Kopeček in *Éra nevinnosti [The Era of Innocence]*, a substantial portion of the populace at the time perceived politics as a positive endeavour and a 'key instrument for the transformation of the country', representing 'a relatively respected and appreciated field of human activity' (Kopeček 2010a: 6).

appeal to some sections of the population unhappy with the progress and results of post-communist transformation, it failed to establish itself permanently and disappeared entirely from Czech politics after the 1998 elections.[20]

The second formative process was the struggle between KSČM and ČSSD, who vied for the dominant position on the left. Between 1990 and 1993, Czech communists undertook several attempts to reform their party, but these all resulted in pro-reform members leaving the party. Thus, KSČM largely preserved its traditional ideological orientation. The price it paid for this was its practically non-existent coalition potential. By contrast, ČSSD was searching for its identity. Its search ended in early 1993 when Miloš Zeman was voted the party's chair and consistently pursued a course of opposition to the ruling right-wing governments.[21] The Social Democrats adopted a critical stance, especially towards the economic transformation implemented by the right-wing government, and gradually established itself as a leading force on the left and an equal to ODS. The position of KSČM, by contrast, remained practically static, both in terms of its electoral support and its position as a largely ostracised player in the party system.[22] This was reflected in election results. While in the 1990 and 1992 elections KSČM polled a significantly larger share of the vote than ČSSD,[23] from 1993 onwards the patterns of electoral support started to reverse.

The third process that substantially contributed to the character of Czech party politics can be described as the 'emptying of the centre'. After the 1992 elections a number of parties sought to establish themselves as an ideological alternative to the right and the left. Practically all failed. Voters of the mid-1990s preferred a clear-cut ideological orientation. The dominant Czech popular position towards party politics and partisanship was an emphasis on their standard character. Non-political politics, extremisms of any kind (with the partial exception of the communists) and nationalism were not widely

---

20 For a long time the SPR-RSČ had been the only far-right party to win parliamentary representation in the Czech Republic. For a more detailed analysis of the SPR-RSČ's functioning, see Mareš 2005; for an analysis of why the extreme right has been unattractive in the Czech Republic, see Mareš 2011.
21 For an analysis of correlations in the developments of the two parties, see in particular Kopeček and Pšeja 2008.
22 For detailed analyses of the development and functioning of KSČM see Fiala, Holzer, Mareš, and Pšeja 1999, Hanley 2001, Kunštát 2013b, Grzymala-Busse 2002, and Pšeja 2008.
23 KSČM polled 13.5 and 14.0 % of the vote, while ČSSD only won 4.1 and 6.5 % respectively.

acceptable to the general public.[24] The 1996 elections (see Table 8.3) thus spelled not just a significant consolidation of the party system, one connected with a decrease in the number of relevant parties, but, in particular, an apparent end to the debates as to whether traditional political parties were or were not the most suitable instrument for mediating the political will of citizens.

Popular trust in political parties started to erode soon after the 1996 elections. The causes were a series of scandals, especially the non-transparent funding of ODS,[25] economic problems which destroyed the notion of a trouble-free transformation,[26] and growing intra-party conflict in ODS and ODA. Altogether these events resulted in an unprecedented political crisis. Its consequences were three-fold: the end of the Civic Democratic Alliance as a relevant party; the split of ODS and the formation of the Freedom Union (US), which strived for a more 'moral' right-wing politics; and, most importantly, the disintegration of the right-wing coalition, the establishment of a "semi-political" caretaker government, and the calling of early parliamentary elections in 1998. Paradoxically, the results of these elections, presented in Table 8.4, showed no great shake-up in popular support for political partisanship. On the contrary, they largely confirmed the patterns of electoral behaviour that were already observable in the 1996 elections. The events of 1997 and early 1998 nevertheless suggested that the majority's belief in the success of the political and economic transformation was shaken. This was the case despite the not-very-convincing electoral result of the Freedom Union and its attempts to establish itself as a critic of Czech politics (Fiala and Mareš 2005: 1563–1578).

8.3. The ups and downs of party politics: 1998–2010

The months before the 1998 parliamentary elections were turbulent. The subsequent electoral term and the first decade of the twenty-first century showed contradictory tendencies in popular views and electoral results. On the one hand, the whole period was stable in terms of electoral support for

---

24 Significant in this respect was the rapid decline of support for Moravian nationalist politics, which ceased to be viable in spring 1991.
25 For a detailed analysis of these cases and their consequences for both parties, see Pšeja 2004b and 2005.
26 A detailed description of this period is offered in Kopeček 2010a: 266–275.

established political parties. Though there was some fluctuation, it did not have fundamental consequences for the relative weight of the individual parties, and more importantly, for the overall workings of the party system. On the other hand, growing anti-party tendencies could be observed among the Czech public from 1999 onwards (Linek 2003), though for the time being they did not have a serious effect on the existing support for political parties or break up established patterns of electoral preference.[27]

It is in a way paradoxical that the key event in the gradual transformation of the popular perception of party politics, and one that in the long term contributed significantly to the destabilising of Czech partisanship, occurred soon after the 1998 parliamentary elections. Although post-election mathematics allowed at least two different possible coalition governments, the equivocations of the Christian Democratic Union – Czechoslovak People's Party (KDU-ČSL) and the Freedom Union, together with personal disputes among the representatives of parliamentary parties, ultimately resulted in a wholly unexpected solution. Post-election negotiations were concluded by a deal between ODS and ČSSD, which became known as the Opposition Agreement and confirmed the dominant position of the two parties (Kopeček 2012b, 2015). This agreement oversaw the creation of a minority ČSSD government supported by ODS. It also elicited very negative responses among other parties and many in the general public, who perceived the Opposition Agreement as a political cartel and an expression of the unwillingness on the part of political elites to respect the will of the electorate. One of the early political consequences of the Opposition Agreement was the creation of the so-called Coalition of Four, uniting KDU-ČSL, US, ODA and the Democratic Union (DEU). The Coalition sought to present itself as a defender of ethical principles in politics and defined itself in contrast to the pragmatism of ODS and ČSSD. In civil society, the displeasure created by the Opposition Agreement was manifest from 1999 to 2001 in a series of civic initiatives such as *Impuls 99* [Impulse 99], *Děkujeme, odejděte* [Thank you, now leave] and *ČT – věc veřejná* [Czech Television – a public matter],[28] which sought to draw

---

27 As Lukáš Linek has noted, it is nonetheless apparent that in the period 1997-1998 not only did the public dissatisfaction with political parties and politics increase, but the general public attitude towards political partisanship changed, as the legitimacy of partisanship weakened. For a detailed analysis of the causes and consequences of this dissatisfaction, see Linek 2010.

28 Common to these initiatives was their inability to achieve their goals. Their social appeal was short-term, as they did not offer a viable alternative. For a more detailed analysis of their activities, see Dvořáková 2003 or Kopeček 2015: 148–152.

upon various visions of non-political politics ultimately originating from the non-Klaus wing of the Civic Forum.

Of fundamental importance were the interconnections created among these responses to the Opposition Agreement. The Coalition of Four, or more precisely, US and KDU-ČSL, cooperated relatively closely with the civic initiatives mentioned above; but this did not result in the emergence of a viable political alternative. In fact, it did just the opposite. The mechanism of the Opposition Agreement survived virtually the whole electoral term, without thereby strengthening the Coalition of Four, the only relevant Czech party to represent the anti-Opposition Agreement sentiments of the Czech populace (except KSČM which, however, continued to be ostracized). The Coalition of Four also faced mounting internal issues, which eventually led to the demise of ODA and the merger of US with DEU, so that ahead of the 2002 elections its name was shortened to 'Coalition', as it comprised only these two parties.[29]

The results of the 2002 elections, presented in Table 8.5 eventually confirmed that the existing patterns of electoral support remained in place and preserved the traditional bipolar scheme of party competition.[30] Thus, rather than elevating the Coalition (of Four), public dissatisfaction and resistance to the political style of the existing party elites translated merely into low voter turnout and an increased vote for the anti-systemic KSČM.[31] This negative trend, which saw greater popular resistance to traditional party politics, also manifested itself more generally in declining satisfaction with the functioning of democratic mechanisms. Whereas in early 1997, before the political crisis and recession, 55 % of the populace were satisfied with the functioning of democracy, two years later it was only 33 % and it hovered around the 40 % mark until the 2002 elections.[32]

---

29 For a more detailed analysis of the disintegration of the Coalition of Four, see Kolář 2003.
30 It cannot be ignored that ČSSD formally terminated the Opposition Agreement shortly before the elections. This and the fact that the party leadership changed in 2001 (Miloš Zeman, who together with Václav Klaus had been an initiator of the Agreement, was replaced as party chair by Vladimír Špidla, an opponent of the Agreement) helped to create the illusion that the party had changed and lent some credence to its claims of pursuing a more transparent politics.
31 At 58 %, voter turnout was more than 15 percentage points lower than in the 1998 elections to the Chamber of Deputies. The 2002 figure remains historically the lowest. In the three subsequent elections electoral participation increased only very modestly and did not exceed 65 %. For KSČM, by contrast, 18.5 % of the vote was its best result since the transition.
32 For a more detailed analysis see Seidlová, Červenka, and Kunštát 2003. An interesting correlation is provided here by opinion polls examining popular satisfaction with the political situation. In 1999, when civic initiatives were gaining ground, the ratio of the satisfied to the

The period 1997–2002 can be considered the first, albeit limited, era of disillusion about political parties, when the public's readiness to view political parties as an appropriate instrument for the realisation of citizens' interests decreased noticeably. This was manifested in the distrust of political parties generally (a trait that was already characteristic of the earlier notion of non-political politics) and, more importantly, in criticisms of the contemporary functioning of political parties. Towards the close of the Opposition Agreement era, it could be observed that the existence of these attitudes 'reflects the discrepancy between the legitimacy of political parties and criticism of (or lack of trust in) them. The first, less widespread dimension of anti-partisanship (held by about 10 % of society) can be described as a rejection of the representative function of political parties and characterised as a stance that considers political parties illegitimate. The second dimension of anti-partisanship can be defined as criticism of current political party behaviour (about 30–40 % of society)' (Linek 2003: 15). The questioning of whether political elites were fit for the purpose[33] gradually resulted in noticeable shifts in voter behaviour.

For most of the first decade of the 2000s, however, this trend did not manifest itself as a vocal rejection of the established parties. It led instead to shifts in electoral support between individual parties and stronger bipolarity. In the 2006 elections (Table 8.6), the two strongest parties together polled more than 67 % of the vote, their highest percentage in the post-communist era. By contrast, the Freedom Union, which had become a member of the coalition government in 2002 and was increasingly helpless in personal and programmatic terms, failed to clear the 5 percent threshold. Although the Green Party (SZ) assumed the position previously occupied by the Freedom Union – a more 'civic' and less political alternative to traditional parties – this implied no serious challenge to the existing party system.

Developments after the 2006 elections likewise did not suggest that a fundamental change in political partisanship was pending, although the new government headed by ODS faced all the usual ailments of Czech coalition governance: lack of a clear majority, allegations of corruption, and disputes

---

dissatisfied was about 20:80. After the 2002 elections it shifted to about 35–40:55–60 (Chludilová 5/2004).

33 Substantially contributing to this was the fact that political scandals affected practically all parties (except KSČM), including their top leadership. An exemplary case was that of the then-prime minister Stanislav Gross (ČSSD), who was forced out of office when he was unable to credibly document the source of funding he had used to buy his apartment.

within the coalition. It was the last of these problems that was instrumental in the government's downfall, embarrassingly during the Czech presidency of the Council of the European Union. The Czech political elite's inability to effectively resolve existing problems and respond to popular demands, together with the global financial crisis, profoundly changed the existing patterns of party competition and electoral support, leading to a transformation of the Czech party system.

The 2010 elections to the Chamber of Deputies therefore stood at the beginning of an era. They introduced new players who sought to define themselves in opposition to traditional parties. It also opened a discussion as to whether a modification in the perception of political parties and partisanship might be underway, one that would be based on the weakening of traditional cleavages (and especially the dominant socio-economic cleavage; see Hloušek and Kopeček 2008) and a strengthening of anti-establishment stances, includeing a revision of the establishment's interpretation of developments since the 1989 regime change.

8.4. Searching for the 'other' way: Czech (non-)partisanship since 2010

The 2010 elections to the Chamber of Deputies (Table 8.7) initiated a trend that has since become a dominant trait of Czech partisanship. Whereas until 2010 attempts at consolidation were observable within the party system and were supported by the public's willingness to hold onto traditional patterns of electoral support, the 2010 elections clearly suggested that a shift in electoral preferences was underway to the benefit of parties that questioned traditional partisanship and ideologies. This development has been manifest both in the substantial decrease in electoral support for established parties and in attempts to find alternatives to them. The shift resulted in electoral losses for all parliamentary parties, with KDU-ČSL and SZ failing to cross the five percent threshold necessary to win seats. The two large parties, ODS and ČSSD, each polled only slightly more than 20 % of the vote, and together lost 25 percentage points compared to the previous elections. KSČM, traditionally stable, lost the least: only about one-and-a-half percentage points. Two entirely new parties were formed, based on different principles. Whereas TOP 09 established itself as a classic party with a strongly conservative orientation,[34] the Public Affairs (VV) party was the first example of an entity with a vague ideology and strong populist traits (Jarmara 2011, Bureš 2012, Hloušek 2012, Havlík and Hloušek 2014).[35] Public Affairs defined themselves in opposition to established parties, whom they accused of incompetence and corruption. A desire for change – though it was not entirely clear what the essence of that change should be – permeated the social mood and found expression in the new government. Though led by ODS, it also included the two new parties.

The initial success of VV was not to last. By early 2011, the party faced accusations of corruption and non-transparent funding. Ultimately, this led to a split in the party: the majority faction left the government, which effectively lost the ability to act. That part of the populace which thought VV to be an entity not linked with traditional parties and their shortcomings was disappointed. Yet the tendency to seek 'new parties' continued as did the weakening of the socio-economic cleavage.[36] This opened up space for the emergence of other populist parties, of which ANO 2011 quickly became the most important.[37] Founded by Andrej Babiš, one of the country's richest businessmen, in late 2011, ANO 2011 built its image on criticising the representatives of established parties, accusing them of incompetence and corruption – as VV previously did. ANO 2011 presented Babiš and itself as a 'non-political' alternative, one that – unlike existing political parties – would be able efficiently to manage the state 'as a business firm' (Němec 2012). The period of VV's disintegration and ANO 2011's emergence was marked by a new wave of public discontent with the political situation. After the 2010 elections the percentage of those dissatisfied was about the same (55 %) as in 2002 (when the first wave of opposition to traditional parties had ebbed). A

---

34 The name refers to the year of the party's formation and its main principles, tradition, responsibility and prosperity.
35 In particular with its proposal of direct democracy as a panacea for the ailments of Czech politics.
36 This tendency also had its roots in the economy (recession, growing unemployment) and politics (ODS's inability to transform its rhetoric into practice). For a comprehensive analysis of volatility and the (non-)transformation and support for political parties, see Deegan-Krause and Haughton 2010, Hanley 2011, or Havlík 2015a.
37 As with TOP 09, the name of the party refers to the year of its inception. The acronym ANO (Action of Dissatisfied Citizens, *Akce nespokojených občanů* in Czech) refers to the 'civic' (i.e., 'non-political', or perhaps 'anti-political') character of the party, while also invoking Obama's 'Yes, we can' (*ano* meaning 'yes' in Czech), to suggest the party's ability to achieve change.

year and a half later it was practically identical with its peak in 1999, exceeding 75 %. During 2012 it increased by a further five percent (Kunštát 2013a). In short, a growing segment of the population no longer accepted traditional political parties and was even losing faith in politics as such. It thus supported 'fresh faces' coming from outside politics – people who distanced themselves from the usual mechanisms of political bargaining. Paradoxically, the government coalition which took power in 2010 enjoyed the largest parliamentary majority in the history of the independent Czech Republic.[38]

Although the government was given a strong mandate, it failed to pursue a clearly formulated and consistent policy, and this quickly increased public dissatisfaction with the political style to date and led to calls for both institutional and personnel change. Public distrust of traditional parties was exacerbated again by allegations of corruption and abuse of offices that caused the downfall of the government and the resignation of Petr Nečas as head of ODS. The subsequent elections, held in October 2013, continued the trends started three years earlier – the weakening of traditional parties and the strengthening of populists (Table 8.8). The break-up of the system's bipolarity was a fundamental change: although ČSSD suffered only modest losses, ODS polled less than eight percent of the vote, by far the worst result in its history and one that denied it a position as one of the party system's two main poles. By contrast, ANO 2011 polled almost 20 % of the vote, becoming the most successful protest party in Czech history. Another new party – Dawn of Direct Democracy – also managed to cross the electoral threshold with almost seven percent of the vote. Formed in the wake the Nečas government's demise, its agenda combined intense anti-establishment rhetoric, xenophobia, and direct democracy, the last being almost *de rigueur* for populist parties. However, direct democracy as advocated by Dawn's representatives often amounted to calls to circumvent parliamentary institutions.

The 2013 elections to the Chamber of Deputies therefore confirmed that the long-standing structure of the Czech party system and voters' electoral preferences are disintegrating. The bipolar tendency of the system has been seriously called into question;[39] several traditional parties have lost their

---

[38] The parties in government were supported by 118 out of the 200 deputies in the Chamber of Deputies. The government with the second highest majority was Václav Klaus's first cabinet, supported by 106 deputies.

[39] It is theoretically possible that ANO 2011 would replace ODS as the system's second pole, thus preserving its formal bipolarity. Such considerations are nonetheless premature and not yet sufficiently grounded in empirical facts, since the strong position of ANO 2011 within the

appeal; and parties that advocate the weakening of parliamentary mechanisms have emerged. The existing patterns of interaction within the system, namely the established coalitional configurations and the system's polarity, including the positions of the relevant parties, have lost much of their validity. This opened the space for a reconfiguration of the prevailing logic of party competition. Previously typical was a structure with two dominant parties (ODS on the right and ČSSD on the left) and two other relevant parties, one at the extreme left (KSČM), the other in the centre (KDU-ČSL), variably complemented by another party, whose position on the left-to-right axis varied (the Greens, US, ODA, TOP 09). Now another arrangement seems to be taking shape. If enduring, it would be less stable and feature a greater number of relevant, though relatively weak, parties, each polling between five and ten percent of the vote. This would also imply less intelligible patterns of potential coalition governments. Some exceptions aside, the most notable being the Opposition Agreement, governments have tended to alternate between centre-right and centre-left coalitions based on ODS or ČSSD respectively.[40] Now coalitions are more likely to be created across the party spectrum and based on a purely pragmatic agreement about the most efficient government mechanism.

8.5. Some concluding remarks about Czech party politics

The trends described above clearly illustrate a trait of Czech politics that has been variously present since the regime change: efforts to find alternatives to traditional political parties. These efforts have changed greatly over time. In the first years of the transition they were characterised by an emphasis on non-political politics, which sought to create loosely organised political entities with horizontally distributed decision-making and participation mechanisms. Starting in the mid-1990s traditional political parties found greater acceptance. The phenomenon of non-political politics did not disappear, but weakened significantly. It was partially revived between 1997 and 2002, but the political entities that emerged were not organisationally similar to those from the early

---

system has not yet been tested. The dynamics of ANO 2011's interactions with the other entities in the system can also be expected to be different from those of ODS.

40 The specific position of KSČM needs to be emphasised. It has traditionally been ostracised by other parties, and excluded from consideration as a potential partner in negotiating government coalitions (Kunštát 2013b: passim).

1990s. Instead, there was an increasing incidence of civic movements operating outside the party system and calling for the existing parties to be rebuilt in a way that would better represent the interests of voters.

The period 2002-2010 witnessed a revival of party politics, albeit with continuing distrust of the parties' ability to fulfil their social function. The economic recession and the political crisis that followed resulted in a new phenomenon best characterised by the term 'anti-politics'.[41] Typical of anti-politics was the rise of populist entities, which largely rejected (or at least questioned) traditional party politics as dysfunctional. The populists argued that problems needed to be resolved either by stronger direct democracy or by establishing managerial-type parties. Thus, the influence of traditional parties, particularly on the right, was reduced. Since the 2013 elections, a significant segment of the population has come to support the anti-politics style, and traditional parties continue to stagnate.[42] However, bearing in mind the trends of recent years, one cannot help concluding that the future of the Czech party system and citizens' attitudes towards partisanship are very difficult to predict.

---

41 However, the use of the term 'anti-politics' here does not draw in a straightforward manner on either of the notions proposed by Andreas Schedler. Instead of 'removing' or 'colonising' politics (Schedler 1997: 14), it would be more fitting to speak of the depoliticisation of politics achievable by various means. While non-political politics emphasises the implementation of politics by means of entities other than parties, but nevertheless fully respects parliamentary mechanisms, Czech anti-politics has a tendency to seek such pathways that, while respecting democracy, strive to simplify the relation between the electorate and government. Thus, it is seeking alternatives, rather than intending to eliminate or appropriate politics as such. Also typical of anti-politics is ideological vagueness or a refusal to assume a clear ideological stance; the ambition to create a non-traditional internal structure of the 'party'; and attempts to present the party as an entity standing more or less outside the existing political establishment. For a discussion of populism in the Czech party system and its growth since 2010, see Havlík 2015b.

42 Since the rift in Dawn, which led to the party's collapse, this support has largely been concentrated around ANO 2011. Of course, Dawn's demise does not preclude the emergence of a similar new entity. Since mid-2014, ANO 2011 has enjoyed about 30 % support in opinion polls. The only traditional party to score similarly has been ČSSD, enjoying the support of slightly more than 25 % of respondents. KSČM's support remains at the same level as its election result in 2013, and the parties of the right – ODS, TOP 09 and KDU-ČSL – score between five and ten percent (Kunštát 2015).

Appendix: Results of elections to the Czech National Council and the Chamber of Deputies of the Parliament of the Czech Republic[43]

Table 8.1: Elections to the Czech National Council held on 8 and 9 June 1990

Party	Vote %	Seats
Civic Forum	49.5	124
Communist Party of Czechoslovakia	13.2	33
Movement for Self-Governing Democracy – Society for Moravia and Silesia	10.0	23
Christian and Democratic Union	8.4	20
Alliance of Farmers and the Countryside	4.1	0
Czechoslovak Social Democracy	4.1	0
Green Party	4.1	0

---

43 Data have been adopted from the website www.volby.cz, which provides the official results as published by the Czech Office for Statistics. Only those parties which polled more than three percent of the vote are included. Figures are rounded to the nearest 0.1 percent. Party names have been translated as faithfully as possible from the original Czech.

Table 8.2: Elections to the Czech National Council held on 5 and 6 June 1992

Party	Vote %	Seats
Coalition of Civic Democratic Party and Christian Democratic Party	29.7	76
Coalition Left Bloc – Communist Party of Bohemia and Moravia, Democratic Left ČSFR	14.1	35
Czechoslovak Social Democracy	6.5	16
Liberal Social Union	6.5	16
Christian Democratic Union – Czechoslovak People's Party	6.3	15
Association for the Republic – Republican Party of Czechoslovakia	6.0	14
Civic Democratic Alliance	5.9	14
Movement for Self-Governing Democracy – Society for Moravia and Silesia	5.9	14
Civic Movement	4.6	0
Movement of Pensioners for Life Security	3.8	0

Table 8.3: Elections to the Chamber of Deputies of the Parliament of the Czech Republic held on 31 May and 1 June 1996

Party	Vote %	Seats
Civic Democratic Party	29.6	68
Czech Social Democratic Party	26.4	61
Communist Party of Bohemia and Moravia	10.3	22
Christian and Democratic Union – Czechoslovak People's Party	8.1	18
Association for the Republic – Republican Party of Czechoslovakia	8.0	18
Civic Democratic Alliance	6.4	13
Pensioners for a Secure Life	3.1	0

Table 8.4: Elections to the Chamber of Deputies of the Parliament of the Czech Republic held on 19 and 20 June 1998

Party	Vote %	Seats
Czech Social Democratic Party	32.3	74
Civic Democratic Party	27.7	63
Communist Party of Bohemia and Moravia	11.0	24
Christian and Democratic Union – Czechoslovak People's Party	9.0	20
Freedom Union	8.6	19
Association for the Republic – Republican Party of Czechoslovakia	3.9	0
Pensioners for a Secure Life	3.1	0

Table 8.5: Elections to the Chamber of Deputies of the Parliament of the Czech Republic held on 14 and 15 June 2002

Party	Vote %	Seats
Czech Social Democratic Party	30.2	70
Civic Democratic Party	24.5	58
Communist Party of Bohemia and Moravia	18.5	41
Coalition of Christian and Democratic Union – Czechoslovak People's Party, Freedom Union – Democratic Union	14.3	31

Table 8.6: Elections to the Chamber of Deputies of the Parliament of the Czech Republic held on 2 and 3 June 2006

Party	Vote %	Seats
Civic Democratic Party	35.4	81
Czech Social Democratic Party	32.3	74
Communist Party of Bohemia and Moravia	12.8	26
Christian and Democratic Union – Czechoslovak People's Party	7.2	13
Green Party	6.3	6

Table 8.7: Elections to the Chamber of Deputies of the Parliament of the Czech Republic held on 28 and 29 May 2010

Party	Vote %	Seats
Czech Social Democratic Party	22.1	56
Civic Democratic Party	20.2	53
TOP 09	16.7	41
Communist Party of Bohemia and Moravia	11.3	26
Public Affairs	10.9	24
Christian and Democratic Union – Czechoslovak People's Party	4.4	0
Party of Civic Rights – Zemanovci	4.3	0
Sovereignty – Jana Bobošíková Bloc	3.7	0

Table 8.8: Elections to the Chamber of Deputies of the Parliament of the Czech Republic held on 25 and 26 October 2013

Party	Vote %	Seats
Czech Social Democratic Party	20.5	50
ANO 2011	18.7	47
Communist Party of Bohemia and Moravia	14.9	33
TOP 09	12.0	26
Civic Democratic Party	7.7	16
Dawn of Direct Democracy	6.9	14
Christian and Democratic Union – Czechoslovak People's Party	6.8	14
Green Party	3.2	0

9. Market reforms, society, and the main features of Czech capitalism

Lubomír Kopeček, Stanislav Balík

The purpose of this chapter is not to provide an exhaustive account of the Czech economy since 1989, but to highlight the key moments and explain how the economic, political, and social spheres influenced each other. The main theme of the chapter is that the character and direction of the 1990s economic reforms were determined not just by economists' ideas about the best way of transforming the centrally-planned economy into a market economy. Equally important were politicians' assessment of the social and political consequences of reforms and what voters were willing to accept. Thus, it was politicians who decided that particular steps of the economic transformation would or would not be carried out and the timing of those steps. The most remarkable example of a political choice was the decision to use voucher privatisation. The postponement of the liberalisation of certain regulated prices exemplified how politicians controlled the timing of reforms. Such logic applied equally later in the transition, but the ability of these governments to push through and implement a well thought-out economic policy was restricted by their short life spans. The Czech market was also formed by determinants independent of politics, in particular, the country's industrial tradition and its geographic position close to Western European and especially German markets. This made the country appealing for foreign investors, another important influence on the nature of Czech capitalism.

This chapter mostly proceeds chronologically, although to facilitate understanding of the context we sometimes add an excursus or point out long-term trends and phenomena. At the end of the chapter we include a discussion of three aspects – budget policy, national debt, and taxes – which were of particular importance to politics.

9.1. Orderly economic decline at the end of the communist era

The story of the genesis and functioning of the market economy in the Czech Republic should begin with an overview of the economy under late communism. The Soviet model of a centrally-planned economy, introduced in Czechoslovakia in the second half of the 1940s and early 1950s, survived without substantial change to the very end of the communist regime. This was a consequence of an extreme rigidity on the part of the Czechoslovak communist leadership, who were afraid to undertake any serious experiments, whether political or economic. The source of these fears in the economic sphere was Šik's reform, a set of measures prepared in the second half of the 1960s that were to introduce market elements into the state economy. In the minds of normalisation-era communists, Šik's reform was intimately linked with the revisionism of the Prague Spring. When the Prague Spring was crushed, the reform was abandoned and its author, Ota Šik, went into exile in Switzerland (Šulc 1996, Berend 2006). This was one of the reasons why the KSČ leadership in the second half of the 1980s viewed Gorbachev's *perestroika* with suspicion. Though they ostensibly supported it out of loyalty, its economic aspects were too close to Šik's ideas for comfort.

The rigid emulation of the Soviet economic model was also the reason the private sector was almost completely absent from the Czechoslovak economy. This contrasted with the country's communist neighbours, Poland and Hungary, who experimented with limited markets. On the eve of the Velvet Revolution, the negative consequences of this situation were even admitted by the general secretary of the KSČ, Miloš Jakeš, who, at a session of party officials, said that in nationalising the economy 'we have overdone things a bit in the past' (Jakeš 1989). A consequence of extreme central planning was inefficient manufacturing and technology that lagged behind Western economies. The managers of state-owned companies were not interested in achieving profit but in bargaining for the least demanding output targets. An enterprise's plan set out what would be made and in what quantity, and the fulfilment of this plan was taken to be the main measure of the enterprise's success and determined the remuneration of the management. The behaviour of company directors in such a deformed system has been succinctly described by the economist Otakar Turek: 'Whoever is stupid enough to accept difficult-to-achieve tasks shall suffer the consequences. Respect, by contrast, is won by "clever" directors who have managed to negotiate a good (that is, easy-to-achieve) plan.' (Turek 1995: 47)

Such an environment bred social frustration and dissatisfaction. The economy was unable to smoothly provide the populace with basic staples, and more importantly, it could not fulfil growing consumerist expectations, a key factor in the erosion of trust in the communist regime. Supply problems were one of the main topics on the agenda of the Presidium of the Central Committee of KSČ. In June 1988, for instance, and not for the first time, a substantial portion of the session was devoted to a shortage of toilet paper (Suk, Cuhra and Koudelka 1999: 34). However, the resolutions adopted by the Central Committee could do little to alleviate the shortages, reflecting the powerlessness of the communist leadership.

The atmosphere of late communism is illustrated by popular jokes from the period. For example, a man walks down Wenceslas Square in the centre of Prague, stops at the meat shop, and says: 'No meat.' Then he goes past the drugstore and says: 'No toilet paper.' Then an officer of the police catches up with him and says: 'Citizen, stop this seditious talk. In the past they would have you shot for it. I am only reprimanding you.' The officer walks away and the man mutters under his breath: 'No bullets either.'

The feeling that the country was lagging behind the West was a significant factor in weakening loyalty towards the communist regime. Citizens remembered the highly developed industrial base from the era of Austria-Hungary and the First Republic. The situation was somewhat different in Slovakia, a largely agrarian country before the communist era. For Slovaks, communism was linked with mass industrialisation and urbanisation, which for a substantial proportion of Slovak society represented modernisation and progress. In the Czech part of the country, the feeling of being left behind was of tremendous importance in the overwhelming public support for a market economy in the first years after the Velvet Revolution. This created a supportive atmosphere for the architects of economic reforms such as Václav Klaus. As aptly noted by the anthropologist Ladislav Holý, 'the market has become a symbol of civilisation towards which Czech society is now once again heading' (Holý 2001: 134).

There is a minor paradox here in that the term 'capitalism' – unlike the word 'market' – was perceived very negatively. In late 1989 opinion polls showed that only 3 % of respondents were inclined towards a 'capitalist path' of future development; more than 40 % preferred a 'socialist path' and even more some sort of 'third way' (Vaněk 1994). Consequently, after the Velvet Revolution politicians and liberal economists tended to avoid the ticklish notion of capitalism, preferring terms such as 'market' and 'market economy'. The clearly negative connotations of the word 'capitalism' were not just a legacy of the communist era, but also of an older, intellectual and political tradition that was strongly left-leaning and memories of the Great Depression. To this day the word 'capitalism' is rarely used by Czech politicians and typically more often by those on the left, who tend to connect it with pejorative adjectives such as 'uncontrolled' or 'selfish'.

The economic rigidity of the Czech communists before 1989 also had a positive side. Unlike most other communist countries of Central and Eastern Europe, where attempts during the 1970s and 1980 to reform their economies ended by destabilising them, Czechoslovakia had a small budget deficit, low inflation, and very little external debt (Švejnar 1997, Holman 2000, Žídek 2006), hence the term 'orderly decline' that has been used to describe the Czechoslovak economy at the end of the communist era (Ježek 2006: 12).

The country's geographic position, next to Austria and especially Germany, was to prove a great advantage for the future. The British economist Martin Myant considered the country's position and its industrial tradition to be crucial for its economic future (Myant 2003 and 2007). The Czechoslovak economy was small and always dependent on exports. Reorientation away from the collapsing Eastern markets – particularly the Soviet one, where most of the pre-1989 exports were sent – and towards the West was vital after the collapse of the Iron Curtain. This reorientation was quickly achieved, and in the very first year of the independent Czech Republic, Germany became its most important trade partner in both exports and imports, more important even than the just-separated Slovakia. German businesses quickly found their feet in the Czech market and, in the words of Tomáš Ježek, 'felt at home' there (Husák 1997: 205).

As early as 1990, the flagship of German investment was Volkswagen's purchase of the largest Czech car manufacturer Škoda Mladá Boleslav. The newly-named Škoda Auto Company soon boasted the largest revenues in the country and today its profitability significantly impacts the whole Czech economy. The Czech-German economic links meant that the country became substantially dependent on the economic fortunes of its large Western neighbour, a fact that naturally brings not only benefits but also risks.

9.2. A limited 'Big Bang'

In considering how centrally planned economies should be reformed into market ones, two basic strategies are usually identified. The 'shock therapy' or 'Big Bang' approach consists of a rapid liberalisation of the economy together with privatisation and assumes that economic actors will quickly adapt. The gradualist or institutional-evolutionary approach involves incremental change and acknowledges the need to create an institutional infrastructure for the market, the importance of social norms, and the specific characteristics of the country (Fisher 2008, Turley and Luke 2011).

There was a debate between supporters of the two approaches in the early 1990s. The divide did not pose insurmountable difficulties, as there was a consensus among economists (and politicians) regarding many of the essential steps that had to be taken and the aim of reforms: to introduce a market economy. Furthermore, finding solutions to many of the problems that arose went beyond the simple logic of deciding between two options. Paradoxically, the divide over the direction of economic reform became much clearer from the mid-1990s onwards when the fundamental steps had already been taken and had produced a number of undesirable effects. By that time, however, the debate shifted from the dispute between supporters of shock therapy and gradualism towards a more general quarrel over the *interpretation of the course and results of the transformation,* a debate that continues – though understandably with lesser intensity – to this day. The figure of Václav Klaus has been at the centre of this controversy. Although Klaus initially managed to create an aura around himself as the 'father' of the economic reform, later he became the main 'culprit' of the failures of transformation.

Let us now turn to the actual course of the transformation. Almost immediately after November 1989 measures were taken which paved the way for private entrepreneurship. The leaders of the Civic Forum assumed that Valtr Komárek, a popular symbol of the revolution and deputy prime minister, would devise and direct the reform. Before the Velvet Revolution, Komárek had been the director of the Prognostics Institute of the Czechoslovak Academy of Sciences, an establishment the communist regime vainly hoped would find a miraculous cure for the ailments of the economy. However, the anticipated architect of the reforms quickly lost the Civic Forum's trust, as he was able neither to create a functional team of economists nor to devise a clear plan. Instead he devoted himself to extensive trips abroad. Thus, by the spring of 1990, he was quietly pushed to the sidelines. After the June 1990 elections he lost his position in the cabinet, yet his reputation as an important economist survived and he became one of the icons of the social democratic left.

In this period two teams of economists vied for primacy in the preparation of the economic reforms. A more radical group formed around the minister of finance in the federal government Václav Klaus. A more gradualist team worked within the Czech (national) government and was led by its deputy prime minister František Vlasák. Klaus, originally a subordinate of Komárek at the Prognostics Institute, during the 1980s contributed much to importing the ideas of classic liberal economists into the country by organising seminars and publishing proceedings, which helped to create intellectual conditions favourable to market reforms. In the clash with his competitors from the Czech government, the forceful and politically agile Klaus made use of his superior position in the federal government, and pushed through his team's proposals for reform (Šulc 1998, Suk 2003, Kopeček 2010a).

At the same time, Klaus worked on raising support within the Civic Forum, out of which he ultimately created his own party, ODS, in 1991. His liberal-economic ethos and slogans appealed to the electorate. He promised to create a market economy 'without adjectives' and suggested that after a few years of material hardship, described in a widespread slogan of the times as a 'belt-tightening', a swift economic expansion would follow.

A key macro-economic measure was a radical devaluation of the Czechoslovak crown. During the communist era, the exchange rate was kept artificially high. This was possible because the crown was not fully convertible and a non-privileged citizen could not legally exchange any significant sum in crowns for foreign currency. However, he could turn to the black market, run by illicit moneychangers, popularly known as *veksláci* (from the German *Wechsler*). The devaluation remedied this situation, and the official exchange rate approached the black-market rate. By way of illustration, in late 1989 a US dollar was officially worth about 15 crowns. Within a year the rate was almost double (Žídek 2006: 52). This radical devaluation led to an undervalued crown, which made exports to the Western markets much cheaper. The negative effect was a decline in real wages. The crown's exchange rate was effectively fixed against a currency basket in which the dollar and Deutschmark dominated, and this contributed to the stabilisation of the economy.

Klaus's strategy of reform also employed other restrictive measures, such as a balanced budget, which meant cuts in state expenditure. For most of the 1990s, the Czech Republic ran a balanced budget, even achieving a slight surplus in some years. This was exceptional not just in post-communist countries, but in Europe as a whole. This thriftiness, which would hardly be conceivable later in the transition, was helped significantly by receipts from the privatisation of state property (Dyba and Švejnar 1997, Holman 2000). Another important restrictive measure, aimed at preventing inflation, was the regulation of wages. Introduced in 1991, it lasted with a brief interruption until the mid-1990s. The Czech Republic thus avoided high inflation not to mention the hyperinflation experienced by the majority of Balkan countries and several post-Soviet republics (Turley and Luke 2011). A short but serious increase in the inflation rate to more than 50 % occurred only in 1991 when prices were liberalised. For most of the 1990s, inflation was around 10 %, an acceptable figure (Neset 2002).

A closer look at Czechoslovakia and the Czech Republic in the first half of the 1990s dispels the notion that a 'pure' form of shock therapy was applied. The economic decline of the early 1990s was much less severe than in Poland, considered the prime example of a 'Big Bang' transformation. Also important was the fact that the Czech reformers made sure that radical economic steps were accompanied by mitigating social measures in order to prevent citizens from dropping below the subsistence level. The public's traditionally strong sense of egalitarianism, whose roots can be traced back to the era of national revival and were much strengthened during the communist era, contributed to this cautious approach. At the end of the 1980s Czech society was among the most egalitarian in the post-communist region and indeed in Europe generally. During the first years of the transformation, social inequalities increased only slowly (Milanovic 1998, Frye 2010).

In short, the radical liberal rhetoric of the right was accompanied by much more careful policies in practice. This divergence became even more prominent when ODS came to power in 1992 with Klaus serving as prime minister. Klaus's cabinets of the years 1992-1997 were increasingly criticised for insufficient reform efforts, whether delays in price liberalisation, the non-privatisation of large banks, or dysfunctional bankruptcy laws which helped to preserve inefficient enterprises.

Attempts to dampen the 'shock' of reform can best be illustrated by the example of price liberalisation, a key reform step without which the market economy could not function. Under the communist regime, all prices were set by the state, and commodities such as bread, butter, or the much-loved bottled beer were sold for exactly the same low price throughout the country, irrespective of costs and quality. In early 1991 most prices were liberalised and retailers could set them as they wished. However, this was accompanied by the introduction of a special subsidy paid by the state to all citizens for the purpose of compensating them for the shock of the rapidly increased prices of most goods. This benefit, popularly named after the minister of finance as *klausovné*, paid off: a survey carried out half a year after the liberalisation of prices indicated that more than four-fifths of Czechs considered it a necessary step. Slovaks were much less satisfied (Žídek 2006: 58).

In considering this acquiescence of the populace it is important to note that the 1991 price liberalisation did not affect some very sensitive items such as housing rents. Even later, under Klaus's cabinets, blanket liberalisation of rents was very slow, with the prime minister referring to the threat of 'social catastrophe' (Kopeček 2010a: 171). Thus, the apartment rental market became increasingly deformed, with a significant portion of the cost of property maintenance effectively subsidised by property owners, in many cases people who had been given their apartment blocks in restitution (see below). The situation was made worse by the rigid legal regulations applying to tenancies. Market rents could only be charged to tenants moving into newly-built or vacant flats. 'Sitting tenants' continued to pay rent at the level they were used to, which was now far below the market rate. In effect, this created two categories of tenants, the 'privileged' and the 'non-privileged', and the differences in rents the two categories paid was often immense (Lux 2009, Lux and Mikeszová 2011).

Under cabinets led by the Social Democrats after 1998 the unwillingness to seriously liberalise rents was even more pronounced. The government even sought to circumvent decisions made by the Constitutional Court, which had favoured the rights of owners. In desirable neighbourhoods, in particular in Prague, the situation led to many disputes between private owners and their tenants and was made worse by the sluggishness of the judiciary. Evictions of even non-paying tenants were very difficult. Private owners sometimes resorted to strong-arming their existing, rent-controlled tenants in a bid to get rid of them. It took nearly two decades for there to be a significant change in legislation concerned with tenancies, and the blanket regulation was finally abandoned only in 2012. In short, a temporary measure to make the transformation more bearable had over time created serious political and social problems because politicians lacked the will to address it.

9.3. 'Small privatisation' and restitution

The most important and also the most discussed part of the market reforms was the privatisation of state property. As in a number of other post-communist countries, 'small privatisation', which typically involved shops and restaurants, proved to be the least controversial. The only significant dispute was whether the employees of these establishments should be given the first option to buy, as advocated by President Václav Havel among others. However, the liberal spirit of the times prevailed and such preferential treatment of a particular group was not adopted when the details of the small privatisations were decided in autumn 1990. The favouring of employees would probably have had serious consequences, as before 1989 many managers of shops selling vegetables and meat as well as those running restaurants belonged to an informal upper class. They had been able to exploit the malfunctioning economy by clandestinely hiking the prices of goods in short supply. A pre-emptive right to buy their shops would have rewarded this wrongdoing.

Thus, the privatisation of small enterprises was achieved through an open auction in which the highest bid won. At the time many questioned the 'purity' of the money used in these auctions and demanded that the source of funds be vetted. This, however, did not take place. If such a measure had been introduced into the privatisation mechanism, the whole process would have been much more complicated and unreasonably delayed. When the privatisation of small enterprises ended in 1993, more than 30,000 business premises had been auctioned off in the Czech Republic, representing the bulk of the country's retail and service sectors (Ježek 2006: 44).

Much more controversial than the privatisation of small enterprises was another form of denationalisation: the restitution of property to people from whom it had been seized by the communist regime. The fact that restitution happened shows that the influence of the 'father of economic reforms' Václav Klaus was sometimes very limited. Klaus did not want a restitution of property, conceding, at most, some sort of financial compensation to the injured parties. He saw restitution as a potential brake on privatisation, as it would have imposed a temporary halt to the privatisation of a vast amount of state property. In this respect he diverged from many on the Czech right – for example, the chief promoter of restitution, the Christian Democrat Václav Benda – who considered restitution a necessary part of dealing with the communist past. Other ministers besides Klaus in the federal government similarly disliked restitution, and the communist left was even more disapproving. Though supported by moral appeals, the attempts to undo the wrongdoings of a bygone past, thus faced opposition from both sides: ideological objections from the left and pragmatic considerations from the right. The adoption of restitution ultimately depended on strong support in the federal parliament, mainly among right-wing deputies, and also on the pressure exerted by some social groups (and their organisations) that had been particularly afflicted by the communist regime.

The scope of restitution was contentious. The cut-off point before which confiscations would not be reversed produced particularly serious disputes. This was because large-scale nationalisation had already been undertaken before the installation of the communist regime. The restitution legislation ultimately adopted only considered the period after 25 February 1948. The choice of this landmark date was informed by attempts to avoid opening the issue of returning property to several million Germans expelled from Czechoslovakia in 1945–1946.[1] Restitution only applied to citizens, original proprietors and their descendants, not to foreigners including people who lost citizenship during the communist era. Companies, or more precisely the overwhelming majority of corporate bodies (see below for specific exceptions including churches), were also excluded. Buildings, land, and agricultural properties were the most frequently restituted objects. The process was accompanied by numerous and complicated legal cases which overloaded the courts, an important drawback to restitution. Many of the cases were decided by the Constitutional Court, which in its interpretation of restitution legislation 'oscillated between a tendency to undo wrongs to the widest possible extent and a tendency to limit restitution claims with respect to the guarantees provided by the principle of legal certainty' (Petrův 2010). The approach taken by many agricultural cooperatives was particularly problematic, as they manifestly obstructed the return of property.

Rough estimates value the returned property at about 780 billion Kč (approx. $31 billion), and this does not include agricultural restitution (Benda 2008). More than half of the agricultural land in the Czech Republic was thus transferred to its original owners or their family members. In the case of forests the proportion was lower at slightly more than one-fifth (Benda 2008). It should be emphasised that these are estimates, as there are no exact data available. The social impact of restitution can likewise only be estimated. It was evidently immense, as it affected the lives of hundreds of thousands, a considerable proportion in a nation of ten million. Even more than the small privatisation, restitution helped to form and stratify Czech society. The role played by restitution in the Czech Republic was extraordinary compared to its postcommunist peers.

---

[1] In April 1992 the Czech parliament extended the deadline to 1945 when it allowed the restitution of agricultural property to those who could prove that they had not committed an offence against the Czechoslovak state during the war years and had acquired Czechoslovak citizenship before 1953 (Kuklík 2010).

There was also a limited restitution of Church property during the 1990s, including, for instance, property owned by Jewish communities and associations. The issue of restitution of Church property was not fully resolved at the time. A consequence was that vast tracts of land were blocked and could not be freely exploited. The main cause of this delay was Czech anti-clericalism, whose historical roots went far beyond the communist era. The discussion about the restitution of Church property, especially the property of the Catholic Church, revived this anti-clericalism. It was not only the communist and social democratic left but also some on the right who opposed restitution. After years of debates and unsuccessful attempts, the centre-right government led by Petr Nečas eventually pushed the restitution through in 2012, alongside a large-scale programme of financial compensation for the loss of property that could not be returned. In exchange for this it was agreed that the state would gradually cease to fund the Churches, a practice with deep historical roots. The contract between the state and the Churches has nevertheless provoked significant political and social resistance.

9.4. Voucher privatisation, the 'Czech way' and the decline of public trust in the transformation

The most serious disputes were those accompanying the privatisation of large enterprises. It was perhaps here that shock therapy – the rapid privatisation of hundreds of enterprises – was carried out most conspicuously. Gradualist economists proposed that state enterprises should be restructured first; they should be 'put on their feet' and only then privatised by direct sales. Yet the idea of a restructuring carried out by the state ran into inevitable resistance from Klaus's liberals. Their decisive argument was that the state had neither the funding nor the managers to restructure hundreds of enterprises. To this were added fears of a 'spontaneous' or 'wild' privatisation, that is, the mis-appropriation or stripping of state-owned enterprises by their management prior to privatisation. The attempt to minimise this period of pre-privatisation 'anarchy' was described expressively by Tomáš Ježek, one of Klaus's original supporters and minister for privatisation in the Czech government, as the need to shorten the march through privatisation's 'valley of death' (Ježek 2006).

Large privatisation worked as follows. In July 1991 lists of enterprises to be privatised in this wave were published. Anyone could propose a privatesation project for any of the enterprises on offer in this 'large' privatisation, detailing how it would be done. The winning projects were selected within the space of only a few weeks by Ježek's ministry for privatesation. The most common method was voucher privatisation. Citizens received vouchers for a nominal price and could use them to bid on shares in these enterprises. The federal government, specifically Klaus as the minister of finance, pressured Ježek's ministry to use the voucher method as much as possible, as it was not within the jurisdiction of the federal ministry of finance to decide on the privatisation of particular enterprises.

For ODS voucher privatisation provided the trump card in the 1992 election. The idea of a people's capitalism, where state property would be given to citizens, was popular and almost six millions Czechs, a majority of the adult population, participated in voucher privatisation. Restitution and voucher privatesation reinforced pro-market attitudes in society, and there was a clear correlation between voucher privatisation and support for centre-right parties (Večerník 1999, Earle and Gehlbach 2003). Although over time faith in privatesation was damaged, it was here that long-term electoral support for ODS and the Czech right generally was born.

Despite the pressure exerted by the federal government, other methods of privatisation beyond the vouchers were used. Chief among them was direct sale to a predetermined foreign buyer – this was used for about 60 large enterprises – and public tender where factors other than price mattered, for instance, a promise to preserve jobs. Some enterprises were privatised using multiple methods. A second wave of voucher privatisation was organised in the independent Czech Republic, and there was a change in the use of the other methods. Klaus's government almost entirely discontinued the sale of state property to foreigners, preferring the 'Czech way', that is, sales to domestic businessmen (Myant 2003, Kaláb 2004). In Klaus's view this was a way of creating well-capitalised domestic entrepreneurs. The fact that the public had a negative view of the sale of enterprises to foreign investors also played a role. The opposition left also opposed these sales. Nonetheless, those enterprises that were privatised into the hands of foreign investors in the early 1990s usually prospered and many became the powerhouses of the Czech economy.

The 'Czech way' was accompanied by growing suspicions of corruption. Even more importantly, many of the enterprises privatised in this way found themselves in serious difficulties and some went bankrupt. To fund their purchases the new owners usually borrowed from banks, and paying back the loans proved too much of a burden for the technologically-backward enterprises. Understandably, the new owners lacked experience in managing a business in a market economy. Sometimes it was hard to determine unequivocally whether an enterprise went bankrupt due to bad management or outright fraud. The best example of a 'Czech way' privatisation coming to grief was the mammoth steel works Poldi Kladno, which employed thousands of workers. At the time of the privatisation Poldi Kladno was already making massive losses. In 1993 the businessman Vladimír Stehlík obtained the enterprise, but only paid the first instalment of the purchase price. This was followed by a long-running dispute with the state, which unsuccessfully sought to regain control over the enterprise. In the end Poldi went bankrupt. Politically, the failure of Poldi Kladno and the problems of other, sometimes even larger, enterprises such as the engineering colossus Škoda Plzeň became an important factor that undermined public trust in ODS and ODA during the second half of the 1990s.

That said, the 'Czech way' and privatisation in general enabled or at least facilitated the rise of several domestic tycoons, of which the most important were Petr Kellner, Karel Komárek, Andrej Babiš, Pavel Tykač, Radovan Vítek, and Zdeněk Bakala. Their influence did not end with privatisation and has grown further over time. These billionaires gradually built economic empires that wield tremendous social and political influence, and several expanded their businesses abroad. When one of them, Andrej Babiš, decided to enter politics directly and founded a successful political party of his own, ANO 2011, the public debate about the influence wielded by these tycoons intensified.

Returning to the 1990s, even more lasting damage to public trust than that caused by the problems of the Czech way was inflicted by tunnelling (*tunelování*), the siphoning off of the assets of companies privatised by the voucher method. Privatisation investment funds were also vulnerable to tunnelling. These funds provided an alternative to personally selecting a company's shares. Their advertising campaigns helped to popularise the voucher programme. In the end the funds managed to obtain about three-fifths of the assets privatised by the voucher method (Ježek 2006: 122). The problem was that there was a significant delay in establishing the legal framework to protect the rights of small shareholders and regulate the investment funds. The most conspicuous example and something of a pirate flagship were the Harvard funds (*Harvardské fondy*), whose founder Viktor Kožený robbed shareholders of their assets and fled to the Bahamas.

Another serious problem was so-called bank socialism. Simply put, several large semi-state banks exercised a relatively benevolent lending policy towards enterprises. The voucher privatisation scheme contributed to the problem, as privatisation investment funds founded by these large banks became the owners of many formerly state-owned enterprises. The fact that the banks owned the privatised enterprises secured them a credit line. The banks often kept the enterprises afloat whether they made money or not. Thus a peculiar situation arose, dubbed by the critics of Klaus not just bank socialism but also 'quasi-private ownership'. The state, or more precisely the politicians, exerted a greater influence in the economy than a first glance would indicate, yet this influence was mostly informal (Mlčoch 2000, Myant 2003).

Klaus defended the delay in privatising large banks by arguing that if they were in private hands, they would act 'entirely against the interests of the transformation and [...] would not grant a loan to anyone at all'. From his perspective, it was essential to 'transform the economy without destroying it' (Klaus 2002: 184). Klaus was very reserved about the necessity of bankruptcies of inefficient enterprises, regarded by many of his critics as desirable as they would have 'cleansed' the economy of such businesses.

These policies created a 'black hole' of bad loans and the banks later had to write off their debts and be compensated by the state. Similar problems with bad loans appeared in many small banks, often tipping them towards bankruptcy, and bailing them out also proved expensive (Venclovský 1999). Here the central bank bore some responsibility as it had granted too many new banking licences in the early 1990s. This negative experience nevertheless had a positive side, as much stricter control was instituted over the banks. The Czech Republic thus avoided the banking crisis which afflicted most of the Western world in 2008.

One more point should be emphasised in connection with bank socialism: its consequences for the labour market and living standards. This was again connected with the reformers' reluctance to apply 'shock therapy'. The communist regime had guaranteed full employment. In fact those who lacked an employer's stamp on their identity cards risked prosecution. Full employment was considered one of the major achievement of the communist regime and a major source of its legitimacy. One of the dangers of the transformation was the emergence of unemployment. Uniquely in East-Central Europe, the Czech Republic was able to maintain unemployment at only 3 % until almost the end of the 1990s (Frýdmanová, Janáček, Mareš, and Sirovátka 1998). This situation was influenced by certain natural factors, such as the expansion of employment in the service sector, which had been underdeveloped under communism, and a boom among small businesses. Bank socialism also played an important role as it limited pressure on enterprises to restructure themselves and hence to lay off unneeded workers. This gave Klaus's governments a good degree of social peace: strikes, for example, were rare in the 1990s and to this day are uncommon.

An important role in the relative social peace was played by the weakness of trade unions, which were only slowly shedding their reputation as the communist regime's 'obedient hand' in enterprises. Low public trust in trade unions after 1989 was manifest in their diminishing membership. While an estimated 84 % of employees were organised in trade unions at the beginning of the transition, by 1995 it was a mere 41 %, and this trend continued even though the image of trade unions gradually improved (Vašková, Kroupa and Hála 2005: 142). Since the early 1990s there was also a functioning tripartite institution, the Council for Economic and Social Agreement, which included representatives of the government, trade unions, and employers. However, the council had a merely consultative role and has been of limited importance (Mansfeldová 2005, Valterová 2006).

Many authors consider voucher privatisation and the 'Czech way' a mistake. They argue that the voucher method of denationalisation is generally inappropriate because it leads to the extreme fragmentation of shareholdings and a problematic role for privatisation funds, which together lay the groundwork for inefficient management (Orenstein 2001, Richter 2005). Defenders of the voucher privatesation scheme respond that fragmented ownership soon becomes concentrated (Tříska 2002, Holman 2002). The broader social and political context also make a difference. Martin Myant has aptly described the intentional laxness during the creation of the regulatory environment, a laxity quietly supported by Klaus in order to facilitate the concentration of property and the rise of a well-capitalised stratum of domestic entrepreneurs (Myant 2008). The evaluation of the situation after voucher privatisation offered by one of the key reformers, Tomáš Ježek, is similar to Myant's: Ježek's chief point of criticism was that the regulation of the behaviour of privatisation investment funds and the capital market came too late (Ježek 2006). This, for a long time, undermined trust in mutual funds and the stock market. Klaus, however, played down the necessity of protecting small shareholders and regulating the capital markets (Klaus 1995: 76).

Figure 9.1: Year-on-year changes in gross domestic product (in percent)

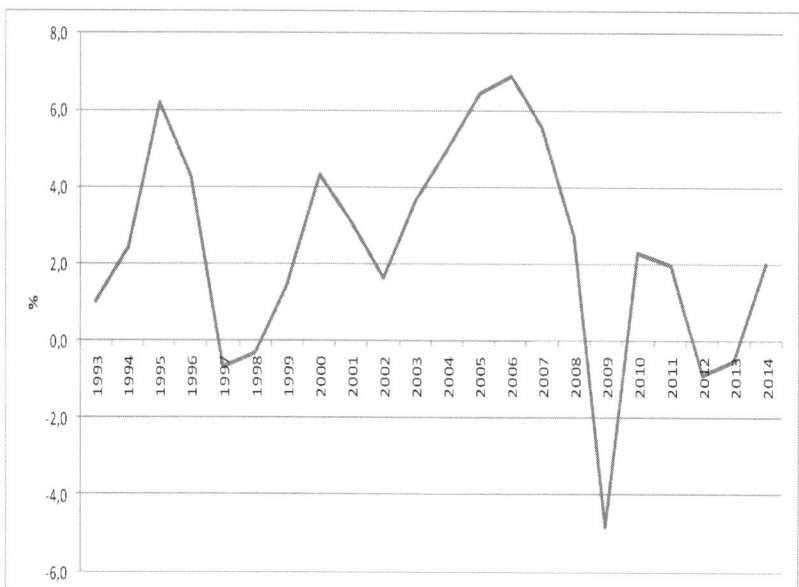

Source: Czech Statistical Office 2015.

Thus, the end of Klaus's era as prime minister was characterised by increasingly negative attitudes towards voucher privatisation and ultimately the economic transformation itself. This also had an impact on trust in the ODS. The end of economic growth exacerbated these problems (see Figure 9.1). Gross domestic product increased by more than 6 % in 1995, but the very next year saw the beginnings of an economic recession. On top of that, in spring 1997 the country faced a currency crisis as foreign speculators launched a concerted attack on the crown. This resulted in a loss of popularity for ODS, the collapse of Klaus's minority government, and ultimately the formation of a social democratic government.

The period was further marked by a discussion about the role of the Czech National Bank. The critics, among whom Klaus was the most vocal, disparaged the central bank for mistakes in monetary policy and unnecessarily restrictive measures, especially the sharp increase in interest rate, which allegedly caused the recession. During the era of the Opposition Agreement (for details see Chapter 8), this criticism also found support with the social democratic prime minister Miloš Zeman. This resulted in an unsuccessful attempt on the part of the two large parties to limit the central bank's independence.

9.5. The era of left-wing governments

In many respects, including the completion of privatisation, Miloš Zeman's social democratic cabinet continued the economic transformation. In privatising or, as the case often was, finishing the privatisation of enterprises where the state was a minority owner, the government tended to seek foreign buyers, although a lot depended on the circumstances. An important element in the social democratic government's strategy was the attempt to implement a large-scale revitalisation of the economy by restructuring loss-making and indebted large enterprises. In doing so the Social Democrats effectively resuscitated an idea that was rejected in the early 1990s by the victorious group of liberal economists concentrated around Klaus. The Minister for Industry and Trade Miroslav Grégr originally envisaged a generous programme that would have involved dozens of private and semi-state enterprises. This idea, however, was opposed within the cabinet on the grounds that it was unrealistic, chiefly because of its enormous cost. In the end, an alternative, scaled-back proposal by Deputy Prime Minister Mertlík, was approved (Bautzová 1999).

The revitalisation programme ultimately affected only nine large enterprises. Yet the government also dealt with issues troubling a number of other enterprises independently of the revitalisation programme. Some evaluations of the programme have been critical, pointing out the lack of transparency in the provision of financial support, which facilitated corruption, and the high costs. Additionally, some of the 'revitalised' enterprises quickly found themselves in serious difficulties again (Myant 2003, Strašáková 2007). The programme nonetheless had a significant political effect: the Zeman government could point to its activities in revitalising the economy and in saving jobs, this at a time when the unemployment rate was on the increase.

More successful was a system of incentives for foreign investors, an idea viewed with reticence by the preceding centre-right cabinets. Thus, about 200 billion Kč (approx. $8 billion) of foreign investment flowed into the country each year from 1999 to 2001, reaching a high of 270 billion Kč (almost $11 billion) in 2002. This was several times larger than the norm under Klaus's governments (Žídek 2008: 152). Although many foreign investors left again once the incentives expired, the programme provided a substantial impetus to the economy, helping to overcome recession and restart growth.

Bank bailouts, which had started during the Klaus era, continued under Zeman. It is somewhat paradoxical that it was a ČSSD government which completed the privatisation of large, semi-state-owned banks and that it privatised them into foreign hands, adopting an approach it originally rejected. In 1999 the state sold its share in the Czechoslovak Trade Bank (*Československá obchodní banka*, ČSOB) to the Belgian KBC Bank. In 2000 the Czech Savings Bank (*Česká spořitelna*) was privatised, with the Austrian Erste Bank becoming the majority shareholder. The next year the Commercial Bank (*Komerční banka*) was sold to the French Société Générale. These privatisations have been viewed positively as an important step towards the stabilisation of the banking sector.

In 2000 the sector experienced a large, albeit one-off, shock, when the central bank took the Investment and Postal Bank (*Investiční a poštovní banka*, IPB) into receivership due to mismanagement. IPB, which had three million clients and wielded enormous influence, effectively went bankrupt. The government supported the central bank's move, and the day after IPB was put into receivership and sold for the symbolic sum of one crown to its competitor, ČSOB. It needs to be noted that IPB had been partially privatised by the voucher method, and it was effectively controlled by its management. Shortly before the Social Democratic government came into power, the state sold its then minority stake to the Japanese bank Nomura which was closely cooperating with IPB's management (Knot 2004). The intervention by the state in IPB was immensely controversial. It was described both as the only possible solution and 'the healing of a sore spot on the Czech economy' (President Václav Havel) and 'daylight robbery' (leader of then oppositional ODS Václav Klaus) (Kopeček 2015: 164 and 166). In the emotionally charged atmosphere surrounding the failure of IPB, the links many politicians had with the banking sector played an important role. The entire case demonstrated the unhealthy connection between economic interests and politics.

At around the mid-term point of Zeman's cabinet came an economic recovery that was reflected, after some delay, in a slowly decreasing unemployment rate and the gradual strengthening of the crown, all accompanied by a low inflation rate that continues to this day. The other governments led by the Social Democrats, with Vladimír Špidla, Stanislav Gross and Jiří Paroubek serving as successive prime ministers (2002–2006), were characterised by three main economic processes: first, continued solid growth;

second, and somewhat paradoxically considering the first, unprecedented growth in national debt (see below); and third, the integration of the Czech Republic into the structures of the single European market.

The Czech Republic joined the European Union in 2004. Chapter 10 discusses this process in more detail, so let us just mention some selected points here. From the time the Zeman government took power, prospective membership became a leitmotif informing many reforms, which have been summarily described as the completion of the transformation. In November 1999, for instance, the Czech government and the European Commission produced a 'Joint Assessment of the Economic Policy Priorities of the Czech Republic', which contained a 'set of medium-term economic policies necessary to advance the country's economic transformation and to prepare it for accession to the European Union'. In reality, this was not so much about finishing the post-communist transformation as about adapting Czech law to EU law. The 'Copenhagen criteria' for EU accession included as conditions a functioning market economy and the ability to cope with competitive pressures within the EU. Also emphasised was the enforceability of law, including property law. EU bodies and member states had to judge that the Czech Republic had met these conditions before it could be admitted. But even before accession the Czech economy had converged with the economies of EU countries. This was not merely a governmental or political decision. Rather it was a consequence of external economic forces, which connected the Czech Republic to the European economy (Hodulák and Krpec 2010: 208–213).

9.6. Post-2008 economic recession and the return of prosperity

Until 2008 the Czech economy enjoyed decent economic growth. This growth, however, coexisted with disregard for many long-term issues including: a growing national debt, structural problems in the pension system, and incomplete healthcare reform. The postponement of serious reform was partly due to government instability: there were six cabinets in the eight years between the 2002 and 2010 elections. Furthermore, there was at the time a relatively widespread belief in continued growth, which encouraged overly generous promises in the competitive 2006 campaign. As a result, there was a leap in benefits paid out by the state (for example, birth grants and parental allowances) and the Czech Republic did not enter the global recession in optimal shape.

When ODS replaced the Social Democrats in government, they hoped to carry out extensive deregulation, undertake reforms of the tax system, healthcare and pensions, and privatise many of the services hitherto provided by the state. If there was a time when neoliberalism was influential in Czech politics, it was during these governments between 2006 and 2009. Even Klaus had not been preparing to privatise services provided by the state. Despite his grand plans, the Prime Minister, Mirek Topolánek, did not manage to push through most of his reforms, in part due to his weak backing in parliament. One that did succeed was the introduction of a flat tax, describe in more detail below. Even the little that was adopted was not necessarily permanent, as these measures could easily be overturned after the next election. Topolánek also had to deal with the so-called 'solar bubble', a sudden increase in photovoltaic power plants due to advantageous electricity prices guaranteed by the state. In reality the problem was a legacy of the preceding era, since the relevant legislation had been passed before 2006 and ODS had opposed it then. It is true, however, that Topolánek's governments were unable to resolve the problem.

The financial crisis and economic recession that hit the world in 2008 was accompanied in Czech politics by effects similar to those experienced a decade earlier. Shortly after the first signs of recession were felt the centre-right government collapsed. Although important, economic problems were not the main trigger of the collapse. As in 1998, a caretaker cabinet took power. Led by Jan Fischer, head of the Statistical Office, the new government relied on the implicit support of both ODS and ČSSD. After a modest delay compared to Western Europe, Czech GDP dropped significantly, which, naturally, led to a decrease in tax receipts and a dramatic increase in the budget deficit. There was, however, no turbulence in the financial markets, and the banking sector withstood the crisis exceptionally well. This was in no small part thanks to the experience with bank failures in the second half of the 1990s – an experience for which the country had already paid dearly (Hodulák and Krpec 2010: 215–217, Zpráva o finanční stabilitě 2014/2015). The central bank sought to mitigate the economic slump by cutting interest rates.

Fischer's caretaker cabinet did not introduce any fundamental reform. Although its minister of finance, the well-respected senior civil servant Eduard Janota, prepared significant budget cuts, the 'Janota package' was rejected by parliament during the negotiations over the 2010 budget. The cabinet also found itself unable to deal with the aforementioned 'solar bubble'. These failures revealed the limits of a caretaker cabinet lacking a real mandate.

With the rise to power of Nečas's centre-right government after the 2010 election, fiscal restraint arrived on the scene, at least rhetorically. The main face of this government's economic policy was Minister of Finance Miroslav Kalousek (TOP 09), who in subsequent years styled himself the guardian of fiscal discipline. This discipline was more symbolic than real. The government did manage to persuade the general public that the future was grim. This resulted in a substantial curtailment of private investment and consumption. Yet the government itself behaved inconsistently. Its cuts in public expenditure were limited. Its pension reform was questioned from the start as the government never secured the support of the opposition and the general public doubted the reform would last. (And the public was right: the next government abolished the most important elements of the pension reform.) The Nečas government was thoroughgoing only in increasing some taxes, most importantly the VAT, and in reintroducing progressivity with a new 'solidarity tax' for those with the highest incomes. It was precisely the combination of inconsistency in cutting public expenditure and increasing taxation that, together with the impact of the recession, conflicts within the government coalition, and general disgust with the political class, helped to undermine public trust in Nečas's government. These factors were also behind the failure of the centre-right parties in the 2013 election.

At that time the country began to see the green shoots of recovery, which soon brought genuine economic growth: in 2014 GDP rose by 2 % and in 2015 by an additional 4.3 %.[2] The new government of the Social Democrats, Andrej Babiš's ANO 2011, and the Christian Democrats reaped significant political capital from the economy. Their agenda was rhetorically focussed on the anti-corruption struggle, which was to improve the budget balance. Another pillar of its agenda was clamping down on tax evasion. The main measures here were tightening control over VAT revenue and the introduction of electronic records of sales.

By contrast, the debate over the introduction of the euro produced no tangible results in either the 2000s or 2010s. Though the Czech Republic committed itself to the euro as part of the terms of its EU accession, during the era of Social Democratic governments support for the euro was merely

---

2   Overall, the two decades from 1995 to 2014 saw dynamic growth with GDP per capita doubling from 11,550 Kč to 22,935 Kč (Český statistický úřad 2015).

symbolic. Indeed, given the serious increase in the deficit the country no longer fulfilled the Maastricht criteria necessary to enter the Eurozone. This remained the case after 2006, when the Euro-sceptic ODS showed little enthusiasm for the euro.

After the global downturn, the euro-caused economic troubles in the countries of Southern Europe contributed to a sharp increase in Czech public resistance to the euro. According to an opinion poll undertaken in 2013, almost four-fifths of the Czechs polled rejected the introduction of the euro (CVVM 2013). Even after the revival of the economy and the elections of 2013, the topic of euro adoption remained politically frozen. This was largely due to the Greek debt crises, in which the euro played a major role. This precluded any serious consideration of adopting the euro.

Having been dormant for more than a decade, the debate about central bank independence was revived in 2013. This resulted from the bank's decision to intervene in the foreign exchange market with the aim of weakening the crown and averting the threat of deflation. The central bank faced severe political and public criticism over this move. Particularly vocal was President Zeman, but many other government politicians sought to distance themselves from the intervention, arguing that they had not been consulted. Yet retrospectively it appears that the devaluation of the crown provided an important impulse for the kick-starting of economic growth.

9.7. Budget policy and the national debt

In the early twenty-first century, the national debt and large budget deficits, especially in the national budget, became the main focus of economic concern in the Czech Republic. Czech budgets had been relatively balanced or in surplus during the first half of the 1990s. The first significant debate about deficits occurred in 1997, when the economy dipped into recession. Public revenue dropped significantly, prompting budget cuts and cost-saving measures. Despite this the 1997 and 1998 budgets ended up in deficit (see Figure 9.2).

The budget for 1999, the first prepared by Zeman's minority government, was pushed through by the Social Democrats in cooperation with the opposition communists and Christian Democrats. For the first time in post-transition history, parliament passed a budget with a large planned deficit. In an extension of the Opposition Agreement, Zeman's government passed the next three budgets with the assistance of ODS. In exchange for the support of ODS on the national budget, the Social Democrats pledged to implement a number of liberal policies favoured by ODS. These included a reform of the pension system, and a halt to increases in the overall tax burden and mandatory spending. In practice, many of these promises remained unfulfilled (Pečinka 2001, Kopeček 2015). The ČSSD also pledged to gradually decrease the budget deficit until it reach balance by 2003. Although ultimately the deficits were larger than the agreed-upon targets, Zeman's government did limit its expenditure as a consequence of the agreement with ODS (see Figure 9.2).

The government's behaviour changed dramatically after the 2002 election. The reversal was emblematically expressed by the chair of the Social Democrats and later prime minister Vladimír Špidla when he declared, during a TV debate with the leader of the ODS and former prime minister Václav Klaus: 'The resources are there' *(Zdroje tu jsou),* which echoed ČSSD's spending promises (Kopeček 2015: 257). The first budget prepared by Špidla's government was a fundamental departure from the previous practice of budget restraint. The year-on-year budget deficit more than doubled and for the first time exceeded the 'magical' threshold of 100 billion Kč. The exceptionality of this deficit was that it was not dictated by Keynesian imperatives about state investment during a recession.

Figure 9.2: Budget balance as a proportion of GDP (in percent)

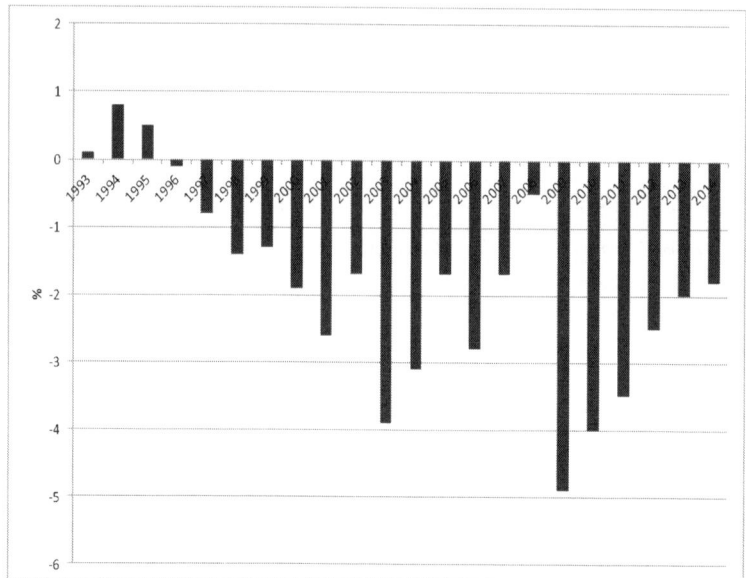

Source: Czech Statistical Office 2015.

The economy was actually growing. In 2004 and 2006 the deficit was again near the 100-billion-Kč threshold, subsequently decreasing until the budget was almost balanced in 2008. However, with the economic recession and a drop in GDP of almost 5 %, the deficit in 2009 reached the unprecedented level of 200 billion Kč. It did not shrink to below 100 billion Kč until 2013. The Maastricht criterion which required budget deficits below 3 % of GDP was not met by the budget in 2003, 2004, or 2009–2011. Budget deficit are characteristic not just of the national government but also of municipal and regional budgets.

In the mid-1990s the debt-to-GDP ratio was only about 10 %. Debt then started to grow substantially: by six percentage points during Zeman's government in 1998–2002 and by a further 8 percentage points during the Social Democratic cabinets that followed in 2002–2006 (see Figure 9.3). It was not until 2013 that debt stopped growing, by then it stood at two-fifths of GDP.

Figure 9.3: Debt as a proportion of GDP (in percent)

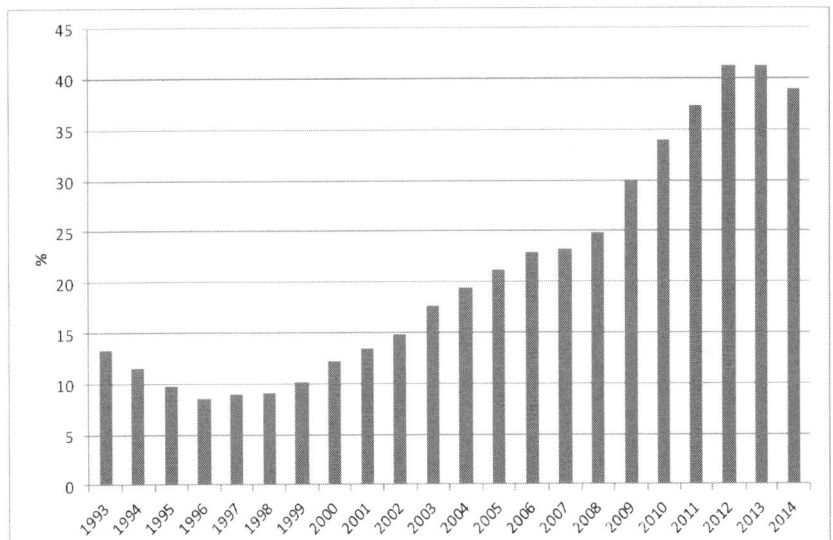

Source: Czech Statistical Office 2015.

Looking now at the structure of expenditures, in 2015 44 % was to be dispensed through the Ministry of Labour and Social Affairs (pensions, welfare, unemployment benefits), 11 % through the Ministry of Education, Youth, and Sports and 3.5 % through the Ministry of Defence (Zákon č. 345/2014 Sb. o státním rozpočtu ČR na rok 2015).

It is also interesting to see how much space the government has for policy manoeuvre. This can be analysed by comparing the share of mandatory and quasi-mandatory spending in total expenditure. Mandatory spending is required by law and chiefly consists of social transfers. Quasi-mandatory spending is not required by law, but is difficult to reduce, as, for example, the wages of public employees. Figure 9.4 shows that in the long term non-mandatory spending in the Czech budget has been at best a third, but mostly about a quarter, of total expenditure. Interestingly this proportion is essentially static, unaffected by changes of government. Thus, the space available to Czech governments for implementing their desired policies has long been very limited.

Figure 9.4: Mandatory and quasi-mandatory spending

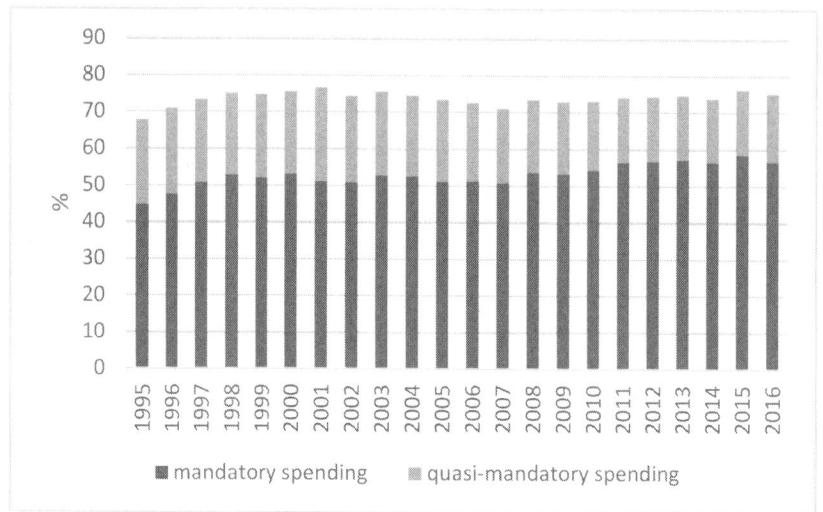

Note: Expressed as a proportion of national budget expenditure (in percent).
Source: Smetanková 2014: 3, updated.

9.8. Taxes

Although taxation is currently an important topic in Czech politics, it was not at the centre of political discussion early in the transition. This was due to that fact that under the communist regime tax policy was of marginal importance to ordinary citizens, and other economic issues dominated public debate. A tax reform did come into effect on 1 January 1993 and fundamentally overhauled the entire tax system (Vítek 2001: 29). The most important changes were the replacement of the turnover tax with a VAT (charged at two rates) and the introduction of excise duties. The general aim of the reform was to increase indirect taxation (such as VAT) relative to direct taxation. Today indirect taxation makes up two-thirds of tax receipts (Klaus 2013: 130).

The level of taxation and even the legitimacy of certain types of taxation (such as inheritance taxes or property taxes) were for a long time not the subject of political discussion. The first signs that this might change appeared in

ODS's 1998 election campaign, but the 2002 elections marked a real watershed. ODS proposed a new flat tax that would remove progressivity from the personal income tax and set the income tax and the VAT at the same level. In the following years taxation became one of the main differences between the right (who defended lower taxes) and the left (who defended the status quo or proposed tax increases).

Topolánek's centre-right government took some steps towards lowering taxes. In particular, progressive taxation was abolished, the corporate tax was lowered, and the inheritance tax was *de facto* almost entirely abolished. The following government, in which budgetary hawk Miroslav Kalousek had a much stronger say, made a remarkable about-face. They prioritised the stabilisation of the public finances rather than low taxation and thus increased a number of taxes.

The level of tax burden (total tax receipts as a percentage of GDP) provides a measure, albeit an imperfect one, of these changes. According to OECD data (see Figure 9.5), the tax burden essentially followed the changes to economic policy outlined earlier: it decreased to a low of 32.5 % in 1998, stagnated for the following three years, and then gradually increased until peaking at 34.7 % in 2004. It then decreased to 32.4 % (its lowest value in post-1989 history), followed by an increase to 34.1 % in 2013.

It is particularly interesting to compare these data with growth rates. The decrease in the tax burden in 2004-2007 was accompanied by a sharp growth in GDP. The real tax burden therefore did not decrease as much as a first glance would suggest. By contrast, the decrease in tax burden in 2008–2009 must be understood in the context of declining GDP during the economic recession which also mitigates the change in the tax burden

A comparison with other countries reveals more interesting facts. The values for the tax burden in the Czech Republic are similar to those in Poland, Germany, and pre-2004 Slovakia. By contrast, in Scandinavia the tax burden is much higher, varying between 40 and 46 % for Norway and Finland, and 44 and 50 % for Sweden and Denmark (OECD 2015).

At present, the Czech tax system does not permit any level of government besides the centre to impose taxes. There are no regional or local taxes. The main taxes are the personal income tax, the corporate tax, the property tax, the road tax, the inheritance tax (now virtually unused), the gift tax, the property transfer tax, and the VAT as well as excise duties.

Figure 9.5: Evolution of tax burden

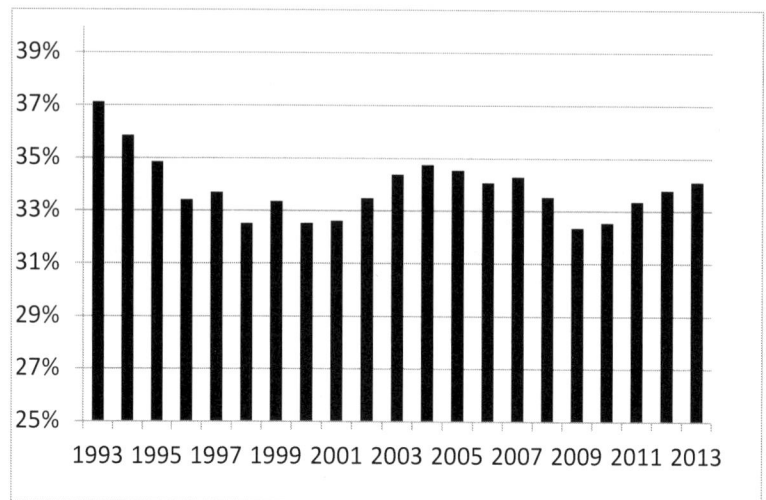

Source: OECD 2015.

9.9. Conclusion: reflections on the Czech transformation and capitalism

After 1989 the Czechs made the great leap from a centrally planned to a market economy. Some of the decisions and steps taken have proved problematic or simply wrong in retrospect. However, in assessing the transformation process, one needs to bear in mind that the reformers lacked experience and were learning on the job. Further, the extent and nature of the transformation was unprecedented. Although 'the Czech way' and voucher privatisation can be criticised in retrospect, it is worth remembering the reasoning behind them. One also needs to bear in mind that nowhere in the post-communist world were the methods and outcomes of the transformation uncontroversial. Mass privatisation in particular, whatever the methods adopted, never brought universal satisfaction. The criticisms levied in other countries were often similar to those documented in this chapter. The 'bad mood' that affected the Czech Republic at the end of the 1990s had its analogues in other countries of the Eastern bloc, and in some of them the accompanying effects – economic chaos, drastic declines in the standard of living, loss of savings due to inflation – were much more dramatic (Turley and Luke 2011).

In assessing the results of the Czech transformation, Martin Myant's (2007) conclusion that it was a qualified success, seems apt. A functional market economy was created, though it was one with limited potential for further growth. One of the main causes of these limitations according to Myant was substantial dependence on foreign-owned companies. Although they were the country's economic powerhouse, the products they manufactured in the Czech Republic were often much 'less sophisticated or cheaper than those made in the most advanced Western countries'. This negatively impacted the potential for innovation in the Czech economy (Myant 2007: 449). The impact of foreign investment thus seems to be a double-edged sword.

If in 1989 the reformers lacked experience, ordinary citizens likewise knew almost nothing about market economies except for communist propaganda. For some of them the 1990s were disappointing and robbed them of their naïve illusions. Yet for many the birth of the market economy provided an opportunity, which they proved able to seize. Thus, the economic transformation, and privatisation and restitution in particular, contributed signifycantly to the stratification of Czech society. The winners and losers of transformation were born.

The political pressures on economic reformers deserve a chapter of their own. As the economist Libor Žídek noted, 'the reformers had to choose between reforms and efforts to maintain [public] support for the process of transformation and for themselves. Their attempts to keep a hold on power are entirely understandable' (Žídek 2006: 263). These pressures were as strong later in the transformation as they were early on. Later Czech governments repeatedly had to face the problems of weak parliamentary backing and their own internal fragility. Understandably, the situation significantly inhibited their ability and desire to push through serious reforms.

The consequence was that many issues went unresolved or only half measures were taken. Combined with the recession that struck the country after 2008, this has revived the 'bad mood' of the late 1990s and led to popular demands for 'competent governments' which, in turn, can explain the political earthquake that shook the Czech Republic in the early 2010s.

Andreas Nölke and Arjan Vliegenthart (2009) have proposed one of the most influential assessments of contemporary Czech capitalism. They have described it, alongside Hungary, Poland, and Slovakia, as a 'dependent market economy'. Although this type is able to produce relatively complex consumer goods, it is dependent on transnational companies, not least in the banking sector. This dependency has a number of consequences, such as the concentration of decision-making in intra-firm hierarchies within transnational enterprises and the transfer of new technologies through these firms, which limits domestic innovation. Also important are limited investment into research and education, as is the fact that relatively skilled, but also relatively cheap, labour is crucial for growth. Connected with this is the weakness of trade unions, which are unable to push for higher wages.

However, it might be questioned whether the core of the argument – the dominance of foreign enterprises – is being gradually undermined by the expansion of several domestic business empires. Only the future can confirm or reject this objection.

10. Europeanising and Westernising

Vít Hloušek

The aim of this chapter is not to give a synoptic yet condensed history of the Czech Republic's international relations, nor is it to show exhaustively how Czech political institutions and actors Europeanised themselves, as a number of excellent studies have already focused on these topics.[1] The subject of this chapter are the key issues of Czech foreign policy, which provided the context for, and, in some respects, framed (and continue to frame) current discussions about Czech domestic policy. It shows the direction Czech (and in the early 1990s Czechoslovak) policy took,[2] from its 'return to Europe' to increasingly directed efforts to integrate the country with the European Union and NATO to the contemporary Europeanisation of Czech politics. It also touches on the contradictions between the attempts by Czech political leaders to establish their country's position in Europe and international politics and the failures and distortions that have been inherent in these attempts.

10.1. Return to Europe: Czechoslovakia and the Czech Republic in Europe and the world during the 1990s

In late 1989 and early 1990 it seemed obvious what foreign policy course the country should take. The slogan 'Return to Europe' expressed, in a sound bite, the desire to escape the Soviet grip, to reconstitute the true international independence of the country and to anchor the new democratic political system

---

1 The most lucid compendium on the evolution of Czechoslovak and Czech foreign policy is Cabada and Waisová (2011). Marek and Baun (2010) have provided a synoptic survey of the Czech Republic's relationship with the European Union. Fiala (2009) has addressed the Europeanisation of Czech politics.
2 For the most part, Czechoslovakia returned to being a full-fledged actor in international relations in the years 1990-1992 (see Table 10.2). It established relations with countries the communist regime ignored (Israel, the Vatican) and became a member of, or renewed its membership in, crucial international organisations such as the IMF (Dejmek 2002: 368–369). When in 1993 the Czech Republic was created as a successor state to Czechoslovakia, it mostly continued the latter's membership of international organisations, recognising and being recognised by countries which previously recognised Czechoslovakia. On 19 January 1993 the Czech Republic was accepted as the 179th member of the United Nations.

in the international community. In the eyes of the Czechoslovak general public and its nascent democratic political elite, this community was the West and its political, economic, and security alliances. While there was near universal agreement (except for the communists) on the need to leave the geopolitical 'East', the question of foreign policy priorities did not admit a similar consensus.

An important factor in the stabilisation of Czechoslovakia's security situation was the withdrawal of the occupying Soviet forces in 1991 and the dissolution of the Warsaw Pact (1 July 1991) and Comecon (28 June 1991).[3] While the makers of Czechoslovak foreign policy agreed that these organisations needed to be shut down, they were not entirely united on the issue of what should fill the security and political vacuum that they would leave behind.

In 1990 it was Minister of Foreign Affairs Jiří Dienstbier who was the most vocal, envisaging a gradual departure from both blocs and the creation of a Europe-wide security structure. His idea was to anchor Czechoslovakia's security within the framework of the Committee on Security and Cooperation in Europe (CSCE) (Dienstbier 1990), that is, outside both the Warsaw Pact and NATO. This idea fell by the wayside when Václav Havel and his close advisers and collaborators clearly prioritised NATO as a guarantor of security and stability. In February 1991 the president's foreign policy adviser Alexandr Vondra first openly and officially declared that Czechoslovakia viewed the preservation of NATO and its expansion eastwards as the ideal scenario. Later he presented an official proposal to the then secretary-general of NATO Manfred Woerner. Given that the Soviet Union still existed, Woerner's response was evasive if not disapproving. Yet the second pillar of Czechoslovak and, later, Czech foreign policy had been laid.

Besides endeavours to integrate into the West, an important dimension of Czech foreign policy in the 1990s were efforts to cooperate within the narrower space of Central Europe. In a way, Czechoslovak and, later, Czech diplomacy picked up the thread of discussions among exiles and domestic dissenters who, following Milan Kundera's well-known essay *'The Tragedy of Central Europe'*, emphasised the difference between Central Europe and Eastern Europe. As early as May 1990, Czechoslovakia became a full member of the

---

3 The last Soviet unit left the territory of Czechoslovakia on 21 June 1991 and the commander of the so-called central group of Soviet forces, Colonel General Eduard Vorobyov, left six days later.

group that was later called the Central European Initiative (CEI). Created at the very end of the Cold War, CEI was a project linking some Western (Italy and Austria) and some Eastern (Yugoslavia and Hungary) countries, but the focus of its activities gradually shifted towards Central and Eastern Europe. Although CEI never created a true international organisation or international regime, in the first half of the 1990s it offered a platform where the Czech Republic could not only cooperate with other countries of the region, but also learn the methods and mechanisms of international cooperation (Dančák 1999: 14–23).

The aims of the Visegrád Group, formed on the basis of Václav Havel's initiatives of 1990 and 1991, corresponded more closely to the crucial objective of participating in Western and Western European political, security, and economic integration. The chief aim of Havel and his collaborators was that Central European cooperation would support the dismantling of the Warsaw Pact and Comecon and, at the same time, move Central European states towards membership in European institutions including the EEC. Thus, the Visegrád Group looked to the future, rather than the past, of Central Europe. The very fact that a group of Central European states came together was a watershed, signalling that a new quality of relations between the nations in this part of Europe had been reached. During the interwar period these states were often at loggerheads, pursuing different priorities in their domestic and foreign policies.

In February 1991 at a summit of foreign ministers of Czechoslovakia, Hungary and Poland the so-called Visegrád Declaration was adopted, laying out the political objectives of this Central European cooperation.[4] An overview of these aims faithfully describes the hopes and fears of Central European countries in the early 1990s and the fundamental course of their foreign policies:

- Full restitution of state sovereignty, democracy, and freedom,

- Elimination of all existing social, economic, and spiritual remnants of the totalitarian system,

---

4 It was officially entitled the 'Declaration on Cooperation between the Czech and Slovak Federal Republic, the Republic of Poland, and the Republic of Hungary in Striving for European Integration'. See *Visegrad Declaration 1991* for an unofficial English translation.

- Construction of parliamentary democracy, rule of law, and respect for human rights and freedoms,
- Creation of a modern free market economy,
- Full involvement in the European political, economic, security, and legal systems.

The obvious similarity between these aims and the subsequent Copenhagen Criteria,[5] formulated by the EU in 1993 as conditions of full membership, was not entirely accidental. Rather, it stemmed from the context in which the Visegrád Declaration was expressed, one that viewed the connection between democratisation and Europeanisation as fundamental. In the early 1990s Czechoslovak diplomacy believed that domestic democratisation and economic reform was linked with the consolidation of the country's international position. The Visegrád Declaration and the early days of the Visegrád cooperation reflect the optimistic outlook of the times, according to which the integration into the European Communities would be swift. By the later part of the 1990s a certain disillusionment had set in. Nonetheless, a clear priority of Czech foreign policy and the need to cooperate with other countries in the efforts at European integration had been established in the early days.

Although, the Czech Republic under Klaus's government sought to portray itself as ahead of everyone else in approaching the West, the multilateral dimension of the Visegrád cooperation did not lose its importance. During the second half of the nineties, it helped to break the international isolation of Slovakia after Mečiar's strongman rule (which was also in the Czech interest); it played a certain coordinating role in the process of Central European accession to the EU (Štastný 2002); and it even maintained its significance after accession, as certain political and security issues continue to be debated on this platform, thus allowing for 'enhanced' cooperation between the Czech Republic and its Central European partners (Dangerfield 2008).

Besides the political dimension of European integration, the Czech Republic also realised the necessity of economic cooperation. Therefore, the

---

5 'Political criteria: stability of institutions guaranteeing democracy, the rule of law, human rights, and respect for and protection of minorities. Economic criteria: a functioning market economy and the capacity to cope with competition and market forces; administrative and institutional capacity to effectively implement the *acquis* and ability to take on the obligations of membership.' See EU – Enlargement – Accession criteria – European Commission.

country was, together with Hungary, Poland, and Slovakia, among the founding members of the Central European Free Trade Agreement (CEFTA), signed in December 1992 with the aim of creating a free trade zone by 2001. In addition to strengthening international trade, thus facilitating economic transformation, CEFTA also had another dimension that was connected with EU integration. It aimed to produce an arrangement very similar to the Single European Market then under construction. Although the workings of CEFTA were not always idyllic (Dančák 1999: 53–58), and tariff and other barriers were removed only gradually, CEFTA not only brought tangible economic advantages to the Czech Republic – ones that were linked with its position as a primarily export-oriented economy – but also reinforced the orientation of Czech politics towards full European integration (see Mostetschnig 2011).

10.2. NATO: providing security and a sense of belonging in the West

If the European Union represented the ultimate goal of Czech political and economic integration, then NATO had been understood by leading Czech politicians as a guarantor of international security ever since the options of neutrality, preservation of the Warsaw Pact, or a Europe-wide security structure based on the OSCE had shown themselves to be illusory in the early 1990s. For the Czechs, this was not only an attempt to secure their fragile and militarily weak young democracy, but also represented a political and cultural manifesto. Membership in NATO was understood as confirmation of belonging in the West, and at least some Czech politicians (such as Václav Havel and Alexander Vondra) considered future NATO membership a mutual commitment to collective security through which the Czech Republic would not only obtain guarantees of its own security, but also actively co-guarantee the security of other member countries.[6]

---

6 Signing the accession document, Václav Havel said: 'After many centuries of the dramatic existence of our state, its security is at last strongly guaranteed, as it becomes an integral part of the security of the whole Euro-American world. Membership of the North Atlantic Treaty Organisation is for us both a hope and a commitment: it gives us hope that our country will never again succumb, nor be sacrificed to, any aggressor; it also expresses our clear resolve to share responsibility for the freedom of nations, human rights, democratic values and peace on our continent.' (Havel 1999: 825)

The chronology and critical junctures of NATO's enlargement to the East are relatively well-known (see Asmus 2002). Vague promises of enlargement and an obvious unwillingness to do so on the part of a number of Western politicians (for example, Margaret Thatcher and François Mitterrand) were only gradually replaced by a clearer perspective on NATO expansion. This was due not only to a geopolitical shift after the disintegration of the Soviet Union, but also to the changing willingness of Western countries to accept their former enemies 'from the East'. An important move from words to action occurred in 1993–1994. Visiting Prague in August 1993, Boris Yeltsin responded to Václav Havel's explanation that the Czech Republic including its military was going West with the words: 'It's your free choice' (Asmus 2002: 39). And when in January 1994 during his visit to Prague Bill Clinton announced the Partnership for Peace (PfP) programme, a structure had finally appeared for intensive dialogue and rapprochement between NATO and those Central European countries, such as the Czech Republic, which were interested in full membership. In 1995 and 1996, the criteria for membership were specified, and at the June 1997 NATO summit in Madrid it was announced that the Czech Republic, Hungary, and Poland would become members of the alliance, which they did on 12 March 1999.

For some of the Czech Republic's political leaders the accession to NATO meant less emphasis on a quick accession to the European Union, as it seemed that the basic security guarantees had already been obtained. The attitude of Czech politicians and the general public towards NATO has been changing since the late 1990s. Although most of the populace continues to approve of NATO membership, this general support is accompanied by scepticism of Czech military potential and by a reluctance to engage in military operations within the Alliance. The general public has long opposed increasing the defence budget and has been critical of some NATO activities such as the bombing of Kosovo in 1999 and the invasion of Iraq in 2003, even though the Czech Republic contributed to the latter. There has been much discussion about the placement of a US radar station in the Brdy mountains military area. Some members of the elite share these misgivings (Řiháčková 2005). The Czech Republic sometimes acts as a free-rider in NATO, benefitting from the guarantees of security without being particularly willing to contribute to the provision of this security. However, with the exception of the communists, no relevant Czech political party questions NATO membership or the country's security orientation towards the West – something which cannot be said about Czech attitudes to European integration.

10.3. The road to the European Union[7]

Full membership in the European Communities (after 1993 the EU) was a natural and, for some political leaders, the most important aspect of the Civic Forum slogan 'Return to Europe'. Characteristic of the initial discussions about the prospects of Czechoslovak EC membership was naïve optimism about the speed of this process. On 16 December 1991, when Czechoslovakia signed the Association Agreement with the European Communities, many Czech politicians thought that gaining membership would be a matter of a few years.[8]

The initial optimism was soon replaced by disenchantment due to the fact that the EC/EU preferred what was called in the jargon of the time a 'deepening' of integration at the expense of its territorial 'widening'. Besides the fact that the political focus was on reforms within the existing Union, economics also played a role, whether it was the potential costs of enlargement into Central Europe or the incompatibilities between the Central European economies and those of existing member states. Against the wishes of Central European politicians, the association agreements did not contain a binding promise of membership. The negotiations over the agreements already suggested that the EC/EU would be the one to set the deadlines and the rules of the game. The option of membership for 'post-communist' Central European countries was confirmed by the Edinburgh summit in December 1992, with the proviso that necessary criteria were to be met first. These criteria were only formulated at the Copenhagen summit the following year (see footnote 4) and in 1995 the additional requirement was made that applicants must adopt the *acquis communautaire*. Czech politicians were frustrated by the lack of a clear roadmap for the EU's eastern enlargement and the existing barriers that hindered the access of products, goods, and services to the emerging Single European Market.

Despite disillusionment and growing Euroscepticism among some prominent politicians (notably Prime Minister Václav Klaus), the Czech Republic submitted an official application for membership in the EU on 17 January 1996. In doing so it was among the last of those 'post-communist'

---

7 For a more detailed description and analysis of the eastern enlargement, see Henderson 1999, O'Brennan 2006, and Vassiliou 2007.
8 Due to the length of the ratification process and the division of Czechoslovakia, this association agreement never came into force. Hence a new Association Agreement with the Czech Republic was signed on 4 October 1993.

countries that were deemed to be the most prepared to join. The position assumed by the EU itself had also evolved: in parallel with the process of approving the Amsterdam Treaty, the Union worked out a more specific plan for eastern enlargement. In July 1997 Agenda 2000 was adopted, where enlargement formed an important part. On the basis of this document, accession negotiations started with the first wave of applicants in 31 March 1998. Despite the growing Euroscepticism of some Czech politicians, the Czech Republic was among them.[9]

It would be overkill to describe in detail the contents of the opinions of the European Commission monitoring the progress of reforms demanded as part of the accession process. These reforms involved the harmonising of the Czech legal system with that of the EU as well as achieving isomorphism between Czech and EU institutions in order for the Czech Republic to be able to adopt the *acquis communautaire*. However, it must be said that the EU set the conditions of this process in their entirety and also evaluated whether and how they were being met. The Europeanisation of Central European countries came about through the process of conditionality (Grabbe 2006). It did not necessarily involve a harmonisation of results, but it left little room for domestic creativity. In the Czech Republic, as in other candidate countries, politicians tended to blame the EU for all unpopular reforms before and after accession, while presenting positive changes as resulting form their own activities and diligence. Seen retrospectively, the progress of pre-accession harmonisation was one-sided and directed by the EU; however, one cannot ignore the fact that in a number of areas, such as the civil service and regulatory institutions, the conditionality of accession led to improvements in state administration, the finalisation of some economic reforms (for example, the privatisation of Czech banks), and overall improvement in the quality and stability of democratic institutions (Vachudova 2005). At least part of the Czech political elite (namely, the Christian Democrats and some politicians of the Civic Democratic Alliance, the Civic Democratic Party and the Freedom Union) admitted that they considered many of the reforms demanded by the EU to be good, not only in the instrumental sense of facilitating accession, but as beneficial for Czech politics generally. However, the uncritical image of the EU as a panacea for all Czech problems and weaknesses led to unrealistic expectations among some members of the general public and frustration after accession to the EU on 1 May 2004.

---

9   Together with Cyprus, Estonia, Hungary, Poland and Slovenia.

10.4. Problems with Europeanisation: European integration as a task and an apple of discord

Many political leaders and a significant portion of the Czech general public were lukewarm or sceptical about the EU at the time of the accession.[10] Over the 1990s, Czech popular opinion stabilised, with 40 to 50 % of respondents in favour of EU accession in opinion polls, a fifth to a quarter against, and the rest vacillating between the two options or not expressing an opinion. In comparison with other Central European countries, support for the EU tended to be lower in the Czech Republic (Hanley 2005: 138; Guerra 2013: 23–31). Ultimately, 77 % voted in favour of EU accession in the June 2003 referendum (with a turnout of 55 %). Long-term public opinion trends, presented in Figure 10.1, indicate that despite the significant scepticism and a relatively low degree of trust in the European Union compared with the rest of Europe (Jerez-Mir, Real-Dato and Vázquez-García 2010), Czech respondents typically trust the EU more than their domestic political institutions (with the exception of the country's president). However, the Czech public is much more sceptical about the potential adoption of the euro, as seen in Figure 10.2.

Thus, at first glance it would seem that the Czech Republic is lukewarm or reserved about European integration, not only due to prominent Eurosceptics among its political elite, but also with respect to the cautious and sceptical attitude of the general public towards many EU policies beginning with the euro and ending with an array of apparently useless regulations. One explanation of this attitude is that the public is not sufficiently versed in the functioning of EU institutions. In other words, people do not know much about the EU and are not particularly interested either. In this the Czech Republic is not an exception. A second, complementary reason is the generally high scepticism of the Czech people towards all political elites, as they tend to be

---

10 The greater part of the Civic Democratic Party (ODS) was sceptical, as was the extreme left (the Communists, KSČM) and the no less extreme right (the Republicans). However, ODS never questioned the priority of EU accession during the campaign and even Václav Klaus did not do so openly, despite his mantras of prosperity and sovereignty. Indeed, even the KSČM did not lead an openly anti-accession campaign; its position during the referendum could be expressed as silent acquiescence to EU membership and subsequently the party lost interest in the EU as a political issue. Mansfeldová and Špicarová Stašková (2010) have provided interesting data on the Euroscepticism of the economic and political elite.

perceived as remote from the issues plaguing ordinary citizens and concerned only with their own interests.

To illustrate the first point we can refer to an opinion poll undertaken during the Czech presidency of the European Council in the first half of 2009. According to a CVVM survey in December 2008, less than a third of respondents were interested, fully or partially, in the upcoming Czech presidency, and almost 71 % of respondents either did not know what the Lisbon Treaty was or only had a vague idea (the ratification of the treaty being the subject of a fierce political struggle at the time). To illustrate the second point, voters for the Eurosceptic Civic Democrats have long shown the greatest support for the EU, whereas the electorate of the pro-integration Social Democrats is much less supportive of the EU. The most likely explanation of this paradox is that the issues of European integration are of little importance for Czech voters.[11]

---

[11] The fact that there is only minimal interest in the elections to the European Parliament supports this argument. In 2004, turnout was 28.3 percent, in 2009 28.2 percent, and in 2014 a mere 18.2 percent.

Figure 10.1: Evolution of public trust in the EU and the most important Czech political institutions (in percent)

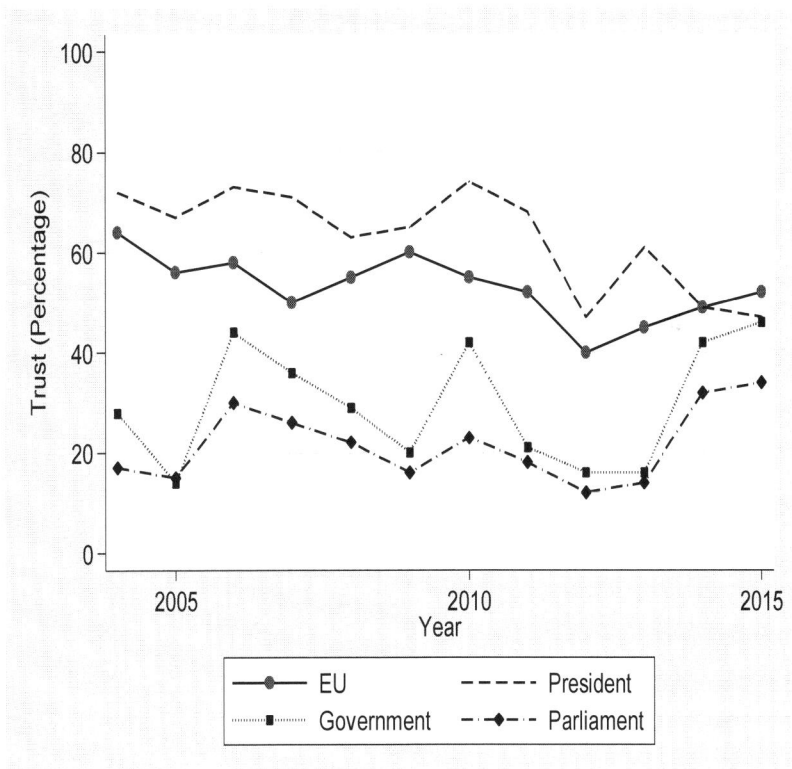

Source: cvvm.soc.cas.cz.

Note: The numbers indicate the percentage of people who 'strongly trust' or 'rather trust' the institution in question.

Figure 10.2: The evolution of Czech public opinion on the introduction of the euro (in percent)

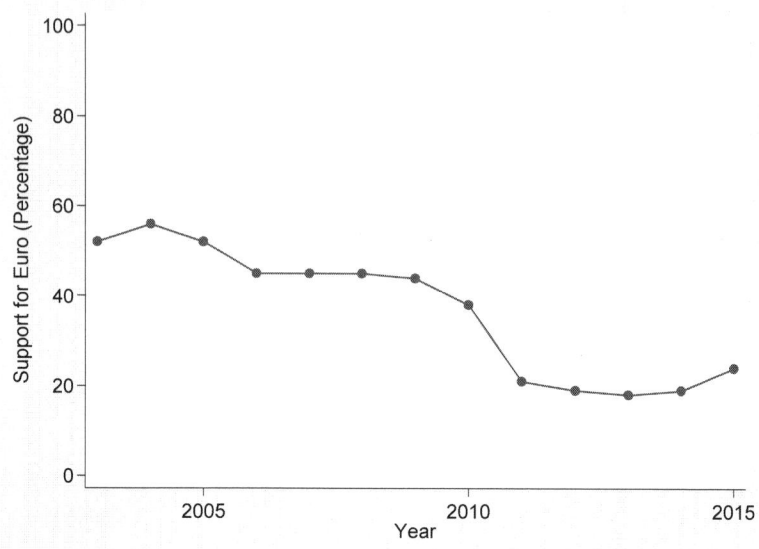

Source: Červenka 2015: 2.

The stance assumed by Czech voters is not particularly surprising. The political discussion about European integration has been superficial. Within Czech political parties, European issues are often not discussed substantially, but rather in order to defame political opponents (Haughton 2009: 1385). Even debates between parties do not amount to a true dialogue. Quite often there is a multitude of monologues whose speakers drown each other out. The result is twofold: a fatal lack of consensus concerning the Czech position and priorities within the EU and an image of the Czech Republic abroad as a confused country, which in its solipsism and selfishness refuses to participate in most of the Union's agenda without offering any reasonable alternatives (Drulák 2012, Šlosarčík 2011: 29).[12] On the other hand, these evaluations are often based

---

[12] The process of ratifying the Lisbon Treaty in the Czech Republic provided a remarkable illustration of this statement. The country (together with Poland) not only obstructed the ratification process, it also showed its lack of internal political consensus and an inability to

more on first impressions than on a deep analysis of the situation. Under the superficial appearance of confusion there lies a professional civil service working in close partnership with the EU that is much less problematic than the utterances of top politicians would suggest.

Returning to Czech political leaders and their attitudes towards European integration, two general traits can be identified. First, their narratives are relatively superficial. They are not well thought-out and dynamic political visions. Second, these narratives were developed in the first half of the 1990s, either in connection with the slogan 'Return to Europe' or in opposition to it. When the EU presented a clearer strategy and a roadmap for enlargement in the late 1990s, Czech parties responded by broadening their 'European' discourses without subjecting them to a substantial, qualitative transformation (Havlík 2011a).

A conceptual map of the Czech political debate about European integration will help us to chart the attitudes currently present in Czech political discourse. The map has two dimensions. The first is based on the simple distinction between Eurosceptic and pro-European ('Europeanist') parties. Naturally, both pro-European and Eurosceptic attitudes can be of varying intensity and based on different logics. Thus we may distinguish 'functional' and 'identity' variants of both attitudes. An identity-based attitude indicates a principal, ideologically-driven approval or disapproval of integration, whereas a functional attitude is more strategic and instrumental (Kaniok 2012). The second dimension considers the historical sources of the attitudes towards the EU displayed by the political party or figure. The attitudes can be either autochthonous, stemming from domestic discussion, or they can be the product of imported ideas and ideologies. This dimension is important if we are to understand the degree to which Czech political parties are willing or able to put European integration within the framework of domestic political discourse. One may assume that parties displaying autochthonous attitudes would make a greater effort at Europeanisation, striving to bring domestic and Union policies together. The sources of a party's attitude or narrative can also be mixed.

On the basis of the dimensions defined above, a schematic breakdown of contemporary Czech political parties is presented in Table 10.1. Several conclusions can be drawn on the basis of this conceptual map. First, the main lines of division are between parties who support integration based on ideology

---

straddle the divide between a government pushing for ratification and a president who opposed the treaty (Rybář 2010: 49–53).

or identity and those who oppose integration for instrumental reasons. Instrumental support for the EU and ideological opposition tend to be taken up by marginal parties.

Table 10.1: Conceptual map of the contemporary Czech debate about European integration

	Autochthonous sources of debate	Mixed sources of debate	Imported sources of debate
Identity Europeanism		Westernising narrative TOP 09	Eurofederalist narrative KDU-ČSL ČSSD SZ
Functional Europeanism		ANO	
Functional Euroscepticism		'Eurorealist' narrative ODS Anti-neoliberal narrative KSČM since 2004	
Identity Euroscepticism		Marginal narratives of the extreme right	Libertarian narrative SSO

Source: Dostál and Hloušek 2014 (simplified).

Second, the narratives of autochthonous origin, which were present in the Czech debate during the 1990s (variants of the slogan 'Return to Europe' and the anti-German isolationist rhetoric of the Communists and the Republicans), have practically disappeared. The Czech debate over the EU is mainly fought using arguments imported from abroad. This appears to be connected with the historical shift of the Czech Republic's geopolitical situation.

Few parties have changed their position on Europe. The only noteworthy ones are the transformation of the majority narrative in the ODS from a Westernising ethos towards a 'Eurorealist' narrative in the second half of the

1990s (Hanley 2004)[13] and the move of the communists from identity Euroscepticism towards functional Euroscepticism. Established parties remain relatively consistent in their opinions without bringing new dynamics to the political debate overall (Hloušek and Kaniok 2014: 168–169). Interest in the topic of European integration peaked in the 2002 elections. Since then politicians and their parties have shown declining concern about European issues in their public statements (Hloušek and Pšeja 2011: 115–118).

The conceptual map suggests that pro-integration narratives prevail. While this is true in purely rhetorical terms, in practice parties such as the ČSSD and ANO do not necessarily link their real politics with the effectively federalist European integration narrative they share with their partners abroad like the Party for European Socialists (PES) and the Alliance of Liberals and Democrats for Europe (ALDE). This is evidenced by the position of the pro-integration government of Bohuslav Sobotka, which strongly opposed the EU aid provided to Greece.

10.5. Conclusion

The Europeanisation and Westernisation of the Czech Republic has been and continues to be ambivalent. On the one hand, the country has managed to fully integrate itself into the projects of European and Western political, economic and security cooperation and, at the economic and administrative level, fulfils the requirements of membership in the EU and NATO without serious issues.

On the other hand, the political role of the Czechs in these institutions is at times unclear. The country tends to act as a reluctant ally whose political representatives are none too keen to contribute to the solution of shared problems. In part this is due to the low awareness among Czechs of the importance of international cooperation is for smaller, economically open, trade-dependent, and geopolitically vulnerable countries like theirs. Leading Czech politicians largely view the international dimension of their activities as a mere accessory to, and quite often as an annoying burden on, their domestic agendas, and they are not willing to even consider a greater integration of

---

13 Important in this has been the changing position of Václav Klaus, who during the second half of the 1990s became more critical of European integration.

international (especially 'European') topics into Czech political discourse.[14] In doing so they accommodate the prevailing political culture of the majority, which can appear parochial. When international topics are introduced into the Czech political discourse, it is too often done in a populist and superficial manner, ultimately damaging the interests of the country.

In a country that has too often been in thrall to other states, one might expect there to be a tendency to view national sovereignty as an essential value. But a more probable cause of the prevailing Czech attitude is that Czech political leaders have little to gain from engagement in international and EU politics and are generally not very competent in these fields.[15] Pinning the blame for unpopular measures on the European Union was a popular sport among Czech politicians even before the country's accession to the EU and this practice has changed little during the first decade of Czech membership. The geopolitical position of the state – with no border external to the EU – has lulled Czechs into a false feeling of invulnerability. One also has to consider the fact that, unlike in Hungary, Poland, and Slovakia, the element of modernisation through Europeanisation has not been prominent in Czech political discourse (Guerra 2013; Chapter 2). Although this has somewhat mitigated unrealistic expectations about the benefits of EU accession, it has also weakened the entirely pragmatic awareness of the true extent of the EU's political and economic importance for the Czech Republic.

Table 10.2: Czech and Czechoslovak membership in selected international organisations

Organisation	Czechoslovakia	Czech Republic
Council of Europe (CE)	1991	1993
European Bank for Reconstruction and Development (EBRD)	1990	1993
European Organization for Nuclear Research (CERN)	1992	1993

---

14 The ouster of Mirek Topolánek's government in the middle of the Czech presidency of the European Council provides a crystal-clear example of the ignorance of the international context. Although the presidency was well-managed in administrative terms and relatively successful in terms of the agenda achieved, it was not well presented by Czech politicians in the media (Kaniok and Smekal 2009).
15 For an up-to-date overview of European integration, see Kovář and Hendrych 2015.

International Atomic Energy Agency (IAEA)	1957	1993
International Bank for Reconstruction and Development (IBRD)	1945	1993
International Civil Aviation Organisation (ICAO)	1944	1993
International Criminal Police Organization (INTERPOL)	1990	1993
International Development Association (IDA)	1990	1993
International Investment Bank (IIB)	1978	1993
International Labour Organisation (ILO)	1949	1993
International Monetary Fund (IMF)	1944	1993
International Organisation for Migration (IOM)	-	1995
International Telecommunication Union (ITU)	1918	1993
North-Atlantic Treaty Organisation (NATO)	-	1999
Organisation for Economic Co-Operation and Development (OECD)	-	1995
Organisation for Security and Cooperation in Europe (OSCE, formerly CSCE)	1975	1993
United Nations Educational Scientific and Cultural Organisation (UNESCO)	1945	1993
United Nations Food and Agriculture Organisation (FAO)	1945	1993
United Nations Industrial Development Organisation (UNIDO)	1967	1993
United Nations (UN)	1945	1993
World Health Organisation (WHO)	1946	1993
World Trade Organisation (WTO, formerly GATT)	1948	1993

Source:http://www.mzv.cz/jnp/cz/zahranicni_vztahy/cr_v_mezinarodnich_organizacich/index.html

11. Five ways of looking at Czech politics

Andrew Roberts

It is doubtful that one theory can explain politics in any country, but Czech politics presents particular problems. It was at once the sole surviving democracy in Central and Eastern Europe between the wars and one of the last remaining bastions of totalitarian rule in the 1980s. Since the revolution it has been both the poster child of democracy and economic reform and, in the view of most citizens today, a cesspit of political opportunism and corruption.

Nevertheless, at the conclusion of this book full of detailed analyses of different aspects of Czech politics, it is worth seeing how much of Czech politics can be accounted for by larger theories. That is the aim of this chapter. It considers four major traditions in Czech politics – nationalism, liberalism, egalitarianism, and democratic humanism – along with one additional perspective – self-interest – and assesses how far they can make sense of Czech politics. What can they explain and what can they not explain?

The answer, as suggested above, is that no one theory can get us all or even most of the way there. This is not just the Rashomon point that one can have different perspectives on Czech politics. It is the deeper point that Czech politics is the product of a number of different traditions. Some of these traditions do more work than others: liberalism and egalitarianism seem to be stronger than nationalism and democratic humanism or other even less central traditions such as Catholic conservatism. Rational self-interest is probably the equal of these forces. But again, these are guides to thinking rather than answers.

This analysis should not be seen as a rigorous empirical investigation, but rather as food for thought. Indeed, it is doubtful that politics can be explained in this form at all. If one wanted to put this analysis in political science form, it might be whether culture or rationality better explains politics, but even that question is poorly posed (Whitefield and Evans 1999). Nevertheless, I hope these perspectives can serve as a useful heuristic for readers who are trying to make sense of the mass of information provided in this book.[1]

---

1 Chapters 1 and 2 also provide similar analyses of Czech political traditions.

11.1. Explaining pre-1989 politics

I begin by applying these perspectives to Czech politics in the period from the national awakening in the nineteenth century to the fall of communism. In the second half of the chapter I turn to the postcommunist period.

11.1.1. Awakening a nation: Nationalism

Without the successful national revival of the nineteenth century, we would probably not be speaking of Czech politics today or we would be speaking of it in a radically different way. In that sense at least, nationalism may be the ur-explanation of Czech politics. The belief that there was a Czech people with a claim to their own state and culture did not exist at the beginning of the modern era. But thanks to the efforts of "awakeners" like Josef Dobrovský, Josef Jungmann, František Palacký, and others, Czech speakers, mostly peasants, acquired a literary language and a self-image that set in motion everything that followed.[2]

It may seem inevitable that there is a Czech nation speaking its own language and with an attachment to particular cultural practices, but scholars of nationalism have persuasively shown that national feeling as we know it today emerged at a specific historical moment in the nineteenth century. The contingency involved may be seen in the famous remark that if a single roof had collapsed in Prague, the Czech nation might not exist, so small was the group of revivalists or awakeners. However, it was not all contingency given that Slovaks developed a national identity under far less auspicious circumstances. As Anderson (1991) and Gellner (1983) have shown, larger structural forces like industrialization and print capitalism created fertile conditions for nationalism.

Nationalism is the ur-explanation in another way – it also partially underlays at least two other traditions. The image of Czechness that emerged in the national revival was one that emphasized certain characteristics that I have included here as separate traditions because they took on or were already living a life of their own. One is the democratic-humanist tradition. Palacký and later Tomáš Masaryk portrayed Czechs as inheritors of a democratic and humanist spirit that extended back to the Hussite era and formed a counterpole

---

2 On this process, see Agnew (2004), Hroch (1999), Macura (1998), Sayer (1998) as well as Chapter 1 of this volume.

to German feudalism. The national revival was also strongly linked to egalitarianism. It created a collective of equals – the people – in opposition to the German-speaking upper class.

While one cannot imagine modern Czech history without nationalism, its explanatory power for political developments is less persuasive. The belief that Czechs deserved their own nation can certainly be found during the Austrian-Hungarian Empire and ultimately did produce independence. However, until a relatively late date most leading politicians, including Masaryk, did not embrace independence and saw their mission as the improvement of the position of Czechs within the empire. Similarly, ordinary citizens were happy to become members of patriotic organizations like Sokol and contribute to the flowering of Czech culture, but active resistance to imperial rule was relatively muted, especially compared to other subject nations like the Serbs. Small, improving work by "little Czechs" was the order of the day.

Nationalism certainly did play a role in the First Republic. The land reform in 1918 was portrayed as undoing the Battle of White Mountain when Czechs were definitively subjected to Habsburg rule, though it is hard to dismiss self-interest whenever property is involved. Despite the presence of significant national minorities like Slovaks, Germans, and Hungarians, interwar Czechoslovakia was in many ways a Czech state featuring Czech national symbols and a dominant position for Czech parties who often took nationalist stances. The general failure to integrate the German minority and their ultimate expulsion in 1945 can similarly be viewed through the lens of nationalist feeling, though it is not hard to describe them equally well as the acts of a majority who had much to gain from expropriating and marginalizing German citizens. Contrary to Heimann's (2009) interpretation, not all blame should be put on Czechs. Prior to the Nazi takeover, minority civil rights if not autonomy were respected to a greater degree than in most states at the time.

On the other side of the ledger, nationalism does less well in making sense of Czechs' embrace of a Czechoslovak (as opposed to Czech) identity. This was a creation out of whole cloth which ultimately came to seem natural to many Czechs. Nationalism also does little to explain the failure to fight in 1938, the almost complete absence of a partisan movement resisting Nazi occupation, and the acceptance of forty years of de facto Soviet rule. While prudence could surely be invoked here, a quick comparison with Poland under both Nazi and communist rule shows the weakness of Czech nationalism.

Finally, the communists found it easy to clothe themselves in nationalist garb. As Sayer (1998) argues, the communist identification of the class struggle with the national struggle was possible because Czechness was constructed as a defence of lower class Czechs against German-speaking aristocrats. But again, while nationalist tropes formed part of the official ideology under communism, it is hard to see how they influenced the actual course of politics. They easily coexisted with internationalism and friendship with socialist neighbours. Those persecuted for bourgeois nationalist deviations were inevitably Slovaks, not Czechs. Nationalism is thus a precondition for Czech politics but a weak driver of politics, something that recurs in the present.[3]

11.1.2. Liberals in a liberal empire: Liberalism

By contrast, liberalism in the sense of commitments to civil rights and free markets can be seen as the presiding ideology of Czech politics both under the Habsburg Empire and in the First Republic.[4] Major nineteenth century figures like Karel Havlíček Borovský and Palacký fit relatively well into the liberal tradition. This may be natural for a well-off subject people under a relatively liberal imperial power. Extending their civil and economic rights was the best that Czechs could expect in relation to a ruling power that held an overwhelming advantage in force. It would enable them to continue to develop both economically and culturally.

The liberal tradition continued in attenuated form during the First Republic. Though no one party represented liberal ideals (the National Democrats came the closest), a number of individuals played major roles in the politics of the time. The main exemplars were the architects of the economy of the day, Alois Rašín and Karel Engliš, both followers of Austrian economics, and an influential group of writers including Karel Čapek and Ferdinand Peroutka who helped to shape public attitudes. The First Republic also stood out in its extension of civil rights to national minorities in a region where such a liberal attitude was unusual

While liberal traditions were relatively strong until 1938, they disappeared under the dual onslaught of fascism and communism. Partially it was the failure of liberal politicians to stand up to these threats and provide effective solutions to the problems of the day which turned the public away from liberalism and towards stronger medicines. The communist regime meanwhile

---

3 The interesting question is why the nationalist tradition is so weak.
4 This section draws on Šíma and Nikodym (2015).

was extremely thorough in eliminating liberal ideas from public discourse and expropriating the property-owning classes who were its natural supporters.

One can see a revival of liberalism in the dissident movement of the seventies and eighties, but this movement was diverse, encompassing religious thinkers, humanists, and reform communists in addition to classical liberals. Their lodestars were only partially in the liberal tradition, though dissidents were able to unite in support of the human rights provisions in the Helsinki Accords. Václav Klaus and a handful of like-minded thinkers attempted to resurrect liberalism with a series of seminars and translations in this same era, but this revival applied to a relatively narrow group of intellectuals. While liberalism had a strong history in Czech politics, its influence looked weak on the eve of 1989.

11.1.3. A plebeian nation: Egalitarianism

Egalitarianism here refers to the levelling impulse inherent in both the social democratic and communist traditions. This egalitarianism has its roots deep in Czech history. Habsburg domination after the Battle of White Mountain led to the elimination of a Czech-speaking nobility and the Germanization of the upper and upwardly mobile classes. Czech culture as it was survived mainly among uneducated peasants. Nationalism thus emerged in a country that mostly lacked an upper-class elite who identified with the linguistic conception of the nation which ultimately triumphed.

It was this state of affairs that the national awakeners tried to correct. And they were successful in resurrecting or simply creating Czech culture. But the fact that they created this culture for mostly lower and middle-class Czechs gave their efforts a strong egalitarian or others would say plebeian flavour. The newly-defined nation lacked an aristocracy or natural upper-class and in turn Czechs tended to view each other as equal or potentially equal.[5]

To this could be added the relatively early industrialization of the Czech lands and the creation of a substantial working class and its associated trade unions and left-wing politics. By the end of Habsburg rule, the Social Democrats were the most popular Czech party eclipsing old-fashioned liberals and nationalists.

---

5 Another interpretation would emphasize the trait that many Czechs view as key to the national character: *závist* or envy.

This trend continued in the First Republic whose first acts included outlawing aristocratic titles and establishing an eight-hour working day and unemployment benefits. Politically, the Social Democratic Party participated in most governments and the Communist Party, despite its radical positions, performed well in elections. Concern for the "social problem" of workers and the poor found expression in other parties particularly the dominant National Socialists as well as with the Castle whose influence was considerable. An important part of the cultural elite similarly inclined to social democratic or communist ideologies, for example, writers like Vitězslav Nezval, Ivan Olbracht, and Vladislav Vančura.

Public support for the left only expanded after the war when right-wing parties were unfairly banned because of their perceived association with fascism. The Communist Party won the free elections of 1946 and the Social Democratic Party also received considerable support. President Edvard Beneš, the main surviving pillar of interwar democracy, gave his blessing to this leftward drift. Though it required a coup and other less than democratic machinations for the communists to take power, it could be argued that Czechoslovakia was the one satellite state where the public largely supported a communist takeover and egalitarian traditions were a major reason why. As mentioned earlier, the equation of Czechness and the people made by the national awakeners fit well with communist ideology and the Communists thus took advantage of almost the entire arsenal of nationalist tropes from Hus to the gloom of the counter-reformation to the national awakening itself.

Though public support obviously faded as the party's totalitarian practices and corruption became apparent, the experience of communism did not eliminate it. Many of the participants in the Prague Spring and the dissident movement wanted only to reform socialism not to end it. Moreover, the general weakness of opposition to communism in the Czech lands could be taken as some testimony to its resonance with much of the population.

11.1.4. The meaning of Czech history: democratic humanism

It is the tradition of democratic humanism that the national awakeners put on a pedestal when they created the modern Czech nation. Their attention was on historical figures like Jan Hus, Petr Chelčický, and Jan Ámos Komenský whose visions of peace and human brotherhood were portrayed as the unique Czech contribution to European and world history. In more standard terminology, one might call this the communitarian tradition. While this idea clearly overlaps with the liberal and nationalist traditions described above, one can see a distinct democratic humanist vision emerging at several key moments in Czech political history.

Masaryk, Alexander Dubček, and Václav Havel are the main exemplars of this tradition. Masaryk's initial engagements in politics seemed to echo Hus's famous slogan "The truth shall prevail." He punctured nationalist illusions in the controversy over the authenticity of supposedly ancient Czech manuscripts and advocated for Leopold Hilsner, a Jew unjustly accused of ritual murder.[6] Masaryk's conception of democracy as discussion among equals who are sincerely searching for truth belongs here as well. One could even include the political system of the First Republic as it relied on broad coalitions and consensus to govern (though it also excluded certain groups).

Dubček is a slightly more problematic case. Though a confirmed communist, it is not a coincidence that he advocated socialism with a "human" face and that this movement rather than a more liberal alternative resonated with Czechs. It is worth emphasizing here the long-standing tradition of viewing the president as a benevolent patron who would stand above politics and directly take care of the people. Democratic humanism means not democracy as the conflict of opposing forces, but munificent governance to the benefit of all.

The dissident movement provides another example. Though it encompassed diverse strands of thinking from Trotskyism through Catholic conservatism, its uniting element was a sense that morality needed to be returned to politics. Havel's "living in truth", again with obvious links to Hus, was central as was his conception of apolitical politics. The major caveat here is that dissent never spread beyond a small group of artists and intellectuals who numbered only a few hundred even as the regime was falling. These ideas however did inspire the Velvet Revolution whose great contribution according to Krapfl (2013) was not any ideology or "ism" but a focus on humaneness or human dignity.

More broadly one can argue that pacifism and non-violence dominate Czech politics from the very start of the modern age. The national awakeners portrayed Czechs and Slavs generally as a dove-like people (*holubičí národ*). With the exception of the Czech legionnaires of World War I, one sees almost nothing but peaceful resistance to the Habsburgs, Nazis, and Communists.

---

6 Masaryk's actual motives appear to be less rooted in humanism than in a desire to protect the image of Czechs as forward-thinking and not in thrall to medieval superstition.

Though it is an anachronism to put it this way, the Czech army has arguably not actively defended the nation since the Battle of White Mountain in 1620.[7] Whether this is motivated by democratic humanism, the weakness of nationalism, or pure self-preservation is a matter of debate.

Of course, it is easy enough to find counterexamples to this humanist tradition whether the undemocratic practices of the leaders of First Republic (often pursued in the name of democracy), the expulsion of the Germans, or enthusiasm, at least initially, for communist repression. This tradition may emerge only at critical moments like 1918, 1968, and 1989 or in exceptional individuals.

11.1.5. The Good Soldier Švejk, Mr. Brouček, and Father Kondelík: Self-Interest

It is probably unfair to consider self-interest a Czech political tradition, but it does have its resonances in folk conceptions of the Czech character whether the concern with comfort (*pohoda*) and peace and quiet (*to chce klid* – take it easy), the national trait of envy, or an avoidance of conflict (*já nic, já muzikant* – I'm just a musician). Classic literary portrayals include Ignát Hermann's hidebound shopkeeper Father Kondelík, Svatopluk Čech's Mr. Brouček who travels through time but remains manifestly his limited self, and Jaroslav Hašek's seemingly dim-witted but self-preserving Švejk (Jedlička 2009). As just mentioned, the lack of resistance to rule by the Habsburgs, Nazis, Communists, and Soviet invaders can all be seen in this light, probably more accurately than as a result of conscious opposition to violence or weakness of national feeling.

One can see these tendencies in the elites of the First Republic who formed a cartel called "The Five" (*Pětka*) and came to prearranged agreements to preserve their own positions. They used this power to extend their tentacles deep into the bureaucracy. The Christian Democratic Party has consistently epitomized this approach where the important thing is not ideology or the public interest but having a seat at the table. The philosopher Jan Patočka identified this tendency in the unwillingness of Czech politicians to make tough, risky decisions (Gellner 1994). The tradition encompasses not just self-interest, but short-term, misguided self-interest.

---

7 At the same time, Havel has claimed that every major European war began in the Czech lands.

Communism which purportedly banished self-interest can also be seen as in fact encouraging a bastardized form of self-interest. One got ahead not by working hard and behaving well but by stealing from the state and informing on one's neighbours and co-workers. The manifest failures of the regime also led citizens to retreat from the public sphere and find fulfilment in private life (Bren 2010).

Indeed, just about every example of policies that illustrate nationalism, liberalism, and egalitarianism can be interpreted as materially benefitting its main drivers. Nationalists would benefit from being able to rise higher in political and cultural spheres if they had a state of their own. Liberals and leftists with their attendant bases in the middle or working classes mostly stood to benefit economically from the policies or the regime they advocated. Democratic humanists may be the exception here in that their benefits were more a matter of prestige than the pocketbook.

***

If one had to rank these influences from weakest to strongest, one might come up with something like the following. Nationalism laid the basis for Czech politics, but appears to be a weaker driver of events than in neighbouring countries. Liberalism and democratic humanism have their moments – before 1938 in the case of liberalism and at a handful of moments for humanism – but they also have their blank spots. Egalitarianism and self-interest, by contrast, are a continuous presence in Czech politics.

11.2. Explaining postcommunist politics

How much do these same traditions help us to understand the Czech present, democratic politics since 1989? Surprisingly, they do relatively well. The egalitarian tradition is still strong while nationalism and democratic humanism mostly remain weak. The most interesting development is the resurgence of liberalism after a period of dormancy, but again this fits well with pre-communist traditions. And few would doubt that the transition provided ample opportunities for self-enrichment that Czech politicians were more than willing to take advantage of.

11.2.1. Latent nationalism?

Even as nationalism remains a precondition for Czech politics, its explanatory power in the post-1989 era remains weak. This contrasts with most of its neighbours who feature not only strong nationalist cleavages but also significant nationalist parties. The Velvet Revolution was certainly seen in terms of national liberation and extracting the country from Soviet hegemony, but it was equally portrayed as a return to Europe. Compared to Slovakia, desire for an independent Czech state was relatively weak, though it was quickly accepted. Giving up Czechoslovakia was felt as a loss to most Czechs albeit not a great one.

The strongest appearance of Czech nationalism came with the success of Miroslav Sládek's xenophobic Republican Party in the elections of 1992 and 1996, but this movement proved to be short-lived and left little residue. There has recently been something of a revival with Tomio Okamura's Dawn Party and its platform of opposition to immigration and foreigners. More lasting and substantial has been Czech support for the Beneš decrees and suspicion of the former Sudeten Germans. Scepticism about the European Union can be included in this category, but despite prominent representatives for this point of view, ordinary Czechs manifest less of the hostility to Europe than can be found in their postcommunist neighbours. Attitudes could better be described as lukewarm. Important parts of each of these trends can be traced more to economic fears than to concerns with sovereignty and national assertion.

Strident expressions of nationalism are all but absent from Czech political discourse. This is not to say that Czechs lack national pride. Rather this pride is expressed more in cultural and scientific achievements than in worries that the nation is threatened by outsiders. Recently, however, there have been signs that nationalism is re-emerging in the rhetoric of the presidential office under both Václav Klaus and Miloš Zeman. It remains to be seen whether the migration crisis which has fanned the most recent outbreak is a temporary blip or a long-term trend.

11.2.2. Liberalism temporarily triumphant?

Possibly the most interesting trend of the postcommunist era is the revival and even for a time the dominance of liberal thought. In one sense this was a reaction against communism. Besides the euphoria of the revolution itself, the most welcome changes from 1989 were a number of basic civil rights. Prime among them were the freedom to travel, the freedom to choose what to read, listen to, and watch, the freedom to start a business, and the freedom to choose where to work (or whether to work). These basic liberal values form the most positive connotations of the new regime and are the things that very few are willing to part with no matter how nostalgic they are for communism.

However, there is a stronger sense in which liberalism triumphed. Here I am referring to neoliberalism, the intention to create a market economy without adjectives. It was Václav Klaus who promoted this vision, first as Minister of Finance and then as Prime Minister. Somewhat surprisingly the public bought into his vision hook, line, and sinker. Klaus's party, the Civic Democrats, contested and won the 1992 elections on a platform of mass privatization, price liberalization, and deregulation (Appel 2004). They managed to put in place much of this liberal vision and uniquely in the region win re-election even after the consequences of reform became clear. Liberalism extended even beyond the economy (though Klaus had less to do with these trends). The Czech Republic has been among the most tolerant states in the region on same-sex relationships, drug use, and sex work (attitudes towards Roma are different).

There are of course caveats. As the chapter on economic reforms outlines, Klaus's government made compromises and some have even labelled his strategy social liberal rather than neoliberal due to the maintenance of many social guarantees and government control of banks (Orenstein 2001). Nevertheless, the fact that an avowedly liberal program could continue in power for the first eight years of the transition and even nearly win elections in 1998 is testament as much to the attractions of liberalism among Czech citizens as to the political genius of Klaus.

There has been some weakening of this liberalism since then. While ODS mostly remained a liberal party, Klaus himself focused more on nationalist and Eurosceptical appeals. The mantle of liberalism thus passed to less dominant parties like Freedom Union and today TOP 09. Meanwhile the Social Democrats, described below, became something closer to the default party of power. Nevertheless, among postcommunist countries, the Czech Republic may be counted, along with the Baltic states, as one where liberalism triumphed.

11.2.3. Egalitarians forever

Though it appeared for a time after the revolution that the egalitarian ethos had disappeared with the defeat of communism, it soon re-emerged. Or possibly never left. Večerník (1996) characterizes that early period as "Think Left, Vote

Right". Citizens continued to believe in social guarantees but nevertheless voted for parties committed to dismantling them because of the obvious failures of communism. This meant that reforms like mass privatization and price liberalization were accompanied by employment protections, rent controls, and a guaranteed minimum income.

Once the defeat of the communist system was confirmed and the Social Democrats managed to resurrect themselves as a democratic alternative, citizens could thus indulge their "left thinking" and vote confidently for the Social Democrats who have since 1998 become something like the party of power, consistently receiving 25 to 30% of votes while other parties, including even ODS, fell by the wayside. And to these results can be added the equally consistent appeal of the Communist Party to something like 10–15 % of the citizenry. If not for the exclusion of the Communists from government and policy making, the Social Democrats would have been even more dominant.

The egalitarian ethos is reflected in policy as well. Although right-wing parties have attempted to roll back the welfare state in areas like healthcare, pensions, and taxes, the result has usually been some version of the status quo or small changes around the edges. The egalitarian ethos in its anticlerical guise meanwhile delayed Church restitution for over two decades and when it finally took place it was at great cost to its right-wing supporters.

The main failure of the egalitarian ethos is in the total isolation of the unreformed Communist Party and a continued attachment of the majority to anti-communist rhetoric. A communist past is still a burden for democratic politicians and lustration laws were among the strongest in the region. It is worth noting as well that Social Democrats were among the most committed supporters of European integration even though this implied many concessions to neoliberal policies.

11.2.4. A philosopher king

For the outside world, the Czech Republic represents the triumph of the democratic humanist ideal. The events of 1989 seemed to exemplify this impression. The transition was velvety – citizens peacefully marched and the regime quietly toppled. In Václav Havel the country had a philosopher president who gave voice to these ideals on an international stage through his defence of Tibetans, Bosnians, and Kosovars. Havel's influence at home was not inconsiderable either, mainly in helping to create a viable opposition to liberal dominance.

The influence of Havel and the Castle bloc more generally can be seen in the drawing of a "thick line" between the communist regime and the present and their efforts were important in getting the Czech Republic into NATO. Finding themselves shut out of domestic politics by the late 1990s, the democratic humanists then spent most of their political capital pushing for entry into the European Union which they saw as a guarantor and supporter of their ideals.

However, many of Havel's dreams were left unfulfilled. Though his brainchild, Civic Forum, dominated the first free elections in 1990, its successors like the Civic Movement and the Democratic Union quickly fell by the wayside. His hopes for a more apolitical politics and for closer links between citizens and their representatives were not included in the new constitution. Instead, it was the liberal vision of democracy as a competition between opposing ideologies that won out, though Havel's vision survived in the influence of the purportedly non-partisan presidency and in a political system that created many checks on power and required broad consensus for important decisions.

Similarly, Havel's advocacy of civil society and civic engagement had only sporadic results in short-lived movements like *Děkujeme, odejděte* (Thank you, now leave), *Impuls 99*, or F—k Communism. Overall civil society has been weak. Instead, once citizens had soured on the ruling parties, they were more likely to turn to technocratic or populist solutions rather than democratic ones.[8] While the democratic humanist ideal was frequently represented in parties like Freedom Union and TOP 09 (and personalities like Karel Schwarzenberg), their influence has been more on the margins than at the centre of Czech politics.

11.2.5. Naked self-interest and nothing but

If citizens were queried today on the main force in Czech politics, it is self-interest which would probably emerge victorious. While the first post-revolutionary decade looked like a classic contest of left and right, the subsequent period has seemed to degenerate into every man for himself. Corruption has become the main symbol of this change and organizations like Transparency International have indeed found worsening levels of corruption

---

8 These technocratic solutions can to be seen as part of this tradition as they draw on the idea of a just and benevolent leader who will rescue the nation.

in the country. And while earlier corruption scandals seemed to be the price of building markets and parties, later corruption appears to be the result of more transparent greed with the prototypical example being the mysterious defection of two Social Democratic MPs to help form a right-wing government in 2006.

It is not just corruption either. Politicians appear to be increasingly willing to say whatever it takes to get elected, leading to a gap between pledges and reality. Again, this is not a new phenomenon and it may be as much due to weak governments as political cynicism, but it has become increasingly salient. Personality conflicts – for example, between Havel and Klaus or more recently Andrej Babiš and Miroslav Kalousek – have similarly stood in the way of reasonable compromises. The symbol of this style of politics is the opposition contract in which the two main left and right-wing parties united simply to eliminate their rivals rather than because of any commonalities in their programmes (Kopeček 2015).

Citizens are not blameless in this problem. They have mostly pursued their private interests rather than engaging in politics. Turnout has declined and other means of participation remain weak. There have been occasional outbursts of dissatisfaction, but they tend to be short-lived and mostly increase distrust in existing parties and politicians instead of creating new viable alternatives. Another problem has been voters' desire for simple solutions and their unwillingness to accept compromises. Few elites or citizens have subscribed to Weber's description of politics as the strong and slow boring of hard boards.

11.3. Do these traditions matter?

It is fun to juxtapose these visions of Czech politics, but a more cynical observer might challenge whether any of them truly matter. As a small nation surrounded by larger ones, the Czech Republic may simply be a pawn. Yes, the skilful actions of Masaryk and others helped to create a Czechoslovak state, but what is the counterfactual? Even groups without such skilful leaders ended up with their own state when empires were dismantled in 1918. Did they really "earn their state" (as the Czech phrase puts it – *zasloužili se o stát*) or did it fall into their lap.

The same goes for the communist takeover. Did it really depend so much on domestic support for the Communists and Social Democrats? Again, can one imagine the counterfactual – a state liberated by the Red Army and reaching the borders of the Soviet Union that was also democratic and maintained good relations with both sides? Could Czechoslovakia have been something like Finland in the heart of Europe?

Even 1989 which is lionized as the triumph of people power seems foreordained. It was not Czechoslovakia which started the dominos falling but Poland or more accurately Gorbachev. Is there any conceivable scenario in which Czechoslovakia remained communist or the revolution took a less velvety form? Did its own decisions matter very much? Petr Fidelius points out the contradiction between Havel's praise of civil society as the motor of revolution and his despair over its weakness (Gellner 1994).

And how much of post-1989 developments are conscious choices? The moves towards democracy and a market economy are something that all of their neighbours made, to be sure at different speeds and with different shadings, but the ultimate outcomes were not so different. As a small economy, the Czech Republic has relatively little room for manoeuvre on economic policy – it is in the words of scholars a "dependent market economy" (Nölke and Vliegenthart 2009). Similarly, in international relations, it was not just the Czech Republic who entered NATO and the EU but all of its neighbours near and far. Yes, things could have turned out a bit worse democratically – witness Slovakia or now Hungary and Poland – or slightly better economically, but it is hard to see dramatically different paths for a country in the Czech Republic's place.

A number of scholars have put this idea to statistical tests and found that geography plays a large role in democracy and economic reform whether through the direct intervention of neighbours or simply exchanges with them (Kopstein and Reilly 2000, Shleifer and Treisman 2014). Of course, geography does not explain everything. If we follow Czech politics with a microscope rather than a telescope – that is, if we focus on day-to-day or even year-to-year happenings – then the traditions described above gain much more traction. But it is worth bearing in mind the limited space in which Czech politics takes place. Indeed, one might argue that its size is precisely the cause of problems, the narcissism of small differences.

11.4. Conclusion

How can we explain postcommunist Czech politics? Bearing in mind the caveat from the previous section that small nations surrounded by great powers work under considerable constraints, we can still draw a number of conclusions. The first is the relatively limited role that nationalism plays in Czech politics. In this the Czech Republic differs from its most similar neighbours. The appeals of the past two presidents to care more about national sovereignty and to resist the intrusions of the European Union have yet to play a major role in politics. Czechs are both secure enough in their national identity and pragmatic enough in their decisions that passionate nationalism has been little more than an attention grabber for marginal politicians.

The same goes for the democratic humanist tradition. Havel and others in this tradition have served as icons for many Czechs, but their example has proved too hard to imitate. Most would concede that the country has been well-served, particularly abroad, by having figures who can act as the nation's conscience, but their influence has again been on the margin rather than at the centre of Czech politics, except at a handful of important moments like 1989.

Liberalism and egalitarianism give us a much better sense of the contours of current Czech politics. The main axis of competition is between right and left, between liberals pushing for a smaller state and lower taxes and social democrats in favour of more social protection. Yes, other issues have occasionally intruded – the Christian Democrats have tried to bring religious issues into the arena and Euroscepticism has played a role – but the liberal and egalitarian traditions have dominated. And this is in keeping with Czech history as these are the traditions that dominated Czech politics before communism and in the case of egalitarianism even during the communist era.[9]

If there is a competitor to these traditions it is self-interest. This is of course a human universal; just try to name the country where politicians do not pursue their own interests. But for many the lack of political idealism after the revolution is striking. It is easy enough to link this tendency to the problems with democracy in the country. Citizens have all but lost faith in their political

---

9 Are any traditions left out of this account? A more complete account would discuss the role of religion in Czech politics. Except for the communist era, traditional-minded Catholics have usually had a small but significant role in governance through the People's Party. Equally significant, however, is the role of anti-clericalism, which comes closer to being a majority belief and can be seen in the strong opposition to Church restitution in the postcommunist era.

leaders and most see Czech democracy as functioning poorly. Czech political scientists have called it an "ineffective regime", a "defective democracy", or "politics as it shouldn't be" (Kubát 2013, Klíma 2015, Fiala 2010).

Can we attribute this problem to the Czech character or to the way that the Czech character was deformed by communism? I am hesitant to go so far. Are the problems in Czech politics so much more severe than its neighbours? Arguably they are less severe and problems caused by ideological commitment (witness Poland) seem worse than those caused by venality.

Context can explain a lot as well. Czech politicians faced greater temptations than their counterparts in the West – an overgrown bureaucracy, an economy almost entirely owned by the state, and underdeveloped courts, police, and media which should serve as counterweights. The country has also had to create a new political class where few had independent sources of wealth that would allow them to ignore these temptations. The point here is not to explain and therefore to forgive. Politics can and should be better, but it is understandable why it is the way it is and it is easy to imagine how it might be worse.

This raises the question of what needs to change for Czech politics to improve. Is it a matter of culture and reducing the degree of short-sighted self-interest in favour of one of the other ideologies? Or is it a matter of fixing the country's institutions so that, as James Madison put it, "ambition can be made to counteract ambition"? These are among the major debates among Czech political observers today.

At least since Peroutka, Czech thinkers have liked to pose the question *"Jací jsme?"* or "What Are We Like?" In politics, at least, we might say that Czechs and their politicians oscillate between the poles of liberalism and social democracy with an unfortunate tendency to put their personal comfort and interests above the national interest. This is not an earth-shattering conclusion, but it is somewhat heartening. It is a vision of "normal" politics, the kind that citizens in the country once envied. Is it enough? Time will tell.

References

Sources

Aktuálne problémy slovenskej spoločnosti, máj 1991. 1992. Bratislava: Ústav pre sociálnu analýzu Univerzity Komenského.
Constitution of the Czech Republic, Constitutional Act No 1/1993 Sb.
Constitutional Law on the Czechoslovak Federation, No. 143/1968 Sb.
CVVM. 2010. *Vztah Čechů k vybraným národnostem – prosinec 2010.* Praha: CVVM (http://cvvm.soc.cas.cz/media/com_form2content/documents/c1/a3816/f3/101094 s_ov110131.pdf; accessed on: 20160505)
CVVM. 2012. *Rozdělení Československa: Dvacet let od vzniku samostatné ČR a SROV.* Praha: CVVM (http://cvvm.soc.cas.cz/media/com_form2content/documents/c1/a6920/f3/po121204d.pdf; accessed on: 20160505).
CVVM. 2013. *Prestiž povolání.* Centrum pro výzkum veřejného mínění, 3. září 2013.
CVVM. 2013. *Občané o přijetí eura – duben 2013.* Centrum pro výzkum veřejného mínění (http://cvvm.soc.cas.cz/media/com_form2content/documents/c1/a7005/f3/pm130503.pdf; accessed on: 20160505).
Czech statistical office. 2015. *Česká republika: hlavní makroekonomické ukazatele* (https://www.czso.cz/documents/10180/20555309/HLMAKRO.xls/c23e8933-37f c-437c-93af-33a8ff1e4266?version=1.0; accessed on: 20160505).
Čarnogurský, Ján. 1997. Prejav na sneme v Žiline 9. novembra 1991. In: *Videné od Dunaja.* Ján Čarnogurský. Bratislava: Kalligram.
Červenka, Jan. 2015. *Občané o přijetí eura a dopadech vstupu ČR do EU, duben 2015.* Praha: CVVM (http://cvvm.soc.cas.cz/media/com_form2content/documents/c1/a7382/f3/pm150512.pdf; accessed on: 20160505).
ČTK. 2014. *Vývoj od listopadu 1989 nesplnil očekávání většiny Čechů i Slováků* (http://www.ceskenoviny.cz/zpravy/vyvoj-od-listopadu-1989-nesplnil-ocekavani-vetsiny-cechu-i-slovaku/1147913; accessed on: 20160505).
Directive No. 176/2015 Coll. (nález Ústavního soudu ze dne 19. května 2015 sp. zn. Pl. ÚS 14/14 ve věci návrhu na zrušení § 47 a § 48 odst. 1 zákona No. 62/2003 Sb., o volbách do Evropského parlamentu a o změně některých zákonů).
EU – Enlargement – Accession criteria – European Commission (http://ec.europa.eu/enlargement/policy/glossary/terms/accession-criteria_en.htm; accessed on: 20160505).
Feierabend, Karel Ladislav. 1994, 1994, 1996. *Politické vzpomínky I.–III.* Brno: Atlantis.
Fierlinger, Zdeněk. 1949. *Ve službách ČSR.* Praha.
Havel, Václav. 1992a. *Vážení občané. Projevy červenec 1990 – červenec 1992.* Praha: Nakladatelství Lidové noviny.

Havel, Václav. 1992b. Několik poznámek na téma české ústavy. In: *Prezident republiky Václav Havel a jeho vliv na československý a český právní řád*. Eds. Brigita Chrastilová and Petr Mikeš. Praha: ASPI.
Havel, Václav. 1993. *The Art of the Impossible: Politics as Morality in Practice*. New York: Knopf.
Havel, Václav. 1999. Spisy VII. Projevy a jiné texty z let 1992–1999. Praha: Torst.
Havelka, Miloš. Ed.; 1995 a 2006. Spor o smysl českých dějin 1. 1895–1938 a 2. 1938–1989. Praha: Torst.
Chludilová, Iva. 2004. *Spokojenost s politickou situací*. Centrum pro výzkum veřejného mínění (CVVM) (http://cvvm.soc.cas.cz/media/com_form2content/documents/c1/a3086/f3/100356s_ps40531.pdf; accessed on: 20160505).
IVVM. 1991. Názory čs. veřejnosti na státoprávní uspořádání a konání referenda, listopad 1991. Praha: IVVM.
IVVM. 1992. Názory čs. veřejnosti na státoprávní uspořádání a na referendum, červen 1992. Praha: IVVM.
Jakeš, Milouš. 1989. *Projev generálního tajemníka ÚV KSČ Miloše Jakeše v Červeném Hrádku dne 17. července 1989* (http://www.totalita.cz/txt/txt_o_jakesm_text_hradek_01.pdf; accessed on: 20160505).
Kunštát, Daniel. 2013a. *Důvěra ústavním institucím a spokojenost s politickou situací*. Centrum pro výzkum veřejného mínění (CVVM) (http://cvvm.soc.cas.cz/media/com_form2content/documents/c1/a6975/f3/pi130327.pdf; accessed on: 20160505).
Kunštát, Daniel. 2015. *Stranické preference a volební model v listopadu 2015*. Centrum pro výzkum veřejného mínění (CVVM) (http://cvvm.soc.cas.cz/media/com_form 2content/documents/c1/a7458/f3/pv151120.pdf; accessed on: 20160505).
Lidové noviny. 1992. Bude snaha o kompromis? *Lidové noviny* 8.12.1992.
Masaryk, Tomáš Garrigue. 1894. *Česká otázka*. Praha.
Motejl, Otakar. 1999. *Záznam z tiskové konference po schůzi vlády ČR ve středu 7. července 1999* (http://www.vlada.cz/cz/clenove-vlady/historie-minulych-vlad/tiskova-konference-po-schuzi-vlady-cr-7--7--1999-1043/; accessed on: 20160505).
Náboženské vyznání obyvatelstva podle výsledků sčítání lidu v letech 1921–1991. 1995. Praha: Český statistický úřad.
Nález Ústavního soudu ze dne 10. 9. 2009, Pl. ÚS 27/09, Kauza Melčák – zkrácení volebního období Poslanecké sněmovny jednorázovým ústavním zákonem.
OECD. 2015. Revenue Statistics – Comparative tables. Total tax revenue 1965–2013 (http://stats.oecd.org/Index.aspx).
Poslední hurá. Tajné stenografické záznamy z posledních zasedání ÚV KSČ v listopadu 1989. 1992. Praha: Cesty.
Přímá volba poslanců (www.primavolbaposlancu.cz; accessed on: 20160505).
Ripka, Hubert. 1995. Únorová tragédie. Svědectví přímého účastníka. Brno: Atlantis.
SLDB 2011 (https://www.czso.cz/csu/sldb; accessed on: 20160505).

Special Eurobarometer, biotechnology. 2010. (http://ec.europa.eu/public_opinion/archives/ebs/ebs_341_en.pdf; accessed on: 20160505).
The Visegrad Group: the Czech Republic, Hungary, Poland and Slovakia. 1991. *Visegrad Declaration.* (http://www.visegradgroup.eu/documents/visegrad-declarations/visegrad-declaration-110412; accessed on: 20160505).
Vládní finanční statistika – 2014. 2014. (http://www.mfcr.cz/cs/verejny-sektor/monitoring/statistika-vladniho-sektoru/2014/vladni-financni-statistika-21676; accessed on: 20160505).
Zákon No. 345/2014 Sb. o státním rozpočtu ČR na rok 2015.
Zpráva o finanční stabilitě 2014/2015. Praha: Česká národní banka (http://www.akatcr.cz/download/3269-fs_2014-2015.pdf; accessed on: 20160505).

Literature

Agnew, Hugh LeCaine. 2004. *The Czechs and the Lands of the Bohemian Crown.* Stanford: Hoover Institution Press.
Almond, Gabriel A. and Verba, Sidney. 1965. *The Civic Culture.* Boston, MA: Little, Brown and Company.
Anderson, Benedict. 1991. Imagined Communities: Reflections on the Origin and Spread of Nationalism. London: Verso.
Appel, Hilary. 2004. A New Capitalist Order: Privatization and Ideology in Russia and Eastern Europe. Pittsburgh: University of Pittsburgh Press.
Asmus, Ronald D. 2002. Opening NATO's Door: How the Alliance Remade Itself for a New Era. New York: Columbia University Press.
Bahýľová, Lenka. 2010. Parlament. In: *Ústava České republiky. Komentář.* Lenka Bahýľová et al. Praha: Linde 2010.
Bakke, Elisabeth. 2004. The making of Czechoslovakism in the First Republic. In: *Loyalitäten im polyethnischen, multikonfessionellen Staat: Die Erste Tschechoslowakische Republik 1918–1938.* Ed. Martin Schulze Wessel. München: Collegium Carolinum.
Balík, Stanislav. 2005. Institucionální stránka krajské politiky. In: *Krajské volby v České republice 2004.* Eds. Stanislav Balík and Jakub Kyloušek. Brno: MU.
Balík, Stanislav. 2009. Komunální politika. Obce, aktéři a cíle místní politiky. Praha: Grada.
Balík, Stanislav. 2010. Neuskutečněné předčasné volby 2009. In: *Volby do Poslanecké sněmovny v roce 2010.* Ed. Stanislav Balík. Brno: Centrum pro studium demokracie a kultury.
Balík, Stanislav. 2012. *Studie ke komunálním volbám 2010.* Brno: Masarykova univerzita.
Balík, Stanislav. 2015. Democratisation in Czechoslovakia. Political and Social Institutions. In: *Helsinki Process, Velvet Revolution of 1989 and the Czech*

Transformation: Lessons for Korean Peninsula? Ed. Alexandr Vondra. Praha: CEVRO Institut Academic Press.

Balík, Stanislav, Lukáš Fasora, Jiří Hanuš and Marek Vlha. 2015 *Český antiklerikalismus v letech 1848–1938*. Praha: Argo.

Balík, Stanislav, Petr Gongala and Kamil Gregor. 2015. *Dvacet let komunálních voleb v ČR*. Brno: Centrum pro studium demokracie a kultury.

Balík, Stanislav and Jiří Hanuš. 2007 *Katolická církev v Československu 1945–1989*. Brno: Centrum pro studium demokracie a kultury.

Balík, Stanislav and Jan Holzer. 2005. Moderní teorie totalitarismu a její česká reflexe. In: *Totalitarismus*. Ed. Ivo T. Budil. Plzeň: FF ZČU.

Balík, Stanislav, Jan Holzer and Lubomír Kopeček. 2008. Czechoslovakia in 1989 – a case of successful transition. *Totalitarismus und Demokratie*, Göttingen, Vol. 5, No. 1.

Balík, Stanislav et al. 2003. *Politický systém českých zemí 1848–1989*. Brno: MU.

Baltl, Hermann and Gernot Kocher. 1997. Österreichische Rechtsgeschichte. Von den Anfängen bis zur Gegenwart. 9. Auflage. Graz: Leykam.

Bartuška, Václav. 1990. *Polojasno*. Praha: Ex libris.

Bautzová, Libuše. 1999. Program hotov, otazníky zůstávají. *Ekonom*. April 22, 1999

Bělohradský, Václav. 2000. Antipolitika v Čechách. In: *Česká konzervativní a liberální politika*. Eds. Petr Fiala and František Mikš. Brno: Centrum pro studium demokracie a kultury.

Benda, Marek. 2008. *Restituční proces v 90-tých letech*. Diplomová práce. Plzeň: Západočeská univerzita v Plzni, Právnická fakulta.

Beneš, Edvard. 1946a. *Demokracie dnes a zítra*. Praha: Čin.

Beneš, Edvard. 1946b. *Šest let exilu a druhé světové války*. Praha: Orbis.

Berend, Ivan T. 2006. *An Economic History of Twntieth-Century*. Los Angeles: University of California.

Boyer, John W. 1986. The End of an Old Regime: Visions of Political Reform in Late Imperial Austria. *The Journal of Modern History*, Vol. 58, No. 1.

Brandes, Detlef. 2002. *Cesta k vyhnání 1938–1945: plány a rozhodnutí o "transferu" Němců z Československa a z Polska*. Praha: Prostor.

Brauneder, Wilhelm. 1987. Parlamentarismus und Parteiensystem in der Österreichisch-Cisleithanischen Reichshälfte 1867–1918. In: *Das Parteienwesen Österreich-Ungarns*. Ed. Gábor Erdődy. Budapest: Akadémiai kiádo.

Brauneder, Wilhelm and Friedrich Lachmayer. 1992. Österreichische Verfassungsgeschichte. 6. durchgesehene und ergänzte Auflage. Vienna: Manz.

Bren, Paulina. 2010. The Greengrocer and his TV: The Culture of Communism after the 1968 Praha Spring. Ithaca: Cornell University Press.

Brokl, Lubomír. 1999. Cleavages and Parties prior to 1989 in the Czech Republic. In: *Cleavages, Parties, and Voters: Studies from Bulgaria, the Czech Republic,*

Hungary, Poland, and Romania. Eds. Kay Lawson, Andrea Römmele, Andrea and Georgi Karasimenov. Westport: Praeger.
Broklová, Eva. 1992. Československá demokracie. Politický systém ČSR 1918–1938. Praha: Slon.
Brunclík, Miloš 2008a. Spory o zahraniční politiku ČR: prezident vs. premiér. In: *Postavení hlavy státu v parlamentních a poloprezidentských režimech: Česká republika v komparativní perspektivě*. Eds. Miroslav Novák and Miloš Brunclík. Praha: Dokořán.
Brunclík, Miloš. 2008b. Role prezidenta při vládních krizích v České republice. In: *Postavení hlavy státu v parlamentních a poloprezidentských režimech: Česká republika v komparativní perspektivě*. Eds. Miroslav Novák and Miloš Brunclík. Praha: Dokořán.
Brunclík, Miloš. 2011. Rozpouštěcí právo v ČR v komparativní perspektivě. *Acta Politologica*, Vol. 3, No. 2.
Brunclík, Miloš. 2013. Mezi Berlínem a Paříží: Kam kráčí politický režim České republiky? In: *O komparativní politologii a současné české politice*. Eds. Michal Kubát, Tomáš Lebeda. Praha: Karolinum.
Bulínová, Marie, Milena Janišová and Karel Kaplan. Eds. 1994. *Církevní komise ÚV KSČ 1949–1951*. Praha: Ústav pro soudobé dějiny AV ČR.
Bunce, Valerie. 1999. Subversive Institutions: The Design and the Destruction of Socialism and the State. New York: Cambridge University Press.
Bunce, Valerie. 2004. Federalism, Nationalism and Secession: The Communist and Postcommunist Experience. In: *Federalism and Territorial Cleavages*. Eds. Ugo M. Amoretti and Nancy Bermeo. Baltimore, MD: Johns Hopkins University.
Bureš, Jan. 2012. Volby 2010 v České republice: fenomén nových stran TOP 09 a VV. *Politics in Central Europe*, Vol. 8, No. 2.
Bútora, Martin and Bútorová, Zora. 2003. Neznesiteľná ľahkost rozchodu. In: *Dělení Československa. Deset let poté...* Ed. Karel Vodička. Praha: Volvox Globator.
Cabada, Ladislav. 2006. Koaliční vládnutí v České republice – teoretická východiska v porovnání s praktickým naplněním. In: *Koalice a koaliční vztahy*. Ed. Ladislav Cabada. Praha: Aleš Čeněk.
Cabada, Ladislav and Šárka Waisová. 2011. *Czechoslovakia and the Czech Republic in World Politics*. Lanham: Lexington Books.
Cigánek, František. 1993. Předlistopadový parlament ve světle archívní dokumentace. In: *Dvě desetiletí před listopadem 89*. Ed. Emanuel Mandler. Praha: Maxdorf.
Claval, Paul. 2000. The European system of capital cities. *GeoJournal*, Vol. 51, No. 1–2.
Cuhra, Jaroslav. 2001. *Československo-vatikánská jednání 1968–1989*. Praha: Ústav pro soudobé dějiny AV ČR.
Cysařová, Jarmila. 1999. Čas přelomu. Garáž OF ČST: 21. listopadu 1989 – 11. ledna 1990, *Soudobé dějiny*, Vol. 9, No. 2–3.

Čaloud, Dalibor, Tomáš Foltýn and Vlastimil Havlík. 2006. Politické strany a jejich systém v období 2002–2006. In: *Volby do Poslanecké sněmovny 2006*. Dalibor Čaloud et al. Brno: Masarykova univerzita.

Čechurová, Jana. 1999. *Česká politická pravice*. Praha: NLN.

Chytilek, Roman, Jakub Šedo, Tomáš Lebeda and Dalibor Čaloud. 2009. *Volební systémy*. Praha: Portál.

Dančák, Břetislav. 1999. Geneze spolupráce ve střední Evropě. In: *Integrační pokusy ve středoevropském prostoru II*. Ed. Břetislav Dančák. Brno: Mezinárodní politologický ústav Masarykovy univerzity.

Dangerfield, Martin. 2008. The Visegrád Group in the Expanded European Union: From Preaccession to Postaccession Cooperation. *East European Politics and Societies*, Vol. 22, No. 3.

Deegan-Krause, Kevin and Timothy Haughton. 2010. A Fragile Stability: The Institutional Roots of Low Party System Volatility in the Czech Republic, 1990–2009. *Czech Journal of Political Science*, Vol. 17, No. 3.

Dejmek, Jindřich. 2002. Československo, jeho sousedé a velmoci ve XX. století (1918 až 1992). Praha: CEP.

Dienstbier, Jiří. 1990. *Snění o Evropě*. Praha: Lidové noviny.

Döring, Holger and Johan Hellström. 2013. Who Gets into Government? Coalition Formation in European Democracies. *West European Politics*, Vol. 36, No. 4.

Doskočil, Zdeněk. 2006. Duben 1969. Anatomie jednoho mocenského zvratu. Brno: Doplněk.

Dostál, Vít and Vít Hloušek. 2014. Narativy evropské politiky v Česku: může být dialog výsledkem změti monologů? (unpublished manuscript).

Dostál, Vladimír V. 1989. *Antonín Švehla*. New York.

Dostál, Vladimír V. 1998. *Agrární strana. Její rozmach a zánik*. Brno: Atlantis.

Drtina, Prokop. 1991. *Československo – můj osud*. Praha: Melantrich.

Drulák, Petr. 2012. *Reinventing Europe: Czech lesson for small countries*. European Council on Foreign Relations (http://ecfr.eu/content/entry/reinventing_europe_czech_lessons_for_small_countries).

Dudek, Antoni. 2002. *Pierwsza lata III Rzeczypospolitej*, Kraków: Arcana.

Durman, Karel. 1998. *Útěk od praporů*. Praha: Karolinum.

Dvořáková, Vladimíra. 2003. Civil Society in the Czech Republic: Impulse 99 and Thank You, Time to Go. In: *Uncivil Society? Contentious Politics in Post-Communist Europe*. Eds. Petr Kopecký and Cas Mudde. London and New York: Routledge.

Dvořáková, Vladimíra and Jiří Kunc. 1994. *O přechodech k demokracii*. Praha: SLON.

Dvořáková, Vladimíra and Jiří Kunc. 1999. Senát? Ano! In: *Senát v České republice – proč a jaký?* Ed. Jan Kysela. Praha: Kancelář Senátu.

Dyba, Karel and Jan Švejnar. 1997. Srovnávací studie ekonomického rozvoje v České republice. In: *Česká republika a ekonomická transformace ve střední a východní Evropě*. Ed. Jan Švejnar. Praha: Academia.

Earle, John S. and Scott Gehlbach. 2003. A spoonful of sugar: privatization and popular support for reform in the Czech Republic. *Economics and Politics*, Vol. 15, No. 1.

Eibl, Otto, Miloš Gregor and Alena Macková. 2013. Témata předvolebních kampaní v programech stran, jejich outdoorových kampaních a médiích. In: *Krajské volby 2013*. Ed. Stanislav Balík. Brno: Munipress.

Eibl, Otto et al. 2009. *Krajské volby 2008*. Brno: Centrum pro studium demokracie a kultury.

Fendrych, Martin and Tomáš Němeček. 1998. Přeji si, aby strany vzkvétaly. *Respekt*, No. 15.

Fiala, Petr. 1995. *Katolicismus a politika. O politické dimensi katolicismu v postmoderní době*. Brno: Centrum pro studium demokracie a kultury.

Fiala, Petr. 2001. Politické strany a stranicko-politické systémy v Československu. *Politologický časopis*, Vol. 3, No. 1.

Fiala, Petr. 2010. *Politika, jaká nemá být*. Brno: Centrum pro studium demokracie a kultury.

Fiala, Petr, Jan Holzer, Miroslav Mareš and Pavel Pšeja. 1999. *Komunismus v České republice*. Brno: MPÚ MU.

Fiala, Petr and Vít Hloušek. 2003. Stranický systém České republiky. In: *Středoevropské systémy politických stran. Česká republika, Maďarsko, Polsko a Slovensko*. Eds. Petr Fiala and Ryszard Herbut. Brno: Masarykova univerzita.

Fiala, Petr and Miroslav Mareš. 2005. Unie svobody-Demokratická unie. In: *Politické strany. Vývoj politických stran a hnutí v českých zemích a Československu. Díl II. 1938–2004*. Eds. Jiří Malíř and Pavel Marek. Brno: Doplněk.

Fiala, Petr and Maxmilián Strmiska. 2001. Kontinuita a diskontinuita českých stranicko-politických systémů. Metodologická východiska a dilemata komparativního výzkumu transformace soustav politických stran v českých zemích. *Středoevropské politické studie*, Vol. 1, No. 1.

Filip, Jan. 2002. Zapomenuté inspirace a aspirace Ústavy ČR. *Časopis pro právní vědu a praxi*, Vol. 10, No. 4.

Filip, Jan. 2010. Čl. 112 Ústavní pořádek České republiky. In: *Ústava České republiky. Komentář*. Lenka Bahýľová et al. Praha: Linde.

Fisher, Sharon. 2008. Re-Creating the Market. In: *Central & East European Politics. From Communism to Democracy*. Eds. Sharon L. Wolschik and Jane L. Curry. Lanham: Rowman & Littlefield Publishers, Inc.

Frýdmanová, Marie, Kamil Janáček, Petr Mareš and Tomáš Sirovátka. 1998. Trh práce a lidské zdroje. In: *Zpráva o vývoji české společnosti 1989–1998*. Ed. Jiří Večerník. Praha: Academia.

Frye, Timothy. 2010. *Building states and markets after communism.* Cambridge: Cambridge University Press.
Garton Ash, T. 1993. *The Magic Lantern. The Revolution of '89.* Witnessed in Warsaw, Budapest, Berlin and Praha. London: Vintage.
Garton Ash, Timothy. 2000. *History of the Present: Essays, Sketches, and Dispatches from Europe in the 1990s.* New York: Random House.
Gellner, Ernest. 1983. *Nations and Nationalism.* Ithaca: Cornell University Press.
Gellner, Ernest. 1994. *Encounters with Nationalism.* Oxford: Blackwell.
Gerloch, Aleš, Jiří Hřebejk and Vladimír Zoubek. 1999. *Ústavní systém České republiky.* Praha: Prospektrum.
Grabbe, Heather. 2006. *The EU's Transformative Power: Europeanization through Conditionality in Central and Eastern Europe.* Basingstoke – New York: Palgrave MacMillan.
Gregorovič, Miroslav. 1995. *Kapitoly o českém fašismu.* Praha: NPN.
Grotz, Florian and Till Weber. 2012. Party Systems and Government Stability in Central and Eastern Europe. *World Politics,* Vol. 64, No. 4.
Grzymala-Busse, Anna. 2002. *Redeeming the Communist Past. The Regeneration of Communist Parties in East Central Europe.* Cambridge: Cambridge University Press.
Guerra, Simona. 2013. *Central and Eastern European Attitudes in the Face of Union.* Basingstoke – New York: Palgrave MacMillan.
Halas, František X. 2004. *Fenomén Vatikán: idea, dějiny a současnost papežství, diplomacie Svatého stolce, České země a Vatikán.* Brno: Centrum pro studium demokracie a kultury.
Hanley, Seán. 2001. Towards Breakthrough or Breakdown? The Consolidation of KSČM as a Neo-Communist Successor Party in the Czech Republic. *Journal of Communist Studies and Transition Politics,* Vol. 17, No. 3.
Hanley, Seán. 2004. From Neo-Liberalism to National Interests: Ideology, Strategy, and Party Development in the Euroscepticism of the Czech Right. *East European Politics & Societies,* Vol. 18, No. 3.
Hanley, Seán. 2005. A Nation of Sceptics? The Czech EU Accession Referendum of 13–14 June 2003. In: *EU Enlargement and Referendums.* Eds. Aleks Szczerbiak and Paul Taggart. Abingdon, Oxon – New York: Routledge.
Hanley, Seán. 2011. Dynamika utváření nových stran v České republice v letech 1996–2010: hledání možných příčin politického zemětřesení, *Czech Sociological Review,* Vol. 47, No. 1.
Hanzel, Vladimír. 1991. *Zrychlený tep dějin. Autentické záznamy jednání představitelů státní moci s delegacemi hnutí Občanské fórum a Veřejnosť pro násiliu v listopadu a prosinci 1989.* Praha: OK Centrum.
Hanzlík, František. 1997. *Únor 1948 – výsledek nerovného zápasu.* Praha: Prewon.

Harna, Josef. 2004. Stranickopolitický systém v Československu v letech 1918–1938. In: *Politické strany. Vývoj politických stran a hnutí v českých zemích a Československu. Díl I. 1938–2004*. Eds. Jiří Malíř and Pavel Marek. Brno: Doplněk.

Haughton, Tim. 2009. For Business, For Pleasure or For Necessity: The Czech Republic's Choices for Europe. *Europe-Asia Studies*, Vol. 61, No. 8.

Havelka, Miloš. 1998. 'Nepolitická politika': kontexty a tradice. *Czech Sociological Review*, Vol. 34, No. 4.

Havlík, Vlastimil and Lubomír Kopeček. 2008. Krize vládnutí v České republice. *Politologický časopis*, Vol. 15, No. 3.

Havlík, Vlastimil and Vít Hloušek. 2014. Dr Jekyll and Mr Hyde. The Story of the Populist Public Affairs Party in the Czech Republic. *Perspectives on European Politics and Society*, Vol. 15, No. 4.

Havlík, Vlastimil. 2011a. A breaking-up of a pro-European consensus: Attitudes of Czech political parties towards the European integration (1998–2010). *Communist and Post-Communist Studies*, Vol. 44, No. 2.

Havlík, Vlastimil. 2011b. Česká republika. In: *Koaliční vládnutí ve střední Evropě (1990–2010)*. Eds. Stanislav Balík and Vlastimil Havlík. Brno: Masarykova univerzita.

Havlík, Vlastimil. 2015a. Stable or not? Patterns of party system dynamics and the rise of the new political parties in the Czech Republic. *Romanian Journal of Political Sciences*, Vol. 15, No. 1.

Havlík, Vlastimil. 2015b. The Economic Crisis in the Shadow of Political Crisis: The Rise of Party Populism in the Czech Republic. In: *European Populism in the Shadow of the Great Recession*. Eds. Hanspeter Kriesi and Takis S. Pappas. Colchester: ECPR Press.

Heimann, Mary. 2009. *Czechoslovakia: The State that Failed*. New Haven: Yale University Press.

Hejl, Vilém. 1990. *Zpráva o organizovaném násilí*. Praha: Univerzum.

Henderson, Karen. Ed. 1999. *Back to Europe: Central and Eastern Europe and the European Union*. London – New York: Routledge.

Heumos, Peter. 1995. Pluralistische Machtorganisation als Garant von Demokratie? Zur Struktur und zum autoritären Potential der Ersten Tschechoslowakischen Republik. In: *Autoritäre Regime in Ostmitteleuropa 1919–1944*. 1995. Eds. Oberlander, Erwin, Rudolf Jaworski, Hans Lemberg and Holm Sundhaussen. Mainz: Institut für Osteuropäische Geschichte.

Hirschl, Ran. 2008. The Judicialization of Mega-Politics and the Rise of Political Courts. *Annual Review of Political Science*, Vol. 11, No. 1.

Hledíková, Zdeňka, Jan Janák and Jan Dobeš. 2005. *Dějiny správy v českých zemích*. Praha: Nakladatelství Lidové noviny.

Hloušek, Vít. 2012. Věci veřejné: politické podnikání strany typu firmy. *Politologický časopis*, Vol. 19, No. 4.

Hloušek, Vít. 2015. Two Types of Presidentialization in the Party Politics of Central Eastern Europe. *Rivista Italiana di Scienza Politica*, Vol. 45, No. 3.

Hloušek, Vít and Petr Kaniok. 2014. Czech Republic. In: *Party Attitudes towards the EU in the Member States: Parties for Europe, parties against Europe*. Ed. Nicolò Conti. London – New York: Routledge.

Hloušek, Vít and Lubomír Kopeček. 2013. Záchrana státu? Úřednické a polopolitické vlády v České republice a Československu. Brno: Barrister & Principal.

Hloušek, Vít and Lubomír Kopeček. 2008. Cleavages in the Contemporary Czech and Slovak Politics Between Persistence and Change. *East European Politics & Societies*, Vol. 22, No. 3.

Hloušek, Vít and Pavel Pšeja. 2011. Europeanization of Political Parties and the Party System in the Czech Republic. In: *Party Politics in Central and Eastern Europe: Does EU Membership Matter?* Ed. Tim Haughton. London – New York: Routledge.

Hodulák, Vladan and Oldřich Krpec. 2010. Hospodářská politika. In: *Veřejné politiky v České republice v letech 1989–2009*. Eds. Stanislav Balík, Ondřej Císař and Petr Fiala. Brno: Centrum pro studium demokracie a kultury.

Holman, Robert. 2000. *Transformace české ekonomiky*. Praha: CEP.

Holman, Robert. 2002. Kupónová privatizace s desetiletým odstupem. In: *Kupónová privatizace*. Ed. Dušan Tříska. Praha: CEP.

Holý, Ladislav. 2001. *Malý český člověk a velký český národ*. Praha: SLON.

Holzer, Jan. 2006. ODS a tradice české politiky. In: *Občanská demokratická strana a česká politika*. Ed. Stanislav Balík. Brno: Centrum pro studium demokracie a kultury.

Holzer, Jan. 2009. Totalitäre Traditionen in der tschechischen Politik. *Bohemia. A Journal of History and Civilisation in East Central Europe*, Vol. 49, No. 2.

Honajzer, Jiří. 1996. Občanské fórum: Vznik, vývoj a rozpad. Praha: Orbis.

Hradecká, Vladimíra. 1998. *Kádrová politika a nomenklatura KSČ 1969–1974*. Praha: Ústav pro soudobé dějiny AV ČR.

Hroch, Miroslav. 1999. Na prahu národní existence: touha a skutečnost. Praha: Mladá fronta.

Hroch, Miroslav. 1999. V národním zájmu. Požadavky a cíle evropských národních hnutí devatenáctého století ve srovnávací perspektivě. Praha: NLN.

Husák, Petr. 1997. Budování kapitalismu v Čechách. Rozhovory s Tomášem Ježkem. Praha: Volvox Globator.

Hye, Hans Peter. 1998. Das politische System in der Habsburgermonarchie. Praha: Karolinum.

Jarmara, Tomáš. 2011. TOP 09 a Věci veřejné v kontextu institucionalizace českých politických stran po roce 1989. *Politologická revue*, Vol. 17, No. 1.

Jászi, Oscar. 1961. *The Dissolution of the Habsburg Monarchy*. Chicago: The University of Chicago Press & Phoenix Books.
Jedlička, Josef. 2009. *České typy a jiné eseje*. Praha: Albatros.
Jerez-Mir, Miguel, José Real-Dato and Rafael Vásquez-García. 2010. Identity and Representation in the Perceptions of Political Elites and Public Opinion: A Comparison between Southern and Post-Communist Central-Eastern Europe. In: *Perceptions of the European Union in New Member States: A Comparative Perspective*. Ed. Gabriela Ilonszki. Abingdon, Oxon – New York: Routledge.
Ježek, Tomáš. 2006. Privatizace české ekonomiky: její kořeny, metody a výsledky. Praha: VŠE.
Jiránek, Vladimír and Bohumil Pečinka. 2000. *To byla léta devadesátá*. Brno: Barrister & Principal.
Just, Petr. 2012. Vývoj ústavních insitucí politického systemu ČR. In: *Česká demokracie po roce 1989*. Jan Bureš et al. Praha: Grada.
Kaláb, Vladimír. 2004. Je česká privatizace jen souhrnem skandálů? In: *Co se stane, když se zhasne?* Ed. Petr Holub. Praha: Prostor.
Kaniok, Petr. 2012. Eurosceptics – enemies or a necessary part of European integration? *Romanian Journal of Political Science*, Vol. 12, No. 2.
Kaniok, Petr and Hubert Smekal. 2009. The Czech Presidency of the EU Council: No Triumph, no Tragedy. *Romanian Journal of European Affairs*, Vol. 9, No. 9.
Kaplan, Karel. 1991. *Československo v letech 1948–1953*. Praha: SPN.
Kaplan, Karel. 1992. *Kádrová politika KSČ 1948–1956*. Praha: Ústav pro soudobé dějiny AV ČR.
Kaplan, Karel. 1993. *Aparát ÚV KSČ v letech 1948–1968*. Praha: Ústav pro soudobé dějiny AV ČR.
Kaplan, Karel. 1994. *O cenzuře v Československu v letech 1945–1956*. Praha: Ústav pro soudobé dějiny AV ČR.
Kaplan, Karel. 1997. *Pět kapitol o Únoru*. Brno: Doplněk.
Kaplan, Karel. 1999. *Nebezpečná bezpečnost. Státní bezpečnost 1948–1956*. Brno: Doplněk.
Kaplan, Karel. 2000, 2002. *Kořeny československé reformy 1968. I.-IV.* Brno: Doplněk.
Kárník, Zdeněk. 2000, 2002, 2003. *České země v éře První republiky I.–III.* Praha: Libri.
Kenny, Padraic. 2003. *A Carnival of Revolution: Central Europe 1989*. Princeton: Princeton University Press.
Kitschelt, Herbert, Zdenka Mansfeldova, Radoslaw Markowski and Gabor Toka. 1999. *Post-Communist Party Systems: Competition, Representation, and Inter-Party Cooperation*. New York: Cambridge University Press.
Klaus, Václav. 1995. Ekonomická teorie a realita transformačních procesů. Praha: Management Press.
Klaus, Václav. 2002. *Občan a obrana jeho státu*. Praha: CEP.

Klaus, Václav. 2013. *Česká republika na rozcestí – Čas rozhodnutí*. Praha: Fragment.
Klaus, Václav and Marek Loužek. Eds. 2006. *Soudcokracie v ČR – fikce nebo realita?* Praha: CEP.
Klíma, Karel. 2008. Prezident České republiky v komparativním pohledu. In: *Postavení prezidenta v ústavním systému České republiky*. Ed. Vojtěch Šimíček. Brno: Masarykova univerzita.
Klimek, Antonín. 1996, 1998. *Boj o Hrad I.–II.* Praha: Panevropa.
Kneblová, Eva. 2010. Využívání preferenčních hlasů. In: *Volby do Poslanecké sněmovny v roce 2010*. Ed. Stanislav Balík. Brno: Centrum pro studium demokracie a kultury.
Kneblová, Eva. 2013. Využívání preferenčních hlasů. In: *Volby do Poslanecké sněmovny 2013*. Ed. Vlastimil Havlík. Brno: Centrum pro studium demokracie a kultury.
Knot, Ondřej. 2004. Proč padl Lev ve světě financí? In: *Co se stane, když se zhasne?* Ed. Petr Holub. Praha: Prostor.
Kocián, Jiří. 2002. *Československá strana národně socialistická v letech 1945–1948. Organizace, program, politika*. Brno: Doplněk.
Kolář, Petr. 2003. Vzestup a pád Čtyř/Koalice. In: *Volby do Poslanecké sněmovny 2002*. Eds. Lukáš Linek, Ladislav Mrklas, Adéla Seidlová and Petr Sokol. Praha: AV ČR.
Kopecký, Petr. 2000. From ,Velvet Revolution' to ,Velvet Split': Consociational Institutions and the Disintegration of Czechoslovakia. In: *Irreconcilable Differences? Explaining Czechoslovakia's Dissolution*. Eds. Michael Kraus and Allison Stanger. Lanham: Rowman & Littlefield Publishers.
Kopeček, Lubomír and Josef Mlejnek. 2013. Different Confessions, Same Sins? Václav Havel and Václav Klaus as Czech Presidents. In: *Presidents above parties? Presidents in Central and Eastern Europe, Their Formal Competencies and Informal Power*. Vít Hloušek et al. Brno: Muni Press.
Kopeček, Lubomír and Jan Petrov. 2016. From Parliament to Courtroom: Judicial Review of Legislation as a Political Tool in the Czech Republic. In: *East European Politics and Societies*, Vol. 30, No. 1.
Kopeček, Lubomír and Pavel Pšeja. 2008. Czech Social Democracy and its cohabitation with the Communist Party: The story of a neglected affair. In: *Communist and Post-Communist Studies*, Vol. 41, No. 3.
Kopeček, Lubomír. 2010a. *Éra nevinnosti. Česká politika 1989–1997*. Brno: Barrister & Principal.
Kopeček, Lubomír. 2010b. Dealing with the communist past: its role in the disintegration of the Czech Civic Forum and in the emergence of the Civic Democratic Party. *Communist and Post-Communist Studies*, Vol. 43, No. 2.
Kopeček, Lubomír. 2012a. *Fenomén Václav Klaus. Politická biografie*. Brno: Barrister & Principal.

Kopeček, Lubomír. 2012b. Jak se zrodila opoziční smlouva. Analýza vzniku jednoho z nejkontroverznějších paktů české politiky. *Soudobé dějiny*, Vol. 19, No. 1.

Kopeček, Lubomír. 2015. *Deformace demokracie? Opoziční smlouva a česká politika 1998–2002*. Brno: Barrister & Principal.

Kopeček, Michal. 2009. *Hledání ztraceného smyslu revoluce. Zrod a počátky marxistického revizionismu ve střední Evropě 1953–1960*. Praha: Argo.

Kopstein, Jeffrey and David Reilly. 2000. Geographic Diffusion and the Transformation of the Postcommunist World. *World Politics*, Vol. 53, No. 1.

Kořalka, Jiří. 1996. Češi v habsburské říši a v Evropě 1815–1914. Praha: Argo.

Koudelka, František. 1993. *Státní bezpečnost v letech 1946–1968*. Praha: Ústav pro soudobé dějiny AV ČR.

Kováč, Dušan. 1997. *Slováci – Češi – dejiny*. Bratislava: Academic Electronic Press.

Kovář, Jan and Lukáš Hendrych. 2015. *Jak české politické strany pracují s unijními tématy?* Praha: Evropské hodnoty (http://www.evropskehodnoty.cz/vyzkum/strany_eu/; accessed on: 20160505).

Kramářův soud nad Benešem. Praha 1938.

Krapfl, James. 2013. *Revolution with a Human Face: Politics, Culture, and Community in Czechoslovakia, 1989–1992*. Ithaca: Cornell University Press.

Křen, Jan. 1996. *Die Konfliktgemeinschaf. Tschechen und Deutsche 1780–1918*. Munich: Oldenbourg Verlag.

Kubát, Michal. 2004. Několik politologických poznámek na margo nálezu Ústavního soudu No. 64/2001 Sb. ze dne 24.1.2001. In: *Volební a stranické systémy ČR v mezinárodním srovnání*. Eds. Miroslav Novák, Tomáš Lebeda. Dobrá Voda u Pelhřimova: Aleš Čeněk.

Kubát, Michal. 2009. Racionalizace parlamentního režimu. Polské zkušenosti jako poučení nejen pro českou politiku. *Politologický časopis*, Vol. 16, No. 2.

Kubát, Michal. 2013. *Současná česká politika. Co s neefektivním režimem?* Brno: Barrister & Principal.

Kühn, Zdeněk. 2009. Důvody zrušení protiústavního "ústavního" zákona No. 195/2009 Sb. *Jiné právo* 16.11.2009 (http://jinepravo.blogspot.cz/2009/09/on-line-symposium-jakub-vosahlo-ustavni.html#Kuhn3; accessed on: 20160505).

Kühn, Zdeněk and Jan Kysela. 2006. Nomination of Constitutional Justices in Post-Communist Countries: Trial, Error, Conflict in the Czech Republic. *European Constitutional Law Review*, Vol. 2, No. 2.

Kuklík, Jan and Jan Němeček. 1999. *Hodža versus Beneš*. Praha: Karolinum.

Kuklík, Jan. 1992. *Sociální demokracie ve Druhé republice*. Praha: Univerzita Karlova.

Kuklík, Jan. 1998. *Londýnský exil a obnova československého státu 1938–1945*. Praha: Karolinum.

Kuklík, Jan. 2010. *Znárodněné Československo*. Praha: Academia.

Kunštát, Daniel. 2013b. *Za rudou oponou. Komunisté a jejich voliči po roce 1989*. Praha: Slon.

Kusák, Alexej. 1998. *Kultura a politika v Československu 1945–1956*. Praha: Torst.
Kysela, Jan. 2004. *Dvoukomorové systémy*. Praha: Eurolex Bohemia.
Kysela, Jan. 2006. Česká republika mezi parlamentním a poloprezidentským režimem? *Politologická revue*, Vol. 12, No. 1.
Kysela, Jan. 2008. Prezident republiky v ústavním systému ČR – perspektiva ústavněprávní. In: *Postavení hlavy státu v parlamentních a poloprezidentských režimech: Česká republika v komparativní perspektivě*. Eds. Miroslav Novák and Miloš Brunclík. Praha: Dokořán.
Kysela, Jan. 2013. Parlament a parlamentarismus. In: *Parlament České republiky*. Petr Kolář et al. Praha: Leges.
Lebeda, Tomáš, Karolína Malcová and Tomáš Lacina. 2009. *Volby do Senátu 1996 až 2008*. Praha: Sociologický ústav Akademie věd.
Leff, Carol Skalnik. 2000. Inevitability, Probability, Possibility: The Legacies of the Czech-Slovak Relationship, 1918–1989, and the Disintegration of the State. In: *Irreconcilable Differences? Explaining Czechoslovakia's Dissolution*. Eds. Michael Kraus and Allison Stanger. Lanham: Rowman & Littlefield Publishers.
Linek, Lukáš. 2003. Dimenze antistranických postojů české veřejnosti. *Naše společnost*, Vol. 1, No. 3–4.
Linek, Lukáš. 2010. *Zrazení snu? Struktura a dynamika postojů k politickému režimu a jeho institucím a jejich důsledky*. Praha: Slon.
Linek, Lukáš. 2013. *Kam se ztratili voliči? Vysvětlení vývoje volební účasti v České republice v letech 1990–2010*. Brno: Centrum pro studium demokracie a kultury.
Linek, Lukáš. 2014. Čistá a celková volební volatilita Česku v letech 1990–2013: stejný koncept, odlišná měření a podobné závěry. *Acta Politologica*, Vol. 6, No. 1.
Linz, Juan J. and Alfred Stepan. 1996. *Problems of Democratic Transition and Consolidation: Southern Europe, South America, and Post-Communist Europe*. Baltimore: The Johns Hopkins University Press.
Lipták, Ľubomír. 1998. *Slovensko v 20. storočí*. Bratislava: Kalligram.
Loewenstein, Bedřich. 1995. Manifest nepolitické politiky. Česká otázka po 45 letech. *Sociologický časopis*, Vol. 31, No. 4.
Lux, Martin. 2009. *Housing policy and housing finance in the Czech Republic during transition*. Delft: Delft University Press.
Lux, Martin and Martina Mikeszová. 2011. Restituce majetku a transformace soukromého nájemního bydlení v České republice. In: *Standardy bydlení 2010/2011*. Ed. Martin Lux. Praha: Sociologický ústav Aakademie věd České republiky.
Macura, Vladimír. 1998. *Český sen*. Praha: Lidové noviny.
Majewski, Piotr M. 2014. *Sudetští Němci 1848–1948. Dějiny jednoho nacionalismu*. Brno: Conditio humana.
Malia, Martin. 2006. *History's Locomotive. Revolutions and the Making of the Modern World*. New Haven: Yale UP.

Malíř, Jiří. 1996. *Od spolků k moderním politickým stranám. Vývoj politických stran na Moravě 1848–1914*. Brno: Masarykova univerzita.
Maňák, Jiří. 1997. *Čistky v Komunistické straně Československa 1969–1970*. Praha: Ústav pro soudobé dějiny AV ČR.
Mansfeldová, Zdenka. 2005. Sociální dialog a jeho budoucnost. In: *Participace a zájmové organizace v České republice*. Eds. Zdenka Mansfeldová a Aleš Kroupa. Praha: Slon.
Mansfeldová, Zdenka and Barbora Špicatová Stašková. 2010. Identity Formation of Elites in Old and New Member States (with a Special Focus on the Czech Republic). In: *Perceptions of the European Union in New Member States: A Comparative Perspective*. Ed. Gabriela Ilonszki. Abingdon, Oxon – New York: Routledge.
Marek, Dan and Michael Baun. 2010. *The Czech Republic and the European Union*. London: Routledge.
Mareš, Miroslav. 2005. Sdružení pro Republiku – Republikánská strana Československa a Republikáni Miroslava Sládka. In: *Politické strany. Vývoj politických stran a hnutí v českých zemích a Československu. Díl II. 1938–2004*. Eds. Jiří Malíř and Pavel Marek. Brno: Doplněk.
Mareš, Miroslav. 2011. Czech extreme right parties an unsuccessful story. *Communist and Post-Communist Studies*, Vol. 44, No. 4.
Mareš, Miroslav and Pavel Pšeja. 2008. Partis agrariens et paysans en République tcheque. In: *Les partis agrariens et paysans en Europe*. Eds. Daniel-Louis Seiler and Jean-Michel de Waele. Bruxelles: Editions de l'Université de Bruxelles.
Mareš, Miroslav and Maxmilián Strmiska. 2005. Moravistické strany a hnutí. In: *Politické strany. Vývoj politických stran a hnutí v českých zemích a Československu 1861–2004*. Eds. Jiří Malíř and Pavel Marek. Brno: Doplněk.
Maršálek, Pavel. 2002. *Protektorát Čechy a Morava*. Praha: Karolinum.
Marušiak, Juraj. 2008. The Normalisation Regime and its Impact on Slovak Domestic Policy after 1970. In: *Europe-Asia Studies*, Vol. 60, No. 10.
Mayer, Francoise. 2009. *Češi a jejich komunismus. Paměť a politická identita*. Praha: Argo.
Měchýř, Jan. 1999. *Velký převrat či snad revoluce sametová?* Praha: Československý spisovatel.
Milanovic, Branko. 1998. *Income, Inequality, and Poverty during the Transition from Planned to Market Economy*. Washington: World Bank.
Miller, Daniel E. 2001. *Antonín Švehla – mistr politických kompromisů*. Praha: Argo.
Mlčoch, Lubomír. 2000. Restrukturalizace vlastnických vztahů: institucionální pohled. In: *Ekonomické a společenské změny v české společnosti po roce 1989*. Eds. Lubomír Mlčoch, Pavel Machonin and Milan Sojka. Praha: Karolinum.
Mlejnek, Josef. 2011. Úvod – potíže s prezidenty. In: *Postavení hlavy státu v postkomunistických zemích*. Ed. Josef Mlejnek. Praha: Univerzita Karlova.

Mlynář, Zdeněk. 1990. *Mráz přichází z Kremlu*. Praha: Mladá fronta.
Molek, Pavel. 2010. Čl. 68 Jmenování vlády. In: *Ústava České republiky. Komentář*. Lenka Bahýľová et al. Praha: Linde.
Mostetchnig, Anna Maria. 2011. *CEFTA and the European Single Market: An appropriate preparatory exercise?* Natolin: College of Europe.
Možný, Ivo. 1991. *Proč tak snadno... Některé rodinné důvody sametové revoluce*. Praha: Slon.
Müller, Wolfgang C. and Kaare Strom. 2000. Conclusion: Coalition Governance in Western Europe. In: *Coalition Governments in Western Europe*. Eds. Wolfgang C. Müller and Kaare Strom. Oxford – New York: Oxford University Press.
Musil, Jiří. 1995. Czech and Slovak Society. In: *The End of Czechoslovakia*. Ed. Jiří Musil. Budapest: Central European University Press.
Musilová, Markéta and Jakub Šedo. 2013. Diskuse o zavedení přímé volby prezidenta v České republice a její schválení. In: *České prezidentské volby v roce 2013*. Ed. Jakub Šedo. Brno: Centrum pro studium demokracie a kultury.
Myant, Martin. 2003. *The Rise and Fall of Czech Capitalism*. Cheltenham: Edward Elgar.
Myant, Martin. 2007. Economic transformation in the Czech Republic – a qualified success. In: *Europe-Asia Studies*, Vol. 59, No. 3.
Myant, Martin. 2008. Podoby kapitalismu v České republice. In: *Kapitoly z dějin české demokracie po roce 1989*. Eds. Adéla Gjuričová and Michal Kopeček. Praha – Litomyšl: Paseka.
Němec, Jan. 2012. Stát se musí řídit jako firma, tvrdí miliardář Babiš. *Aktuálně.cz* (http://zpravy.aktualne.cz/domaci/stat-se-musi-ridit-jako-firma-tvrdi-miliardar-babis/r~i:article:760923/; accessed on: 20160505).
Němeček, Tomáš. 2010. *Vojtěch Cepl*. Praha: Leges.
Neset, Pavel. 2002. Inflace v České republice – nabídkové faktory. In: *Transformace české transformace. Politické, ekonomické a sociální aspekty*. Ed. Vojtěch Spěváček. Praha: Linde.
Nölke, Andreas and Arjan Vliegenthart. 2009. Enlarging the Varieties of Capitalism: The Emergence of Dependent Market Economies in East Central Europe. In: *World Politics*, Vol. 61, No. 4.
Novák, Miroslav. 1996. Volby do Poslanecké sněmovny, vládní nestabilita a perspektivy demokracie v ČR. In: *Sociologický časopis*, Vol. 32, No. 4.
Novák, Miroslav. 2004. Typy vlád a jejich utváření v komparativní perspektivě. In: *Volební a stranické systémy*. Miroslav Novák and Tomáš Lebeda et al. Dobrá Voda u Pelhřimova: Aleš Čeněk.
Novák, Miroslav. 2008. Prezident, premiér a snahy o posílení výkonné moci. In: *Postavení prezidenta v ústavním systému České republiky*. Ed. Vojtěch Šimíček. Brno: Masarykova univerzita.

Novák, Miroslav and Miloš Brunclík. Eds. 2008. *Postavení hlavy státu v parlamentních a poloprezidentských režimech: Česká republika v komparativní perspektivě.* Praha: Dokořán.

O'Brennan, John. Ed. 2006. *The Eastern Enlargement of the European Union.* Abingdon, Oxon – New York: Routledge.

Olivová, Věra. 2000. *Dějiny první republiky.* Praha: Karolinum.

Orenstein, Mitchell. 2001. *Out of the Red: Building Capitalism and Democracy in Postcommunist Europe.* Ann Arbor: University of Michigan Press.

Otáhal, Milan. 1993. První fáze opozice proti takzvané normalizaci (1969–72). In: *Dvě desetiletí před listopadem 89.* Praha: Ústav pro soudobé dějiny AV ČR.

Otáhal, Milan. 1994. *Opozice, moc, společnost 1969/1989.* Praha: Ústav pro soudobé dějiny AV ČR.

Otáhal, Milan. 1998. O nepolitické politice. *Sociologický časopis*, Vol. 34, No. 4.

Otáhal, Milan. 1999. *Podíl tvůrčí inteligence na pádu komunismu.* Brno: Doplněk.

Otáhal, Milan. 2011. *Opoziční proudy v české společnosti 1969–1989.* Praha: Ústav pro soudobé dějiny AV ČR.

Palouš, Martin. 1993. Poznámky ke generačním sporům v Chartě 77 v druhé polovině osmdesátých let. In: *Dvě desetiletí před Listopadem 89.* Praha: Ústav pro soudobé dějiny AV ČR.

Pasák, Tomáš. 1997. *JUDr. Emil Hácha (1938–1945).* Praha: Horizont.

Pasák, Tomáš. 1998. *Pod ochranou Říše.* Praha: Práh.

Pavlíček, Václav and Jiří Hřebejk. 1998. *Ústava a ústavní řád České republiky*, sv. I. Praha: Linde.

Pečinka, Bohumil. 2001. Příliš toleranční patent. *Revue politika*, No. 2 (http://www.revuepolitika.cz/clanky/1050/komentar-prilis-tolerancni-patent; accessed on: 20160505).

Pehr, Michal. 2011. *Zápas o nové Československo 1939–1946.* Praha: NLN.

Pekař, Josef. 1995. Smysl českých dějin. In: *Spor o smysl českých dějin 1895–1938.* Ed. Miloš Havelka. Praha: Torst.

Pěkný, Tomáš. 2001. *Historie Židů v Čechách a na Moravě.* Praha: Sefer.

Pernes, Jiří. 1996. *Pod moravskou orlicí aneb Dějiny moravanství.* Brno: Barrister & Principal.

Pernes, Jiří. 2005. *Nejen rudé prapory aneb Pravda o revolučním roce 1905 v českých zemích.* Brno: Stilus.

Petrův, Helena. 2010. Judikatura Ústavního soudu k restitucím židovského majetku. *Jurisprudence*, No. 8.

Pithart, Petr. 1990. *Osmašedesátý.* Praha: Rozmluvy.

Pithart, Petr. 1999. Senát jako stabilizující prvek politického systému. In: *Senát v České republice – proč a jaký?* Ed. Jan Kysela. Praha: Kancelář Senátu.

Podiven 1991. *Češi v dějinách nové doby (1848–1939).* Praha: Rozmluvy.

Procházka, Theodore. 1981. *The Second Republic: The Disintegration of Post-Munich Czechoslovakia (October 1938–March 1939).* New York, Boulder: Columbia UP.

Przeworski, Adam. 1992. *Democracy and the Market. Political and Economic Reforms in Eastern Europe and Latin America.* Cambridge: Cambridge University Press.

Přibáň, Jiří. 2002. Judicial Power v. Democratic Representation: Culture of Constitutionalism and Human Rights in the Czech Legal System. In: *Constitutional Justice: East and West.* Eds. Wojciech Sadurski and Jan Zielonka. Dordrecht: Kluwer Academic Publisher.

Příhoda, Petr. 1995. Mutual Perceptions in Czech-Slovak Relationships. In: *The End of Czechoslovakia.* Ed. Jiří Musil. Budapest: Central European University Press.

Pšeja, Pavel. 2004a. Občanské fórum jako katalysátor vývoje stranického systému ČR. *Politologický časopis*, Vol. 11, No. 3.

Pšeja, Pavel. 2004b. Občanská demokratická strana jako hlavní ‚dědic' OF a ‚agens' stranického systému ČR (1991–1998). *Politologický časopis*, Vol. 11, No. 4.

Pšeja, Pavel. 2005. *Stranický systém České republiky.* Brno: Centrum pro studium demokracie a kultury.

Pšeja, Pavel. 2008. Holding the Ground: Communism and Political Parties in the Post-Communist Czech Republic. In: *Totalitarismus und Transformation. Defizite der Demokratiekonsolidierung in Mittel- und Osteuropa.* Eds. Uwe Backes, Tytus Jaskulowski and Abel Polese. Göttingen: Vandenhoeck & Ruprecht.

Rataj, J. 1997. *O autoritativní národní stát. Ideologické proměny české politiky v druhé republice 1938–1939.* Praha: Karolinum.

Reif, Karlheinz and Hermann Schmitt. 1980. Nine Second Order National Elections: A Conceptual Framework for the Analysis of European Election Results. *European Journal of Political Research*, Vol. 8, No. 1.

Reiman, Michal. 2000. *O komunistickém totalitarismu a o tom, co s ním souvisí.* Praha: Karolinum.

Renner, J. 1999. *Československá strana lidová 1945–1948.* Brno: Prius.

Richter, Tomáš. 2005. *Kuponová privatizace a její vlivy na správu a financování českých akciových společností.* Praha: Karolinum.

Rokkan, Stein. 1999a. Mass Politics. In: *State Formation, Nation-Building, and Mass Politics in Europe. The Theory of Stein Rokkan.* Eds. Peter Flora, Stein Kuhnle and Derek Urwin. Oxford: Oxford University Press.

Rokkan, Stein. 1999b. State Formation and Nation-Building. In: *State Formation, Nation-Building, and Mass Politics in Europe. The Theory of Stein Rokkan.* Eds. Peter Flora, Stein Kuhnle and Derek Urwin. Oxford: Oxford University Press.

Rupnik, Jacques. 2002. *Dějiny Komunistické strany Československa. Od počátků do převzetí moci.* Praha: Academia.

Rybář, Marek. 2010. Domestic Politics and National Preferences in the European Union. In: *From Listening to Action? New Member States in the European Union.* Ed. Darina Malová. Bratislava: Devin Printing House.

Rychlík, Jan. 2000. The Possibilities for Czech-Slovak Compromise, 1989–1992. In: *Irreconcilable Differences? Explaining Czechoslovakia's Dissolution.* Eds. Michael Kraus and Allison Stanger. Lanham: Rowman & Littlefield Publishers.
Rychlík, Jan. 2002. *Rozpad Československa. Česko-slovenské vztahy 1989–1992.* Bratislava: Academic Electronic Press.
Řepa, Milan. 2001. *Moravané nebo Češi? Vývoj českého národního vědomí na Moravě v 19. století.* Praha: Doplněk.
Riháčková, Věra. 2005. Czech Republic: 'Europeanization' of a hesitant Atlanticist? *Europeum Working paper.* Praha: Europeum (http://www.europeum.org/doc/arch_eur/Czech_attitudes_towards_the_US.pdf; accessed on: 20160505).
Sadurski, Wojciech. 2009. Judicial Review in Central and Eastern Europe: Rationales or Rationalizations? In: *Israel Law Review*, Vol. 42, No. 3.
Sadurski, Wojciech. 2010. Constitutional Courts and Constitutional Culture in Central and Eastern European Countries. In: *Central and Eastern Europe after Transition: Towards a New Socio-Legal Semantics.* Eds. Alberto Febbrajo and Wojciech Sadursky. Farnham: Ashgate.
Sartori, Giovanni. 1994. *Comparative Constitutional Engineering.* Houndmills: Palgrave MacMillan.
Sayer, Derek. 1998. *The Coasts of Bohemia: A Czech History.* Princeton: Princeton University Press.
Schedler, Andreas. 1997. Introduction: Antipolitics – Closing and Colonizing the Public Sphere. In: *The End of Politics? Explorations into Modern Antipolitics.* Ed. Andreas Schedler. Houndmills: Macmillan Press.
Schleifer, Andrei and Daniel Tresiman. 2014. Normal Countries: The East 25 Years After Communism. *Foreign Affairs,* November/December.
Schorm, Vít. 1999. Senát českého Parlamentu – jedna z obětí institucionální nerovnováhy. In: *Senát v České republice – proč a jaký?* Ed. Jan Kysela. Praha: Kancelář Senátu.
Schwartz, Herman. 2000. *The Struggle for Constitutional Justice in Post-Communist Europe.* Chicago and London: Chicago University Press.
Seidlová, Adéla, Jan Červenka, Daniel Kunštát. 2003. Voliči a nevoliči. In: *Volby do Poslanecké sněmovny 2002.* Eds. Lukáš Linek, Ladislav Mrklas, Adéla Seidlová and Petr Sokol. Praha: Akademie věd České republiky.
Smekal, Hubert and Ivo Pospíšil et al. 2013. *Soudcokracie nebo judicializace politiky? Vztah práva a politiky (nejen) v časech krize.* Brno: Masarykova univerzita.
Smetanková, Daša. 2014. *Mandatorní výdaje státního rozpočtu.* Praha: Parlamentní institut (http://www.psp.cz/sqw/text/orig2.sqw?idd=100870; accessed on: 20160505).
Soubigou, Alain. 2004. *Tomáš Garrigue Masaryk.* Praha – Litomyšl: Paseka.
Soudní perzekuce politické povahy v Československu 1948–1989. 1993. Praha: ÚSD AV.

Springerová, Pavlína. 2010. *Analýza vývoje a činnosti moravistických politických subjektů v letech 1989–2005*. Brno: Centrum pro studium demokracie a kultury.

Staněk, Tomáš. 1991. *Odsun Němců z Československa 1945–1947*. Praha: Academia – Naše vojsko.

Stein, Eric. 1997. *Czecho/Slovakia. Ethnic Conflict, Constitutional Fissure, Negotiated Breakup*. Ann Arbor: University of Michigan Press.

Stone Sweet, Alec. 1992. *The Birth of Judicial Politics in France: The Constitutional Council in Comparative Perspective*. New York: Oxford University Press.

Stone Sweet, Alec. 2000. *Governing with Judges: Constitutional Politics in Europe*. New York: Oxford University Press.

Stone Sweet, Alec. 2012. Constitutional Courts. In: *The Oxford Handbook of Comparative Constitutional Law*. Eds. Michel Rosenfeld and András Sajó. Oxford: Oxford University Press.

Strašáková, Iva. 2007. *Strukturální politika v ČR*. Diplomová práce. Brno: Masarykova univerzita, Ekonomicko-správní fakulta.

Stropnický, Matěj. 2013. *Myslet socialismus bez tanků. Svoboda slova ve střed/tu zájmů československého roku 1968*. Praha: Scriptorium.

Suk, Jiří, Jaroslav Cuhra and František Koudelka. 1999. *Chronologie zániku komunistického režimu v Československu 1985–1990*. Praha: Ústav pro soudobé dějiny AV ČR.

Suk, Jiří. 1997a. *Občanské fórum. 1. díl, Události*. Praha – Brno: Doplněk.

Suk, Jiří. 1997b. *Občanské fórum. 2. díl, Dokumenty*. Praha – Brno: Doplněk.

Suk, Jiří. 2003. *Labyrintem revoluce: aktéři, zápletky a křižovatky jedné politické krize (od listopadu 1989 do června 1990)*. Praha: Prostor.

Suk, Jiří. 2004. 'Vidím vám všem až do žaludku'. Sesazování Gustáva Husáka v roce 1987. In: *Dějiny a současnost*, Vol. 26, No. 4.

Syllová, Jindřiška. 2013. Legislativní činnost parlamentu. In: *Parlament České republiky*. Ed. Petr Kolář et al. Praha: Leges.

Szomolányi, Soňa. 1999. *Kľukatá cesta Slovenska k demokracii*. Bratislava: Stimul.

Šaradín, Pavel and Jan Outlý, J. Eds. 2004. *Studie o volbách do zastupitelstev v obcích*, Olomouc: UP.

Šíma, Josef and Tomáš Nikodym. 2015. Classical Liberalism in the Czech Republic. In: *Econ Journal Watch*, Vol. 12, No. 2.

Šimíček, Vojtěch. 2001. Ústavní postavení krajů a některé problémy s ním spojené. In: *Krajské volby 2000. Fakta, názory, komentáře*. Ed. Ladislav Mrklas. Praha: Cevro.

Šimíček, Vojtěch. 2003a. Právní zakotvení institutu referenda v ústavním pořádku České republiky. *Politologický časopis*, Vol. 10, No. 2.

Šimíček, Vojtěch. 2003b. Ústavněprávní pravidla sestavování vlády po volbách a jeho praxe. In: *Volby do Poslanecké sněmovny 2002*. Ed. Lukáš, Linek et al. Praha: Sociologický ústav AV ČR.

Šimíček, Vojtěch. Ed. 2008. *Postavení prezidenta v ústavním systému České republiky.* Brno: MPÚ MU.

Šimíček, Vojtěch. 2009. Materiální ohnisko ústavního pořádku, jeho ochrana a nález Ústavního soudu ve věci M. Melčáka. In: *Liber Amicorum. In memoriam emeritního soudce Ústavního soudu.* Eds. Ivo Pospíšil and Eliška Wagnerová, Praha: Linde.

Šimíček, Vojtěch. 2013. Soudní přezkumy politických procesů. In: *Soudcokracie nebo judicializace politiky? Vztah práva a politiky (nejen) v časech krize.* Eds. Hubert Smekal and Ivo Pospíšil. Brno: Masarykova univerzita.

Šlosarčík, Ivo. 2011. The Czech Republic – impacts of and experience with EU membership. *Eastern Journal of European Studies*, Vol. 2, No. 2.

Štaif, Jiří. 2005. *Obezřetná elita. Česká společnost mezi tradicí a revolucí 1830–1851.* Praha: Dokořán.

Šťastný, Marek. Ed. 2002. *Visegrad Countries in an Enlarged Trans-Atlantic Community.* Bratislava: Institute for Public Affairs.

Štefek, Martin. 2014. *Za fasádou jednoty. KSČ a SED po roce 1985.* Červený Kostelec: Pavel Mervart.

Šulc, Zdislav. 1998. *Stručné dějiny ekonomických reforem v Československu. České republice) 1945–1995.* Brno: Doplněk.

Šustrová, Petruška and Josef Mlejnek. 2014. *Zaostřeno na komunismus.* Praha: Euroslavica.

Šútovec, Milan. 1999. *Semióza ako politikum alebo "Pomlčková vojna".* Bratislava: Kalligram.

Švejnar, Jan. 1997. Úvod a celkový přehled. In: *Česká republika a ekonomická transformace ve střední a východní Evropě.* Ed. Jan Švejnar. Praha: Academia.

Táborský, Eduard. 1993. *Prezident Beneš mezi Západem a Východem.* Praha: MF.

Tesař, Jan. 2000. *Mnichovský komplex. Jeho příčiny a důsledky.* Praha: Prostor.

Trávníček, Jiří. Ed. 2009. *V kleštích dějin. Střední Evropa jako pojem a problém.* Brno: Host.

Trávníček, Matěj. 2012. Pokus o reformu volebního systému pro volby do PS PČR z let 2007 až 2009. In: *Acta Politologica*, Vol. 4, No. 1.

Tříska, Dušan. 2002. Východiska, cíle a principy provedení kupónové privatizace. In: *Kupónová privatizace.* Ed. Dušan Tříska. Praha: CEP.

Tsebelis, George. 2002. *Veto Players: How Political Institutions Work.* Princeton: Princeton University Press.

Tůma, Oldřich. 1999. 9.00, Praha-Libeň, horní nádraží. Exodus východních Němců přes Prahu v září 1989.In: *Soudobé dějiny*, Vol. 6, No. 2–3.

Turek, Otakar. 1995. *Podíl ekonomiky na pádu komunismu v Československu.* Praha: Ústav pro soudobé dějiny AV ČR

Turley, Gerard and Peter J. Luke. 2011. *Transition economics. Two decades on.* London – New York: Routledge.

Urban, Otto. 1982. *Česká společnost 1848–1918*. Praha: Svoboda.
Urbášek, Pavel. 2008. *Vysokoškolský vzdělávací systém v letech tzv. normalizace*. Olomouc: UP.
Vachudova, Milada Anna. 2005. *Europe Undivided: Democracy. Leverage & Integration After Communism*. Oxford – New York: Oxford University Press.
Valenta, Aleš. 2002. *Politické dějiny českých zemí a habsburské monarchie 1848–1914*. Hradec Králové: Gaudeamus.
Vallinder, Torbjörn. 1995. When the Courts Go Marching. In: *The Global Expansion of Judicial Power*. Eds. Neal C. Tate and Torbjörn Vallinder. New York: New York University Press.
Valterová, Aneta. 2006. Česká tripartita v evropském kontextu. In: *Central European Political Studies Review*, Vol. 8, No. 4.
Vančura, Jiří. 1990. *Naděje a zklamání. Pražské jaro 1968*. Praha: Mladá fronta.
Vaněk, Miroslav. 1994. *Veřejné mínění o socialismu před listopadem 1989*. Praha: Maxdorf.
Vaněk, Miroslav. 2006. Proč přišli o moc? Pád socialismu v Československu očima protagonistů komunistického režimu. In: *Mocní a bezmocní? Politické elity a disent v období tzv. normalizace*. Ed. Miroslav Vaněk. Praha: Prostor.
Vassiliou, George. Ed. 2007. *The Access Story: The EU from 15 to 25 Countries*. Oxford – New York: Oxford University Press.
Vašková, Renáta, Kroupa, Aleš, Hála, Jaroslav. 2005. Možnosti a bariéry členství v odborech. In: *Participace a zájmové organizace v České republice*. Eds. Zdenka Mansfeldová and Aleš Kroupa. Praha: Slon.
Veber, Václav. 2008. *Osudové únorové dny*. Praha: Nakladatelství Lidové noviny.
Večerník, Jiří. 1996. *Markets and People. The Czech Reform Experience in a Comparative Perspective*. Aldershot: Avebury.
Večerník, Jiří. 1998. Kapitalistická obnova: privatizace a podnikání. In: *Zpráva o vývoji české společnosti 1989–1998*. Ed. Jiří Večerník. Praha: Academia.
Venclovský, František a kol. 1999. *Dějiny bankovnictví v českých zemích*. Praha: Bankovní institut.
Vítek, Leoš. 2001. *Daňová politika České republiky: historický vývoj, současnost a perspektivy zdanění na území ČR s ohledem na integraci českého hospodářství do světového ekonomického společenství*. Praha: Národohospodářský ústav Josefa Hlávky.
Výborný, Miroslav. 2003. K okolnostem vzniku Ústavy ČR z parlamentní perspektivy. In: *Deset let Ústavy ČR*. Ed. Jan Kysela. Praha: Eurolex Bohemia.
Vyhnánek, Ladislav. 2010. Čl. 63 Pravomoci vázané na součinnost vlády. In: *Ústava České republiky. Komentář*. Lenka Bahýľová et al. Praha: Linde.
Vykoukal, Jiří, Bohuslav Litera and Miroslav Tejchman. 2000. *Východ. Vznik, vývoj a rozpad sovětského bloku*. Praha: Libri.

Whitefield, Stephen and Geoffrey Evans. 1999. Political Culture Versus Rational Choice: Explaining Responses to Transition in the Czech Republic and Slovakia. In: *British Journal of Political Science*, Vol. 29, No. 1.
Wintr, Jan. 2008. Prezident republiky jako reprezentant státu, garant řádu a moderátor politických sporů. In: *Postavení prezidenta v ústavním systému České republiky.* Ed. Vojtěch Šimíček. Brno: MU.
Wintr, Jan. 2010. *Česká parlamentní kultura.* Praha: Auditorium.
Wolf, Karol. 1998. *Podruhé a naposled aneb mírové dělení Československa.* Praha: G plus G.
Wolchik, Sharon. 2000. The Impact of Institutional Factors on the Breakup of the Czechoslovak Federation. In: *Irreconcilable Differences? Explaining Czechoslovakia's Dissolution.* Eds. Michael Kraus and Allison Stanger. Lanham: Rowman & Littlefield Publishers.
Zakaria, Faared. 2005. *Budoucnost svobody. Neliberální demokracie v USA i ve světě.* Praha: Academia.
Žídek, Libor. 2006. *Transformace české ekonomiky 1989–2004.* Praha: C. H. Beck.

List of Abbreviations

ALDE	Alliance of Liberals and Democrats for Europe
CE	Council of Europe
CEFTA	Central European Free Trade Agreement
CEI	Central European Initiative
CERN	European Organization for Nuclear Research
ČNV	Czechoslovak National Committee
CSCE	Committee on Security and Cooperation in Europe
ČSDSD	Czechoslovak Social Democratic Workers' Party
ČSL	Czechoslovak People's Party
ČSNS	Czech National Socialist Party
ČSS	Czechoslovak Socialist Party
ČSSD	Czech Social Democratic Party
DEU	Democratic Union
DNSAP	German National Socialist Workers' Party
EBRD	European Bank for Reconstruction and Development
EC	European Communities
EEC	European Economic Community
EPP	European People's Party
EU	European Union
FAO	United Nations Food and Agriculture Organisation
GDP	Gross Domestic Product
HSD-SMS	Movement for Autonomous Democracy – Society for Moravia and Silesia
HSĹS	Hlinka's Slovak People's Party
HZDS	Movement for Democratic Slovakia
IAEA	International Atomic Energy Agency
IBRD	International Bank for Reconstruction and Development
ICAO	International Civil Aviation Organisation
IDA	International Development Association
IIB	International Investment Bank
ILO	International Labour Organisation
IMF	International Monetary Fund
INTERPOL	International Criminal Police Organization
IOM	International Organisation for Migration
IPB	Investment and Postal Bank

ITU	International Telecommunication Union
K231	Club of Former Political Prisoners
KAN	Club of Committed Non-Party Members
Kč	Czech crown
KDU-ČSL	Christian Democratic Union – Czechoslovak People's Party
KSČ	Communist Party of Czechoslovakia
KSČM	Communist Party of Bohemia and Moravia
KSS	Communist Party of Slovakia
MEP	Member of European Parliament
MP	Member of Parliament
NATO	North-Atlantic Treaty Organisation
NF	National Front
NSP	National Party of Work
ODA	Civic Democratic Alliance
ODS	Civic Democratic Party
OECD	Organisation for Economic Co-Operation and Development
OF	Civic Forum
OH	Civic Movement
OSCE	Organisation for Security and Cooperation in Europe
PES	Party for European Socialists
PfP	Partnership for Peace
PM	Prime Minister
PVVZ	Petition Committee We Shall Remain Faithfull
RČS	Republika československá
S&D	Socialists & Democrats
SdP	Sudetendeutsche Partei
SNJ	Party of National Unity
SPR-RSČ	Association for the Republic – Republican Party of Czechoslovakia
SZ	Green Party
UAE	United Arab Emirates
UN	United Nations
UNESCO	United Nations Educational Scientific and Cultural Organisation
UNIDO	United Nations Industrial Development Organisation
USA	United States of America
US	Freedom Union

ÚV KSČ	Central Committee of the Communist Party of Czechoslovakia
ÚVOD	Central Leadership of Home Resistance
VAT	Value Added Tax
VPN	Public Against Violence
VV	Public Affairs
WHO	World Health Organisation
WTO	World Trade Organisation
WWI	World War I

Tables and Figures

Tables

Table 6.1: Governmernts in the Czech Republic since 1992...................124

Table 8.1: Elections to the Czech National Council held on 8 and
9 June 1990 ....…..................................178

Table 8.2: Elections to the Czech National Council held on
5 and 6 June 1992..179

Table 8.3: Elections to the Chamber of Deputies of the Parliament of
the Czech Republic held on 31 May and 1 June 1996..............179

Table 8.4: Elections to the Chamber of Deputies of the Parliament
of the Czech Republic held on 19 and 20 June 1998...............180

Table 8.5: Elections to the Chamber of Deputies of the Parliament
of the Czech Republic held on 14 and 15 June 2002...............180

Table 8.6: Elections to the Chamber of Deputies of the Parliament
of the Czech Republic held on 2 and 3 June 2006...................181

Table 8.7: Elections to the Chamber of Deputies of the Parliament
of the Czech Republic held on 28 and 29 May 2010...............181

Table 8.8: Elections to the Chamber of Deputies of the Parliament
of the Czech Republic held on 25 and 26 October 2013..........182

Table 10.1: Conceptual map of the contemporary Czech debate about
European integration 226

Table 10.2: Czech and Czechoslovak membership in selected
international organisations 228

Figures

Figure 7.1: Evolution of voter turnout in the Czech Republic,
1990–2014 148

Figure 9.1: Year-on-year changes in gross domestic product 198

Figure 9.2: Budget balance as a proportion of GDP 206

Figure 9.3: Debt as a proportion of GDP 207

Figure 9.4: Mandatory and quasi-mandatory spending 208

Figure 9.5: Evolution of tax burden 210

Figure 10.1: Evolution of public trust in the EU and the most
important Czech political institutions 223

Figure 10.2: The evolution of Czech public opinion on the
introduction of the euro 224

Politics in Europe

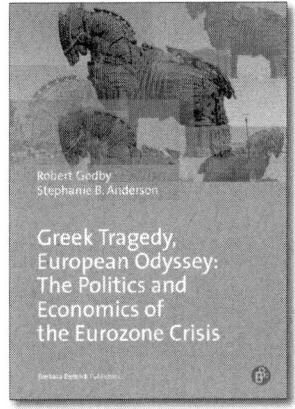

Robert Godby
Stephanie B. Anderson

Ingi Iusmen
Helen Stalford (eds.)

Greek Tragedy, European Odyssey: The Politics and Economics of the Eurozone Crisis

The EU as a Children's Rights Actor
Law, Policy and Structural Dimensions

2016. 209 pp. Pb. 28,00 € (D), GBP 24.95, US$40.00
ISBN 978-3-8474-0618-1
eISBN 978-3-8474-0431-6

2016. 331 pp. Pb. 42,00 € (D), US$58.00, GBP 36.95
ISBN 978-3-8474-0193-3
eISBN 978-3-8474-0412-5

 Order now: www.shop.budrich-academic.de • info@budrich.de

Political Science

Kia Lindroos
Frank Möller (eds.)
Art as a Political Witness

2017. 239 pp. Pb. 48,00 € (D), GBP 43.95, US$63.00
ISBN 978-3-8474-0580-1

The book explores the concept of artistic witnessing as political activity. In which ways may art and artists bear witness to political events? The Contributors engage with dance, film, photography, performance, poetry and theatre and explore artistic witnessing as political activity in a wide variety of case studies.

Kari Palonen
The Politics of Parliamentary Procedure
The Formation of the Westminster Procedure as a Parliamentary Ideal Type

2016. 274 pp. Pb. 34,90 € (D), GBP 31.95, US$49.95
ISBN 978-3-8474-0787-4

Currently, parliament as a political institution does not enjoy the best reputation. This book aims to recover less known political resources of the parliamentary mode of proceeding. The parliamentary procedure relies on regulating debates in a fair way and on constructing opposed perspectives on the agenda items.

 www.shop.budrich-academic.de